A COMPLEX FATE

A Complex Fate

Gustav Stickley

AND THE

Craftsman Movement

BARRY SANDERS

PRESERVATION PRESS

JOHN WILEY & SONS, INC.

NEW YORK • CHICHESTER • BRISBANE • TORONTO • SINGAPORE

This text is printed on acid-free paper.

Copyright © 1996 by Barry Sanders.
Published by John Wiley & Sons, Inc.

Library of Congress Cataloging in Publication Data:
Sanders, Barry, 1938–
  A complex fate : Gustav Stickley and the Craftsman Movement /
Barry Sanders.
   p. cm.
  ISBN 0-471-14392-8 (cloth : alk. paper)
   1. Stickley, Gustav, 1858–1942 — Criticism and interpretation.
  2. Arts and crafts movement—New York (State) I. Title.
  N6537.S74S26 1996
  749.213–dc20   95-46177

Printed in the United States of America

10 9 8 7 6 5 4 3 2 1

It's a complex fate, being an American.

—*Henry James*

CONTENTS

PHOTO CREDITS

STICKLEY
PRODUCTS

INTRODUCTION

Smoke, darkness, noise: the clashing of car bells, engine bells, steamer bells; the grating of endless trolleys as they dash along the street, the shriek of the AMERICAN VOICE trying to make itself heard above the uproar. The rattle and thunder of the elevated railway, the unearthly buzzing of electric cabs, and the thudding power houses that shake a whole street."[1] So wrote C. R. Ashbee, a key figure in the Arts and Crafts Movement in England, on his first visit to Chicago in 1900. The thunderclap of noise that overwhelmed Ashbee that year in America—the sounds of power as the twentieth century rolled to life—was only just beginning.

Three short years after Ashbee's visit, Orville Wright was airborne at Kitty Hawk, North Carolina. Alfred Stieglitz opened his "291" Gallery and introduced the works of Rodin, Picasso, and Toulouse-Lautrec to America in 1905, the same year the Ziegfeld Follies opened. The Ashcan School of painting exhibited in New York in 1908, just when George Herriman started drawing Krazy Kat. By 1911, Henry Ford had swung open the doors to his first automobile plant in Highland Park, Michigan. Two years later, W. C. Handy's "Memphis Blues" and Irving Berlin's "Alexander's Ragtime Band" blared above the rhythms of Ford's conveyor belts, gravity slides, and overhead monorails.

The mature years of the Arts and Crafts Movement, 1901 to 1914, were exceedingly significant for American literature. During that period Henry James published his major works: *The Sacred Fount*, *The Wings of the Dove*, *The Ambassadors*, and *The Golden Bowl*. Stephen Crane, Ambrose Bierce, O. Henry, W. D. Howells, Willa Cather, Theodore Dreiser, Edith Wharton, and Gertrude Stein were all building solid reputations. By 1912, Ezra Pound had published seven volumes of poetry. Vachel Lindsay, Marianne Moore, William Carlos Williams, Amy Lowell, Wallace Stevens, Edwin Arlington Robinson, Robinson

Jeffers, Carl Sandburg, and Robert Frost published major poetry between 1901 and 1914. Audiences watched plays by Eugene O'Neill and marveled at D. W. Griffith's *Greed, Intolerance*, and the aptly titled *Birth of a Nation*.

In the midst of Ezra Pound's experiments with poetic form, and Gertrude Stein's with language, as automobiles banged noisily along cobbled streets and planes miraculously left the ground—that is, in an intense period of literary creation and technological innovation—a movement dedicated to simple living began to take shape. As if from some remote past, craftspeople were busily hammering metal, turning clay, hand finishing furniture, and cranking printing presses. An unknown cabinetmaker, Gustav Stickley, became the most vocal spokesman in America for this quirky revolution in aesthetics, known as the Arts and Crafts Movement.

Marked by contradictions, America pushed and shoved its way into the Modern Age. Ralph Waldo Emerson caught the contradictory spirit of Americans in a single, powerful line: "A foolish consistency is the hobgoblin of little minds." Gustav Stickley could not have been accused of holding to a foolish consistency. At first glance his designs and philosophy seem archaic and anachronistic for twentieth-century America. But people bought his furniture in large part because he got them to believe they were acquiring the absolutely new and modern. The idea found appeal in the country of *New* Orleans, *New* York, *New* London, and *New* Mexico. He offered America's own, new furniture. Stickley, who referred to himself as a modern and an innovator, introduced his simple, stark, hand-built cabinets as objects modern enough to take their place alongside planes and automobiles. His ingenuity paid off: in a short time, he enjoyed staggering financial success and wide popularity. But that success lasted only briefly—less than two decades. He wound up a bankrupt and broken man.

Stickley was one of the first Americans to try to hammer out a viable aesthetic for modern society. In a world fast becoming more technological and commercial, Stickley formulated a philosophy for a fulfilling, aesthetic, and, at times, communal country life. At heart, Stickley proved a thoroughly modern baron of this new age, hungry for power and money. But he professed a beneficence and a concern for communal good. He quickly saw that he could satisfy his own desires by giving the people what they wanted: a sense that his pieces of furniture were handcrafted one at a time (the goods were actually die cut by machines and mass produced) and an assurance that Stickley himself produced each piece (in fact, he had very little to do with them). But no one could call him an out-and-out liar: his furniture was the most solid, durable, and carefully constructed of any around.

Stickley did not have the artistic genius of Frank Lloyd Wright. He lacked Wright's uncanny sense of design, his mastery of form and space. But Stickley had something else: savvy and nerve. He had a genius for marketing ideas. Stickley's precipitous rise and fall speaks less to social, political, or economic change than it does to his own desire to amass a fortune at the expense of practically all else—even, according to one daughter, his own family.

Stickley's furniture was rediscovered during the economic boom of the 1980s and can now be found in a good many museums across the country, as well as in the homes of the wealthy and the hip. I do not conceive of Stickley as a lonely aberration but as a man who embodies the American ethos. Michael Milken and Donald Trump, the business tycoons who rose and fell in the 1980s, represent the same ethos, only the stakes were higher and the goods less tangible. Although what Stickley sold was far from junk, there is the sense of the huckster about him. We might find comparisons, as well, with the TV evangelists of the 1980s who also rose to great popularity, only to fall into scandal and bankruptcy.

Contradictions did not seem to bother him. In fact, both worlds—the premodern and the modern—were familiar to him, for though he had grown up in the nineteenth century, he came to maturity in the twentieth. Adopting William Morris as his mentor, Stickley argued that modern life could be ennobled and made holy through honest, worthwhile labor. Based on this premise, he articulated an entire self-styled philosophy. Early in his career he even held that America's economic structure had to be radically changed before workers could pursue decent labor and produce what he called "democratic art." Before his political ardor cooled, he argued that the most effective way to change society was through socialism. For Stickley, dignified labor was art, and art was essential for a healthy and spiritual life. He maintained that people should surround their lives with beauty—in furniture, home accessories, and especially architecture. He wanted beautiful cities, lush gardens, and plentiful parks. Finally, he counseled people to lead simple lives, to cut themselves loose from superfluous, nonutilitarian gadgets that merely encumbered their lives.

The best way to experience invigorating simplicity, for Stickley, lay in a life lived close to the soil. Utopian communities such as Brook Farm and experiences such as Thoreau described in *Walden* appealed to his romantic nature.[2] What a bountiful land, what freedom and happiness abounded, what opportunity! Surely America was destined to be a new utopia. So Stickley insisted that by combining farming and handicrafts Americans could live the ideal life. To spread the word, he briefly contemplated a summer school to train boys in crafts and farming, called Craftsman Farms. Utility, simplicity, beauty: these were the leitmotifs of Stickley's Arts and Crafts Movement.

Stickley's philosophy sought to integrate his own social theory, political commitment, and aesthetic designs, which resulted in furniture, metal accessories, and architectural designs, all of a quality usually found only in insulated communities such as Shaker villages. As his model, Stickley adopted the medieval craftsman, who paid strict attention to the smallest, seemingly most insignificant details.

INTRODUCTION

Moreover, medieval artists represented to him models of the deepest integrity, since they designed their own objects and then executed those designs.

The world, according to Stickley's view, had fallen from the moral and aesthetic heights of the twelfth century. So he set out to save the world (he had at one time wanted to be a minister). The Arts and Crafts Movement, like all movements, aimed at effecting wholesale change. And Stickley, like the leaders of most movements, possessed remarkable charisma and an uncommon ego.

Every person, Stickley announced, was capable of producing art that rivaled medieval standards of quality and craftsmanship. All people possessed artistic ability, but the routine of labor prevented them from expressing their true artistic nature. And people responded. As the machine dominating more and more of daily life, people sought ways of achieving self-expression. Would-be artists formed societies in order to produce their own art: housewives, retired and frustrated businessmen, factory workers, all eager to find expression through metalwork, ceramics, jewelry, leatherwork, or furniture making. Like the Middle Ages, the early twentieth century offered a chance at collectivism—through unions, workshops, associations, and guilds. In Arts and Crafts societies, people sacrificed self and personality in the name of art.

Diverse groups such as the Rhode Island School of Design, the Industrial Art League in Chicago, the Guild of Arts and Crafts in San Francisco, the Women's Club in Michigan, the Society of Arts and Crafts in Ohio, the Boston Arts and Crafts Society, and hundreds of others staged numerous exhibitions during the period. Classes in the manual arts began to appear with some frequency in high schools and colleges. Some colleges devoted themselves almost exclusively to the manual arts, the most notable probably Throop University, now the California Institute of Technology, in Pasadena. Many of these guilds and societies, classes and clubs, developed high-caliber artists. Firms such as the Rookwood Studios, Marblehead, Arequipa, and Newcomb College started as amateur operations and went on to become important potteries. The Arts and Crafts aesthetic not only changed the shape of pottery, but also affected metalwork, jewelry, bookbinding, leatherwork, architecture, and, of course, furniture. This crafts movement, the first of the twentieth century, carried its audience to an orchestrated crescendo. Infused with William Morris's vision of a "society in which all men would enjoy the freedom to be creative," Stickley, the maestro, sought to spread his message to as many people as possible. He hit on a practical and profitable solution.

Stickley popularized the Arts and Crafts Movement by starting his own magazine, *The Craftsman*. In its pages, Stickley exposed his readers to the ideas of Thomas Carlyle, Louis Sullivan, John Ruskin, William Morris, Charles Voysey, Oscar Lovell Triggs, Charles and Henry Greene, Irving Gill, and countless other prominent figures in the arts. Readers who had perhaps only heard the term "Gothic architecture" discovered in *The Craftsman* that the art of building carried great importance for their spiritual lives. But Stickley also gave them the practical; he published plans and lumber lists for virtually all the furniture he manufactured commercially. He possessed remarkable entrepreneurial talent, coupled with a peculiarly American drive. An innovator, Stickley could take ideas from here and there and put his own mark on them. His imagination was synthetic. He promoted himself in his magazine as Mark Twain did by touring the country, speaking to small-town audiences. Gustav Stickley conjured himself out of backwoods thin air, and Americans, who were used to chautauquas, traveling circuses, and a good deal of hokum, ate it up.

By 1909, Stickley sold his Craftsman furniture in forty-two cities across the country and had plans to expand. When he incorporated in 1912, he issued capital stock valued at $300,000, a huge sum in 1912. When he moved his retail sales office to New York City, he paid $5,000 a month in rent, an astronomical amount for the period. Stickley began measuring his success in numbers—dollars, office floors, and pieces of furniture in his catalog. According to one of his daughters, Stickley leased a penthouse apartment on the upper east side of Manhattan and spent less and less time with his family, whom he had left behind in Eastwood, New York. He hobnobbed with opera stars, actresses, and wealthy businesspeople, frequenting the best restaurants and picking up the tab.

Gustav Stickley became an overnight sensation in the normally mundane field of furniture, but he demanded that the world also see him as an artist, aesthetic revolutionary, and philosopher. Hadn't Emerson, one of his heroes, called himself a philosopher? And America responded. Just as Morris had been venerated in England and Mackintosh in Scotland, in America Stickley became synonymous with the Arts and Crafts Movement itself.

In a real and important sense, Stickley liberated the artisan—the craftsperson—and elevated him or her to the level of artist. From his time on, the maligned plate decorator or china painter would be taken seriously. Many of those working in these crafts were women, and Stickley wrote article after article in the cause of their liberation. He established himself as one of the earliest figures who worked toward the liberation of all the marginalized in society—most notably toward the liberation of women.

A New York bank delivered the death blow to the Arts and Crafts Movement in America when Stickley was finally forced to declare bankruptcy. Ironically, the movement was initially motivated by one of Morris's most important pecuniary tenets: "Good decoration, involving rather the luxury of taste than the luxury of costliness, will be found to be much less expensive than is generally supposed." Since the closing of Stickley's workshops, with a few singular exceptions, aesthetics in America have been grounded primarily in money: cheap, expendable, flashy, affordable, fashionable—these have become the guides for contemporary household furnishings and architecture. And though *quality* is probably the most fre-

INTRODUCTION

quently used word in contemporary advertising, finished products often seem shoddily made. Stickley supported the ideals of quality and beauty month after month in *The Craftsman*, and in piece after piece in his workshops. Sit on a 1910 Stickley dining chair today: it is still astonishingly solid.

In the chapters that follow, I trace the development of Stickley's philosophy and work. Stickley's life is a difficult one to organize, since he dabbled in so many areas, but it is possible to distinguish three phases. The first covers the years 1900 to 1904, beginning with his early furniture business, the United Crafts, and culminating in his massive Arts and Crafts exhibition. In the second phase, he dissolves the United Crafts, expands his interests to include more of the arts, and changes the name of his business to the Craftsman Workshops. His work becomes heavily influenced by Harvey Ellis, a designer and architect. This period climaxes with Stickley's decision to further expand and to move his offices to New York City. The last part of Stickley's career takes place in a grand, twelve-story office building in Manhattan called the Craftsman Building, where, in 1916, Stickley finally declares bankruptcy.

This book is not weighed down with pictures, for Stickley's work has been endlessly photographed, described, auctioned, and collected.

Gustav Stickley's fame and popularity were short-lived, lasting only fifteen years. But in that time he exerted a tremendous influence on aesthetics in America. As Ashbee described it, this was an age of speed and acceleration. Ultimately, Stickley ended where he began—in Eastwood—penniless and living with his daughter. But he left his mark. Because of his work, historians and lay people alike often refer to the Arts and Crafts Movement by the name he gave it, the Craftsman Movement. It seems odd that Stickley should have been involved in so much—furniture, architecture, metalwork, needlework, leatherwork, education, farming, homebuilding, landscaping, editing, writing, lecturing, promoting, running a restaurant—when his philosophy was founded on the principle of simplicity. In a way this book traces Stickley's departure from that guiding principle, from what his first catalog called "Holy Simplicity" to his pursuit of a "complex fate."

1

THE BEGINNINGS

IN 1812, GUSTAV STICKLEY'S GRANDPARENTS, the Stoeckels, emigrated from Dresden, Germany, to America and settled in Osceola, Wisconsin, a town that had a large German population. Leopold Stoeckel, Gustav's father, was probably born in Osceola. It was Leopold who changed the family name to the more American-sounding Stickley, because people in the midwest made fun of the name Stoeckel. Barbara Schlaegel, Gustav's mother, whose own parents came from Germany, was born in Brandt, Pennsylvania. As a young woman, she traveled from Brandt with one of her brothers, an itinerant minister, to the German settlement in Osceola. There she met Leopold Stickley, and they married. They had eleven children: Louise, Christine, Mary, Emma, and Julie; Leopold, Jr., Julius George, Albert, Charles, George, and Gustav, their eldest son, born March 9, 1858.[1]

Gustav's father, Leopold, was a farmer. He seems to have been a man who avoided facing problems and difficulties. Refusing to accept the hard work that farming entailed, he made life on the farm a struggle for the whole family, and particularly for Gustav, who as the eldest son was forced to carry much of the load. Besides attending school, Gustav also performed tough daily chores that increased in number during the summer and in difficulty during the winter:

> *Country-born on a small farm in the Middle West, where most of the land was yet heavily timbered, I found myself, at the age of twelve, called upon to do all kinds of farm work in the summer, and to chop wood and draw it to the nearest market in the winter. With few aids other than natural resources we were obliged to depend on ourselves for the commonest needs and comforts of life.*[2]

Gustav learned important lessons growing up on a farm—independence, perseverance, the value of grueling work. Those adolescent years working the land in Wisconsin also made him aware that he could never pursue a life totally devoted

1

to the hard routine of farm work. He continually advocated a much more genteel, less arduous farm experience than the one he had known. But he never dropped the idea of life on the land. Indeed, in later years he would argue that youngsters could find the most vigorous, fulfilling education in a curriculum that combined handicrafts with farming.

Gustav's father fled the rigors of farm life early. Shortly after Gustav turned twelve, Leopold Stickley moved the family across the St. Croix River to Stillwater, Minnesota, where he took up life as a stonemason. Stonemasonry provided an easier life, with better pay. And he seemed to learn the craft well: Leopold is credited with shaping the stones for the First Presbyterian Church in Stillwater.[3] Leopold also had his son apprenticed as a stonemason to bring more money into the family, but the young Gustav expressed a strong dislike for it. Stone resisted too much; it took too much hacking and banging away to give it shape. Gustav loved the more resilient, responsive character of wood. As an older man, Gustav recalled the Wisconsin farm where he first became acquainted with the special qualities of wood:

> *I had always been interested in wood, even before I became interested in furniture, for as a farm boy in Wisconsin I used to make ax helves, yokes for the oxen, runners for the sleigh—whatever happened to be needed for the task at hand. In fact, in the making of these rough farm implements lay the germ of what I have accomplished in later years. After the farming I took up stonemasonry, and it was the hard daily labor with this stubborn material that made me appreciate so keenly the responsive, sympathetic qualities of wood when I began afterward, at the age of sixteen, to learn the cabinet-makers' trade. It was like being with an old friend, to work in wood again. I began to study its beauty more carefully, to note its varied grains and textures, the way it lent itself to sturdy forms and soft finishes, and these things filled me with enthusiasm for the work.[4]*

The family had been in Stillwater only a few years when Leopold abandoned them, sometime in the early 1870s.[5] For Gustav, just entering his teens, life became even harder. Barbara Stickley simply could not afford to feed eleven children on her own. So Gustav gave up any idea of childhood pleasures and worked full time as a stonemason to support the remaining twelve members of the family. But he disliked working with stone:

> *It was heavy and tedious labor, much too hard for a boy of my age, and being put to it so early gave me an intense dislike for it. Had I been older and stronger, I might not have realized so keenly its disagreeable features, but as it was, the feeling of the lime and the grinding of the trowel over stone and mortar was especially repugnant to me, and the toil itself meant the utmost physical strain and fatigue[6]*

So he went after other jobs, landing one finally, at a saw mill. The eldest child, he viewed himself as the mainstay of the family. The loss of his father may have

Sideboard of fumed oak with iron hardware (40″ high, 54″ wide, 18″ deep). Circa 1904.

helped determine the course of his career, for in later years he wrote time and again about the sanctity of the family. He designed his furniture with traditional family activities in mind, and he even planned a school for boys that would serve as a large family for them.

Jacob Schlaegel, Gustav's uncle, offered to bring the struggling family to Laynesboro, Pennsylvania. Jacob owned a chair factory nearby Brandt, Pennsylvania, and promised the sons jobs at the factory. But Gustav's mother, a proud and independent woman, initially refused and thought the family should make it on their own.[7] During those years in the early 1870s, according to John Crosby Freeman, "the family's subsistence often depended on him [Gustav] and what he could make hauling huge logs by wagon during long, lonely nights in order to meet the mill with the rising sun."[8] He dropped out of school in the eighth grade in order to put in more hours. Finally, Barbara could no longer bear the heavy toll on her young son, and in 1873, when Gustav was fifteen years old, she relented and accepted Jacob's offer. Her other brother, the minister, came to Stillwater to retrieve the family. A widely read man, he had studied theology at Princeton University and, once back in Brandt, committed himself to educating the Stickley children. He devoted special attention to Gustav, tutoring him in the arts and let-

Roll-top desk of fumed oak, with copper hardware (46″ high, 60″ wide, 32″ deep). Circa 1909.

ters, philosophy and religion. The lessons must have taken, for, as one of Gustav's daughters recalls, "Gus read everything he could lay his hands on" and took special delight in Emerson, Thoreau, Whitman, and William Morris.[9]

More important than Stickley's reading was his training in the art of cabinet-making at the Brandt Chair Company. The experience delighted the young boy. Now sixteen years old, he realized that labor could be pleasurable: "We made the plain wooden and cane-seated chairs so much used in those days. . . . It was the most common-place of stereotyped work, yet from it I can date my love for working in wood and my appreciation of the beauty and interest to be found in its natural color, texture and grain."[10] The Brandt Chair Company, a small factory, produced simple chairs made by hand from old broom handles and sold door-to-door throughout Susquehanna County, Pennsylvania, and Broome County, New York. Although Gustav initially knew nothing about the furniture business, he rose quickly in the firm. Not only was he industrious and efficient, but his personality demanded that he be boss. Stickley could not work long for anyone else. As one of his daughters says, "Gus [as everyone in the family called him] was a Bavarian—stubborn, independent. He had to be the leader. He was not only a dreamer, but if things didn't go his way, he wouldn't do them at all."[11] But Stickley usually made certain that things went his way. In four short years Gustav moved from inexperienced assembly worker to foreman of the company. At the same time, he was planning ahead: he was saving his money to open his own furniture manufacturing company.

THE BEGINNINGS

He also needed money to start his own family. On one of his business trips to Susquehanna County, Gustav had met Eda Ann Simmons, daughter of John Simmons of Susquehanna. When his wife died, John placed Eda Ann in a Susquehanna convent that took in children. How Gustav and Eda met remains a mystery to everyone in the family. Susquehanna was situated, however, next to Brandt. Eda and Gustav began to correspond, using the local milkman as an intermediary. Finally, one morning, she sneaked out of the convent in the milk wagon, and on September 12, 1883, Gustav Stickley and Eda Simmons were married.[12]

One of Eda's daughters describes her as a gentle woman who spent most of her time raising her six children: five girls and one boy. She had an aristocratic and regal beauty, a handsome woman.[13] As she cared for her family's needs at home,[14] Stickley devoted attention to his business aspirations.

In 1884, one year after their marriage, Gustav, his wife, and two of his brothers, George and Charles, left Brandt, Pennsylvania, and made the short move to Binghamton, New York. Financed by a local businessman, Schuyler Brandt, the three brothers planned to establish a retail outlet for the Brandt Chair Company. The new store, known as Stickley Brothers, also carried a wide line of furniture manufactured in Grand Rapids, Michigan. Then known as the furniture capital of the world, Grand Rapids was famous for producing inexpensive, machine-made period imitations. Stickley Brothers repaired and upholstered furniture and, according to advertisements in the Binghamton *Daily Republican* for October 24, 1885, sold mattresses. Their principal business, however, involved the retail sales of a wide variety of contemporary American furniture: "We have just received a carload of cheap and medium priced Walnut Chamber Suites from the West;"[15] "Cherry Suites from Grand Rapids, Michigan;"[16] "We are the only house in the city that can sell a Shaker Rocker, upholstered in good silk plush, and hand polished frames, for eight dollars."[17] But Stickley did not feel satisfied, for he still devoted his time and talent to manufacturing someone else's furniture.

In addition, the young firm of Stickley Brothers did not meet with much success. Because Binghamton had developed an efficient and advanced commercial transportation system early on, the small town attracted many manufacturing plants that could easily ship their goods across the country. Lumber supplies also existed close at hand. So Binghamton boasted a large number of well-established furniture manufacturers and retailers. Because of keen competition, by 1886 Stickley Brothers was on the verge of closing. At that point, perhaps persuaded by Gustav, a local investor presented Stickley Brothers with the opportunity to manufacture their own chairs.

Though he had never designed furniture, Gustav boldly took charge of designing the new chairs for Stickley Brothers. Shaker designs had always provided the models for sturdy, functional chairs. His daughters recall visiting the Shaker community of New Lebanon many times with their father and remember his talk-

5

ing about the beautiful simplicity of Shaker furniture. But, according to Stickley, economic circumstances forced upon him the design for his first chair:

> *We had no money to buy machinery. I went to a maker of broom handles who had a good turning lathe . . . and with it blocked out the plainer parts of some very simple chairs made after the "Shaker" model. The rest of them I made by hand, with the aid of a few simple and inexpensive machines which were placed in the loft of the store. All we had was a hand-lathe, boring machine, framing saw and chuck, and the power was transmitted by rope from a neighboring establishment. The wood in shape was dried in the sun on the tin roof of the building. The very primitiveness of this equipment, made necessary by lack of means, furnished what was really a golden opportunity to break away from the monotony of commercial forms, and I turned my attention to reproducing by hand some of the simplest and best models of the old Colonial, Windsor and other plain chairs, and to a study of this period as a foundation for original work along the same lines.*[18]

Without knowing it, Stickley found the philosophical foundation for all his future furniture designs: simplicity. But even the "golden opportunity" for doing original work Gustav did not find compelling enough to keep him at the new firm.

Library table of fumed oak (46" high, 36" wide, 66" long). Circa 1912.
On top of table, Dirk Van Erp hammered copper lamp with mica shade.

Clipped-corner table of fumed oak (29″ high; top: 24″ x 24″).
Circa 1902.

He had a difficult time working with his opinionated brother George, even though Charles usually played the role of conciliator and mediator. (The family affectionately called him "Charlie Darling.") So Gustav, now thirty years old, left the Stickley Brothers Company in 1888. Albert and Charles continued to operate the Binghamton wholesale and retail outlet under the name Stickley Brothers until 1889. At that time, Charles joined Schuyler Brandt in forming the Stickley-Brandt Company.[19] Gustav liked Charles very much, and the two remained friends throughout life, whereas relations were contentious between Gustav and his other brothers. Charles was the only brother to attend college—the Binghamton Business College—for which Gustav admired him. In fact, Gustav surrounded himself his entire life with educated, cultured people.[20]

In 1888, when Gustav left the Stickley Brothers Company, Binghamton was developing an elaborate electric railway system, using a method pioneered by Frank J. Sprague, an electrical engineer and inventor. Stickley went to work for the city, helping to develop the system. The Binghamton Street Railway was formally organized in 1890 with Gustav Stickley as vice president; he supervised the first electric streetcar system in the state of New York. That Stickley could, once again, quickly assume a position of authority in a new field says a good deal about his confidence, his daring, his outspoken nature, and his intelligence. Throughout his life Stickley had the ability to convince people of his ideas—in later years, he would talk bank presidents into loaning him large sums of money; convince creditors to wait for payment; persuade people to buy Craftsman furnishings; and even

7

entice his reluctant, opinionated brothers to work for him in the furniture manufacturing business.

Even with his amazing success with the Binghamton railway, Stickley missed
working with wood and wanted desperately to return to furniture making. So in
1890 he and his wife left Binghamton for Auburn, New York. By June of that year,
Stickley had formed a partnership for the manufacture of furniture in Auburn with
Elgin A. Simonds. The new firm, the Stickley and Simonds Company, issued
$50,000 of capital stock on August 28, 1890, a substantial amount for a small, local
company, the equivalent of almost $660,000 today. Stickley assumed the presi-
dency. The new company listed as stockholders Elgin A. Simonds (twenty-five
shares), Jennie Simonds (twenty-five shares), Eda Stickley (forty-nine shares), and
Gustav Stickley (one share).[21]

Shortly after the Stickley and Simonds Company began operations, the pair
decided to expand by purchasing some land in Eastwood, a suburb of Syracuse, for
a new factory. To raise funds for the fledgling company, Stickley persuaded the au-
thorities at the New York State Prison in Auburn to hire him as director of manufacturing operations, a position he held from 1892 to 1894. He had already been
aware of progressive prison reform in Stillwater, Minnesota. It was a historic time
to be at the Auburn prison: on June 4, 1888, New York had adopted electrocution
for capital punishment, the first state to do so. The first criminal to be executed by
electricity was William Kemmler, at Auburn prison, on August 6, 1890, two years
before Stickley arrived at the prison. The electrical components of the electrocution system were devised by Edwin F. Davis, the first state electrician for New
York, whom Stickley most likely met when he was vice president of the
Binghamton Street Railway. Since Binghamton's electric streetcar had become a
transportation model for the entire country, the state electrician would have taken
an active role in its development. After the turn of the century, Stickley designed
a chair for Auburn prison that could accommodate a variety of electrical equipment; it became the standard electric chair. Since he wrote many articles later in
his life on the subject of prison reform and rehabilitation in general, he may have
believed, as many people did at the turn of the century, that prisons could execute
criminals more humanely through electrocution than by hanging.

His position as director of manufacturing operations at Auburn prison helped
to impress the president of the Syracuse Savings Bank, for in 1892 the bank loaned
the now-called Stickley and Simonds Company the money to purchase twenty-
eight lots of land in Eastwood, New York, for their factory, the site that would
later house Stickley's own Craftsman Workshops. That same year Stickley persuaded two other brothers, Leopold and Julius George, to come to work at the
new factory. They would later grow into his keenest competitors. John C.
Freeman described the first few months of the operation in Eastwood:
"Financially, it was a very bumpy road to Eastwood and within three months a

legal suit was brought against the Syracuse Savings Bank and the Stickley and Simonds Company for the foreclosure of its mortgage by a pair of unpaid workmen. The suit did not topple the company and the court cancelled the charges of record on August 23, 1920."[22] That lawsuit might never have been brought if Gustav had not been spending so much time at the prison, for his charm might have smoothed things over.

While employed at the prison, Stickley commuted from Auburn to Eastwood to take care of legal matters with Elgin Simonds and to discuss their line of furniture. It was a hectic time for Stickley: "Activities in Eastwood soon required lengthy sojourns and Stickley in 1893 took a temporary residence for himself in Syracuse at the Yates Hotel. After completing his contract with the New York State Prison he moved his entire family in 1894 to Syracuse."[23] The Stickley and Simonds Company achieved a fair level of success, even though the furniture imitated, in the most uninspired way, Louis XIV and Italian Renaissance models. In 1895 and 1896, the trade journal *Decorator and Furnisher* showed several Stickley and Simonds chairs that were nothing more than reproductions of Chippendale reproductions.[24] Stickley continued manufacturing these Chippendale copies until 1898, the crucial year of his life and the most important year for the Arts and Crafts Movement in America.

2

THE UNITED CRAFTS

IN 1898, GUSTAV STICKLEY launched his own career in the Arts and Crafts Movement. It entailed, initially, a change in attitude. He knew he no longer wanted to produce slavish imitations of Chippendale designs, but he had not yet settled on a precise alternative. His love of Shaker furniture led him to respect uncluttered, elemental, functional forms. Yet he wanted to produce something unique. For Stickley, that kind of furniture could not be found in America. Certain models existed—but nothing that met his exacting standards. He, however, had been reading the English writer and artist William Morris. The Arts and Crafts Movement had crystallized in England in the 1860s when Morris, Edward Burne-Jones, and Dante Gabriel Rossetti had begun exhibiting their early designs in the household arts through an association eventually known as Morris and Company. Morris had revolted against the shoddy, Victorian objects being produced by the new machines; he wanted the decorative arts returned to the elevated position they had occupied during the Middle Ages, and argued for simplicity and function in all such arts. Stickley may have seen Morris's artwork in the Morris showrooms in New York when they opened in 1881, or later in Boston and Chicago. By 1898, Morris's philosophy, aesthetics, and handicrafts had made themselves so visible in America that *House Beautiful* complained: "William Morris's influence is almost too apparent. . . . It is well not to make too much of a fetish of Mr. Morris, nor to follow him blindly into all the clumsiness and discomfort which his love of the medieval has foisted upon the latter half of the nineteenth century."[1]

Despite such criticism, many decorative artists in America recognized Morris's genius and were inspired by his designs. Louis Tiffany, whom one historian called "the William Morris of this century"[2] (although he may have been more accurately one "of this country"), opened his studios in 1878. Other art studios followed. In 1880, the Rookwood Pottery Studios were founded. Chelsea Pottery, in 1891, opened next. Walter Crane, the prominent English designer and painter, associate of Morris, and member of the Arts and Crafts Exhibition Society, visited the United States in 1890; he gave impetus to the American Arts and Crafts Movement when he lectured at the Art Institute in Chicago in 1892. The following year, the English magazine *Studio* appeared in America as *International Studio* and explored every aspect of English arts and crafts. Grueby Faience and Newcomb College, two of the major art potteries during the Arts and Crafts period in America, opened for business in 1895. The first issue of *House Beautiful*, one of America's most important arbiters of taste in household furnishings, arrived in 1896 and included articles and designs by proponents of the burgeoning Arts and Crafts Movement. The momentum continued. Dedham Pottery reorganized that same year under the direction of Hugh C. Robertson, one of the principal Arts and Crafts potters. America was so receptive to the ideas of the Arts and Crafts Movement that even the prominent British designer, silversmith, and jeweler C. R. Ashbee decided to visit New York and Philadelphia in 1896.

Rural craftspeople, without aiming to become nationally known artists, also contributed to the growth of the Arts and Crafts aesthetic. They were working in a folk tradition totally unaware of anything called the Arts and Crafts Movement:

> *This was true, of course, particularly in the Southern mountains or other rural or remote areas. Some organization of these folk elements is illustrated by the work of Mrs. Sarah Avery Leeds of Avery's Island, Louisiana, who energetically sponsored the weaving of cotton fabrics in traditional designs by Creole women. Too, Berea College in Kentucky pioneered in stressing sales of regional products to aid in supporting the students and the institution. And all over the country, book-binders, rug-hookers, basket-weavers, and potters set up shop singly or in small groups to produce and market useful objects with some aesthetic appeal.*[3]

These small groups developed into societies. In 1897, Copley Hall, in Boston, housed the first major Arts and Crafts exhibition. That exhibition gave birth to the Boston Society of Arts and Crafts; the Society elected Charles Eliot Norton, a friend of John Ruskin's, as president. Ruskin wrote two important books on architecture, *The Seven Lamps of Architecture* (1849) and *The Stones of Venice* (1851–1853), as part of his struggle against competition and self-interest and his desire to pursue the medieval, heroic ideals that he found in feudalism and the Christian communitarian life. The Boston Society was only one of a multitude of important Arts and Crafts societies that evolved toward the end of the century. The most energetic, innovative, and influential of these was the Chicago Arts and Crafts Society, founded in 1897 under the direction of Jane Addams at Hull House. Within six months of its founding, the society totaled 128 members. Jane Addams was, of course, an agitator for social reform, but she assumed just as much importance in the reform of art. David Hanks describes how Morris's ideas took shape in Chicago:

Morris's prosperous business led him to an increasing awareness of and concern about the exclusiveness of his beautiful handwrought products. Rather than compromise with the perfection of his works, he felt that the system of distribution of goods through profiteering had to change. His philosophy of socialism was based on the ideal of art as redeeming and civilizing man. These socialistic principles were also to travel to Chicago, where Oscar Lovell Triggs was one of the most eloquent defenders of these beliefs. More famous as social reformers were Jane Addams and Ellen Gates Starr, whose Hull House was to become a center for the movement in Chicago. Hull House, on Chicago's West Side, itself was based on Toynbee Hall in London, which Jane Addams visited before establishing the pioneer settlement house in 1889.

It was at Hull House that the movement, modeled on the English prototype, was finally institutionalized on October 22, 1897, when the Chicago Arts and Crafts Society was organized. One of the charter members of the society was "F. Wright." Wright's own concern about the decline in craftsmanship and the generally poor quality of design was shared by his fellow members of the society.[4]

House Beautiful reported on one of these early meetings at Hull House in 1898: "At a recent meeting of the Chicago Arts and Crafts Society, a spirited discussion took place as to whether the public taste or the manufacturer's obduracy was most to blame for the shocking commercial furniture in all the large stores, and the fact that it is almost impossible to purchase, for example, a really good chair for a small sum of money."[5] Stickley probably saw this article since, according to his daughter, Mrs. Wiles, he read *House Beautiful* avidly; he probably also recognized the business potential that lay hidden in the article. He decided to produce that chair for America.

When Morris died in October 1896, Stickley despaired that he had not met the great man. Morris's death seemed to decide the issue for Stickley: he would travel to Europe to meet with the rest of the artists still working within Morris's principles. In 1898, Stickley arrived in England, where the movement had been flourishing for thirty years. He met with C. R. Ashbee; Samuel Bing, owner of the influential Paris salon Galeries d'Art Nouveau; T. J. Cobden-Sanderson, owner of the Doves Bindery in England and the man credited with joining the words "arts" and "crafts"; William R. Lethaby, architect, designer, teacher, and president of the Arts and Crafts Exhibition Society; Barry Parker and Raymond Unwin, architects; Ambrose Heal, furniture designer; and J. S. Henry, furniture maker. But most important, Stickley met with Charles F. A. Voysey, architect, designer, typographer, and a member of the Art Workers' Guild.

Voysey's work had been shown in American journals in the early 1890s, and the Boston Architectural Club had exhibited his furniture in 1891. *International Studio* had featured his cabinetwork in 1893. He designed not only furniture, but also all the distinctive, hammered metalwork for his cabinets. Perhaps borrowing the idea from Voysey, Stickley would later incorporate metal trim into his own cabinet designs, Voysey pursued an aesthetic committed to simple, unornamented furniture—except for some inlaid animal silhouettes—and to a plain building style in architecture. In 1897, *House Beautiful* commented that, in his cabinetwork, Voysey "almost ignores ornament, especially of the sort that is applied so lavishly to distract attention from faulty workmanship and unsound material." Stickley returned home from his European trip with one of Voysey's rugs, which he used for display in his Marshall Field showroom in Chicago. He also bought several pieces of Voysey's furniture.[6] But he brought back something more significant: Gustav Stickley, the unknown chair manufacturer, carried the philosophy and spirit of the English Arts and Crafts Movement to the United States, shaped and ordered by his imagination and charged by his spirit. In a short time he would make the movement amazingly popular. Everything Stickley did was carefully planned and calculated: with deliberation, he launched his trip, entered his career, and set out to create his reputation.

In 1898, when he returned from Europe, Stickley had just turned forty. He had a fairly large family to support: five daughters—Barbara, Marion, Mildred,

Writing desk of fumed oak, with copper hardware
(43″ high, 36″ wide, 14″ deep). Circa 1909.

Settle of fumed oak (back: 39″ high; seat: 18″ high, 72″ long, 23″ deep). Circa 1909.

Eda Ann—and one son, Gustav, Jr. He had known hardship and had, as a boy, failed to support a family. Now he seemed determined to live in a grand style. After seeing Morris's accomplishments, he was ready to take a huge leap: "[Morris] changed the look of half the houses in London, and substituted beauty for ugliness all over the kingdom."[7] Stickley dedicated himself to accomplish for America what Morris had for England: "My enthusiasm remained with me, lapsing into a steady courage which tided me over all disappointments. I felt that I was serving the people, in company with many others in various walks of life whom I saw preaching, teaching and practising what I venture to call the gospel of simplicity."[8]

Stickley embraced the movement with religious fervor; he used words such as "preach" and "gospel" whenever he talked about the Arts and Crafts Movement. As a child, he had thought about becoming a minister—perhaps influenced by his minister uncle—and one of his daughters remembers his sitting in the living room after dinner reading from the Bible. Though he "took a couple of nips each day,"[9] throughout his life he acted like a missionary determined to save the world. Though he was not yet a successful businessman in 1898, he dressed the part: three-piece wool suit, bow tie, carefully cropped hair, gold chain draped across his vest. He continually smoked a pipe and even sported a pince-nez. As one granddaughter proudly recalls, he talked like a poet, his sentences filled with magic and metaphor, delivered with all the intensity of a Broadway actor.[10]

Stickley returned from Europe not merely filled with a desire to revolutionize the design of home furnishings, but just as important for his career, determined to revolutionize the organizations that made those products. Guilds and unions had

15

characterized artistic production in England for some time: Stickley had the model of William Morris's spiritual group, the Pre-Raphaelite Brotherhood, as well as his commercial venture, Morris, Marshall and Company. Other artists, such as Mackmurdo, had started the Century Guild in 1882, the students of Richard Norman Shaw had put together the Art Workers Guild in 1884, and C. R. Ashbee had founded his Guild of Handicraft in 1888. Even the name of the Movement itself, Arts and Crafts, coined by T. J. Cobden-Sanderson in 1888, forged a union of two separate activities. (The initial name of the Guild of Handicraft, "The Combined Arts Society," made the idea of union more apparent.)

But Stickley wanted to do it better and larger. He envisioned organizing every chair manufacturer in the United States into one grand union, which he proposed calling the United Chair Manufacturers. In statements to the Syracuse *Post-Standard* on May 14, 1899, Stickley announced that such a union, renamed the American Chair Company, would be incorporated at the staggering amount of $25 million. The company appears to have been financed by Charles Flint, whom the *National Cyclopedia of American Biography* calls the "father of trusts." One can only imagine how Stickley met Flint and then convinced him of his scheme. Perhaps they met because of mutual interests and goals. Flint had been instrumental in consolidating the streetcar railroads in Syracuse and, in fact, chaired the group. Stickley, as mentioned earlier, had run the streetcar railroad in Binghamton. Discussions went on in private.

The next thing the public knew about the project was what they read on September 16, 1899, in the Syracuse *Post-Standard*, which ran its second and final article on the idea for the American Chair Company: 90 percent of the chair manufacturers in the country had agreed to join the amalgamation. Then, suddenly, something happened. The *Post-Standard* carried not one more word of the monster merger. Apparently, the deal was off.

Stickley rebounded; he approached a New York bank to loan him money for his own business. Remarkably, the bank agreed. So in 1899 Stickley bought out his partner, Elgin A. Simonds, and formed his own business, the Gustave Stickley Company, in Eastwood, New York.[11] The firm would manufacture Stickley's unique kind of Mission furniture. Stickley once again demonstrated his ability to transform disappointment, or even failure, into success.

3

INFLUENCES

IN THE MID-NINETEENTH CENTURY, Emerson and Thoreau began planting the philosophical seeds for a return to simple living in America. That movement toward simplicity greatly influenced the decorative arts in the 1870s. In 1877, Charles Scribner's published a collection of important drawings and essays Clarence Cook had written for *Scribner's Monthly*, titled "The House Beautiful: Essays on Beds and Tables, Stools and Candlesticks."[1] Clarence Cook, a thoroughly American figure, who had written for the *New York Tribune* and had spent some time abroad as that paper's correspondent, focused his attention on the aesthetics, the theory, and the philosophy of the Pre-Raphaelites—Morris, Edward Burne-Jones, and Dante Gabriel Rossetti. From 1864 to 1892, he edited the influential *Studio* magazine, creating a bridge between the key figures in the Arts and Crafts Movement and the educated in the United States. In his insistence on simplicity and good taste, Cook prefigured the Arts and Crafts Movement in America. He summarized the growing fascination in America around the turn of the century for plain living and simplicity:

> *A change is coming over the spirit of our time, which has its origin partly, no doubt, in the memorial epoch through which we are passing, but which is also a proof that our taste is getting a root in a healthier and more native soil. All of this resuscitation of "old furniture" and revival of old simplicity . . . is in reality much more sensible than it seems to be to those who look upon it as only another phase of the "centennial" mania. It is a fashion, so far as it is a fashion, that has been for twenty years working its way down from a circle of rich cultivated people, to a wider circle of people who are educated, who have natural good taste, but who have not so much money as they could wish.*[2]

His ideas on furniture recall those of William Morris: "Let us begin with the principle, that every piece of furniture in the room must have a good and clear rea-

Left: Dining chair of fumed oak, with rush seat
(height of back from floor, 40″; height of seat from floor, 18″). Circa 1904.
Right: Desk chair of fumed oak, with leather seat (height of back from floor, 40″;
height of seat from floor, 18″). Circa 1909.

son for being there . . . nothing that cannot justify its presence by some actual service it renders to those occupants"[2]. Cook preferred furniture free of any superfluous ornamentation, recommending "the beauty of simplicity in form; the pleasures to be had from lines well thought out; the agreeableness of unbroken surfaces where there is no gain in breaking them; harmony in color"[3]. Cook pointed out that a person had trouble finding any object that did not suffer from "over-ornament." "That terrible word 'bare'," Cook said, "seems to have frightened us all, and driven us to cover the nakedness of things with whatever comes to hand. We cover our note-paper with clumsy water-marks, we put 'monograms' . . . on our bed linen, on our books and title-pages, on our carriages and silver"[2].

Cook argued for the sanctity of the fireplace, warned against the health hazards of carpeting, and stressed the utility of rush seats and the need for muted colors and decorative brads. He lamented cheap imitations and extolled the virtues of ancient craftspeople. Cook's theories about coloring wood suggest Stickley's fuming technique: ". . . a strong decoction of tobacco (which gives a good brown and brings out the grain of the wood) and then shellacing, not varnishing—NEVER USE VARNISH ON FURNITURE"[2].

Stickley's theoretical writings about decoration and furniture echo all of these ideas. In addition, Cook's furniture designs foreshadow the cabinetwork of Stickley's company, the United Crafts. Modify slightly Cook's keyed mortise and tenon joint, eliminate the wood turnings, and straighten the legs, and his "criss-cross" table comes directly out of the United Crafts catalog. His library table becomes, with slight modification, one of Stickley's trestle tables. Cook's combination writing desk and book shelf transforms into a Stickley piece when the curved lines and the scalloped gables are straightened. The brass hinges, the key plates, and the closing rings then dominate the cabinet, instead of competing with the slight carving. In other words, twenty years after Cook created his designs, Stickley gave them a slight twist and made them uniquely his own.

But Stickley did not have to read Cook to find ideas for simple living and plain furniture, for both were available in the summer cottages in the mountains of upstate New York. Only in summer cottages, *House Beautiful* maintained, could a person find "in his house furnishings, as well as in his recreation, [that] he desires whatever is conducive to strength and simplicity." The author of that article, H. Isabelle Williams, pointed out that "for many years in numerous Adirondack camps striking articles of furniture characterized by these qualities [strength and simplicity] have attracted the attention of the newcomer."[3]

Clarence Cook's criss-cross table.

A Complex Fate

Isabelle Williams was describing the furniture of Henry Swan, who began hand building furniture in the 1870s in Wadham Mills, New York. According to Margaret Edgewood, "In this country [the Arts and Crafts Movement] . . . found expression first in the furniture of the Arts and Crafts Society, later in the work of such men as Henry Swan and Charles Rohlfs."[4] Stickley clearly used Henry Swan's plain "Adirondack camp furniture" as one of the models for his early Mission designs. Swan's Great Settle reminds one of a United Crafts settle in its feeling for material and construction, if not in exact detail. Stickley adopted the technique that Swan had revived, of using "wooden pegs . . . to secure parts already carefully mortised together."[5] Swan's oak table became one of Stickley's basic dining room table designs.

Swan worked in a genre of simple, rustic-looking utilitarian furniture for mountain cabins and retreats, and in the 1890s pictures of this rustic furniture filled the pages of *House Beautiful*. "All the pieces of furniture, or nearly all, were made to occupy the various spaces in which you see them in the illustrations . . . have a half-dull finish . . . designed for everyday comfort and use."[6] That is, they were functional, simple, and finished in a modest color—just like the furniture produced by United Crafts almost a decade later.

Swan offered some of these hand-built pieces for sale to the public, but most of it he made to order. Other persons began making hand-built furniture at about the same time. The Chicago Arts and Crafts Society, for instance, offered some

Sideboard of fumed oak, with iron hardware
(38″ high, 48″ wide, 18″ deep). Circa 1909.

20

Footstool, fumed oak and leather, with iron brads
(15″ high; seat: 20″ x 16″). Circa 1909.

pieces made at Hull House for sale in June 1899. Louise C. Anderson sold her furniture through Arts and Crafts societies. Ida J. Burgess showed a Mission oak library table in her shop at the Marshall Field Building in 1899,[7] and W. F. Halstrick presented a "hand-made reproduction of an Antique Dutch chair finished in Flemish Oak, with cane or leather seats" at the turn of the century in his shop in Chicago.[8] Stickley could choose from a wide range of popularly available furniture designs when he decided to produce his own Mission furniture.

But Stickley could find other, more important, figures from whom he could borrow his designs. He of course saw an abundance of British Arts and Crafts furniture when he traveled to Europe in 1898, and knew particularly well the simple, cottage furniture produced by Morris and Company. It is certain that he read closely the *International Studio*, for he reviewed issues of it in *The Craftsman*. In America, Frank Lloyd Wright's early furniture also provided a model for anyone designing furniture—especially for Stickley. Wright had already used square, simple lines in 1893–1894 for the entry bench in the Winslow House. In 1895 he designed high-back dining chairs for his own house, using spindles to create the illusion of even greater lift. In another ten years, Stickley would incorporate those same design elements into his most elegant and most expensive furniture.

There is an even more striking example of such borrowing. A photograph from the Research Center of the Frank Lloyd Wright Home and Studio Foundation shows the dining chairs Wright designed as early as 1889 or 1890. They illustrate Wright's characteristic square shape and have very high backs and wide top rails. They appear to be built of oak. In their design and details, these chairs provided a pattern for the best of Stickley's that he introduced in 1900.

Desk chair of fumed oak, with leather cushion
(height of back from floor, 33″; height of seat from floor, 14″). Circa 1904.

These similarities between Stickley and Wright speak of something other than mere accident. Stickley chose his model well. Wright expressed a genius in all his designs; no one—especially a beginning furniture designer—could escape or ignore his commanding presence. For instance, Gustav Stickley's early Morris chairs look very similar to the fumed oak chairs Wright had designed for the B. Hardley House before 1900. David Hanks, in his superb *Decorative Designs of Frank Lloyd Wright*, points out that "Gustav Stickley's Craftsman furniture like that manufactured by his brothers and competitors L. and J. G. Stickley were appropriate choices for Wright's interiors if the client could not afford all custom-design furniture."[9] Wright recommended the brothers, but he did not recommend Gustav Stickley's furniture.

And Stickley remained strangely silent about Wright. According to John Crosby Freeman, one of Stickley's daughters, Mildred Stickley Cruess, remembers Wright's visiting Syracuse on three occasions and lecturing twice at the Craftsman Building. But Stickley advertised all the lectures given there in *The Craftsman*, and he never mentioned a lecture by Frank Lloyed Wright. Bruce Pfeiffer, director of archives at Taliesen in Arizona, reports that Wright typed all of his speeches in advance.[10] A search of documents at the Frank Lloyd Wright

Home and Studio Foundation archives in Oak Park, Illinois, as well as the archives in Arizona, revealed no speech by Wright at the Craftsman Building. He delivered most of his lectures during the United Crafts period, in fact, in the Midwest. If Wright did lecture in Syracuse, Stickley surely would have announced it, for he thrived on publicity. No record exists of Wright's ever having visited Stickley at any location, though Wright visited Elbert Hubbard, a leader in the Arts and Crafts Movement and a competitor of Stickley's, around 1903.[11] No articles by Wright ever appeared in *The Craftsman*. In spite of Freeman's claim that Stickley had "meetings and dinner parties with known associates, such as Theodore Roosevelt, Frank Lloyd Wright, and Henry Ford,"[12] *The Craftsman* never mentioned Wright's name. Stickley mentioned friends and associates in editorials and articles whenever he could. If Wright had befriended Stickley, the world would have heard about it—from Stickley himself.

Similarly, no mention of Stickley exists in any of Frank Lloyd Wright's letters. And aside from one small comment, Wright never referred to Stickley's furniture. In his autobiography, however, Wright made a crucial distinction: "Plainness was not necessarily simplicity. That was evident. Crude furniture of the Roycroft-Stickley-Mission style, which came along later, was offensively plain, plain as a barn door—but was never simple in any true sense."[13] Wright may be suggesting that Stickley, in copying his early designs, did not get it right. Wright's designs startle through their startling proportional relationships—carried out in both elongations and truncations. Behind Wright's seeming simplicity lies astounding sophistication. While Stickley designed well, he played it safe, his furniture remaining well within the parameters set by the Arts and Crafts aesthetic. Wright equated plainness with crudeness. Simplicity revealed genius.

Stickley did not invent simple furniture, but through his ingenuity he made the style popular. Stickley himself acknowledged that he "adopted" the designs of others. One thing above everything else mattered to him—getting his furniture on the market—and in that process, he borrowed bits and snatches of design elements. At the end of the century, craftspeople and designers scattered around the country had started to hand produce and sell simple furniture. They quickly turned "simplicity" into a catchword in the philosophical movements of the period. Stickley saw the possibility of bringing these various threads together in a furniture style that would have broad, commercial appeal. This style came to be popularly known as Mission furniture.

4

A MISSIONARY ZEAL

THE FIRST PIECES of Craftsman furniture were completed in 1898 and then for two years I worked steadily over the development of forms, the adjustment of proportions and the search for a finish which would protect the wood and mellow it in color without sacrificing its natural woody quality."[1] Stickley wrote those lines in the heyday of his career—1910—and he recalls a time, still partners with Elgin Simonds, when he began to evolve his own style.

Resolving to make radical changes from his earlier Chippendale furniture designs, Stickley adopted the medieval design theory that Morris had resurrected: Form must contribute to function. Ornamentation could no longer be added to a piece of furniture in order to attract the eye; ornamentation must be an integral and organic part of the desk or chair or table:

> I thus clearly recognized the dangers of applied ornament and advanced a step from which I have never retrograded. I endeavored to turn such structural devices as the mortise and tenon to ornamental use; to employ them in such a way as to force them to give accent and variety to the outlines of the objects in which they occurred.[2]

The result was straight-lined, hand-finished, well-made furniture, "constructed on primitive lines," as Stickley said, "planned for comfort, durability and beauty, and expressing the true spirit of democracy." According to Stickley's philosophy, he intended his furniture to be set in place and not moved about, so he made each piece unusually heavy. Aside from a few pieces of inlaid furniture that he manufactured for only one year in 1903, Stickley's furniture carried no trace of applied decoration. As Stickley himself said of his chair designs: "The piece is . . . first, last and all the time a chair, and not an imitation of a throne, not an exhibit of snakes and dragons in a wild riot of misapplied wood-carving."[3]

Stickley introduced his concept in furniture design in July 1900 at the Pythian Temple, in Grand Rapids, Michigan. Furniture manufacturers typically previewed their designs at the annual Grand Rapids Furniture Exposition, and Stickley first tried this standard, commercial route to gain notice. The trade publication, *American Cabinet Maker and Upholsterer,* announced Stickley's arrival:

> *The Gustave Stickley Company will show a beautiful line of diners and rockers at Grand Rapids. They will be represented by Lee Stickley. . . . Mr. Gustave Stickley has devoted much of his time to the new finish in wax called Austrian Oak, and has succeeded in turning out some handsome designs that cannot fail to impress the buyers of fine goods favorably. The line will contain a variety of novelties, some finished in an exquisite shade of green, greatly resembling gun metal.*[4]

Margaret Edgewood, an authority on European and American furniture trends and styles, favorably reviewed Stickley's first showing, in *House Beautiful.* She expressed delight with Stickley's work: "This furniture comes at an opportune time. The day of cheap veneer, of jig-saw ornament, of poor imitations of French periods, is happily over"; this "sensible furniture," as she called it, ushered in a "new era in furniture-making . . . marked by the endeavor to place honest workmanship within reach of the masses."[5] Though the article did not mention Stickley's name, it featured five of his new designs. Edgewood compared his Poppy table and Celandine tabourette with those inspired by Charles Rennie Mackintosh and the Glasgow School. But in particular she favored the heavier, "severely plain" designs that smacked of a "medieval quality." The furniture trade, however, with its less sophisticated outlook and commercial interests, did not immediately take to Stickley's new furniture. An anonymous writer in *The Craftsman* in 1902 recalled that Stickley's early work "produced dismay among the furniture dealers, when it was first shown at the annual exposition two years ago."[6] The *Grand Rapids Furniture Record* hinted at the reluctance of furniture dealers to accept Stickley's strange designs:

> *The furniture merchant must give more attention to the intelligent presentation of new goods and styles in his community. We all recall when the so-called "Mission" style was brought out. It received scant attention and recognition from the furniture buyers and merchants, and had it not been for the general publicity to the consumer of this style by a few manufacturers, the style would never have been perpetrated. It is in spite of, rather than through the furniture dealers as a whole, that any kind of furniture, or new style or new finish or new wood, is popularized.*[7]

But one dealer, the Tobey Furniture Company of Chicago, did take notice. Tobey took out a series of ads in October of 1900 in Chicago newspapers introducing "The New Furniture." The ads show six or seven of Stickley's designs—transitional pieces, really, between Art Nouveau and Arts and Crafts—but the ads never mention Stickley by name. The December 1900 issue of *House Beautiful* also carried Stickley's designs in its Tobey advertisement. Again, Stickley went unmentioned.

If Tobey had agreed to distribute Stickley's furniture, the association did not last long. How could it? Such a silent arrangement could not gratify a person with Stickley's ego. His affiliation with Tobey could not have lasted more than a couple of months at most. For on December 22, 1900, *American Cabinet Maker and Upholsterer* announced that Stickley had rented a well-known stable, called the Crouse Stables, to use as a showroom and office space. He renamed it the Craftsman Building. Not in the least pedestrian, the stables had a size and a design that made them resemble some grand mansion in size and style, and that suited Stickley fine:

> The Crouse Stables, located at 207 South State Street in Syracuse, had been built in 1887–88 to the design of Archimedes Russell, a noted local architect, for D. Edgar

Armchair of fumed oak, with leather seat and iron brads
(37″ high, 20″ wide, 19″ deep). Circa 1902–1903.

Crouse, a wealthy man about town. The $200,000 Queen Anne structure contained elegant bachelor quarters decorated by Herter Brothers of New York for the owner and brass-trimmed porcelain feed bowls for the horses. The prominent location of the Crouse Stables, facing Fayette Park along with expensive houses owned by the upper crust of Syracuse, made the picturesquely asymmetrical stables an important local building.[8]

The Crouse Stables provided a base, a foundation for Stickley's furniture manufacturing. He no longer had to answer to a partner, or any retailer. He needed only to figure out a way to advertise and distribute his furniture himself. He would do just that, shortly, and he would do it by becoming an amalgamation unto himself. That is, he would move to a solid independence.

Unlike his father, Stickley handled criticism well: he either ignored it completely or turned it to his own advantage. In either case, he did not let it destroy him. In response to the poor reception from the furniture trade, he decided to seek acceptance and recognition through less traditional means, by advertising in his own magazine, which he founded in 1901.[9] He also dreamed up another idea: a cooperative exhibit with the Grueby Faience Company of Boston. Grueby pottery, probably the finest U.S. pottery of the period, first showed its art pottery at the Boston Arts and Crafts Society Exhibition in 1897, and "from this introduction, recognition of the artistic merit of the pottery was immediate at home and abroad."[10] In 1900, Grueby showed 100 pieces of art pottery at the Paris Exposition and won two gold medals and one silver. Early in 1901 the company won another gold medal in St. Petersburg, Russia. People paid high prices for Grueby's pottery; some large decorated pieces cost as much as $50 in 1900 (the equivalent of about $600 today). In March 1901, Stickley arranged to show several rooms of his furniture in a cooperative exhibit with Grueby at the prestigious Pan American International Exposition in Buffalo, New York. By arranging this joint exhibit, Stickley not only guaranteed himself an audience, but also associated his furniture with the leading art pottery of the day. Stickley chose well: the quality of his furniture was every bit as high as that of Grueby art pottery, and the exhibit put Stickley's cabinetwork in the category of art furniture. The public responded favorably. By the beginning of the following year, 1902, Stickley could boast of what he called "warerooms"—independent display areas—in forty-one stores in as many cities across the country.

Perhaps prompted by his cooperative venture with Grueby, and remembering the model Morris had presented for a cooperative of artisans, Stickley put into practice his own version of the medieval, profit-sharing guild, which he called the United Crafts, determined "to substitute the luxury of taste for the luxury of costliness; to teach that beauty does not imply elaboration or ornament; to employ only those forms and materials which make for simplicity, individuality, and dignity of effect."[11] In addition, Stickley promised his workmen conditions that would make them neither "over-wearisome nor over-anxious."

The idea even caught the attention of the local newspaper, the *Post-Standard*, which ran a piece on September 15, 1901, describing Stickley's aim as "the raising of the general intelligence of the worker, by the increase of his leisure and the multiplication of his means of pleasure and culture, the endeavor to substitute the luxury of taste for the luxury of costliness, and to do something along the Morris idea that all men shall have work to do which shall be worth doing, and be pleased to do it." The newspaper ran another story on January 2, 1902, designed, it seems, to dismiss those skeptical of Stickley's profit-sharing plan. The newspaper reported on the dramatic and quirky way—I can find no accounting for the exact amounts of individual payments—Stickley involved his workers in his profit-sharing: On New Year's Day, 1902, Stickley gathered everyone together in the Crouse Stables—that is, the Craftsman Building—and distributed $2,000 in gold coins, like Father Christmas, to each and every one of them. No pay envelope, no checks, no posting of payments. Stickley, the consummate showman, chose to hand out bright gold coins!

The United Crafts operation lasted from 1901 to 1904, at which time Stickley changed the name of his business once again, to the Craftsman Workshops. The

Server of fumed oak, with copper hardware (38″ high, 24″ wide, 17½″ deep).
Circa 1905–1907.

Sewing table of fumed oak, with copper hardware; top drawer fitted with cedar tray
(28″ high; top closed: 18″ square; top open: 38″ x 18″). Circa 1912.

guild, and profit-sharing along with it, no longer interested him. His business was much too successful now. As if to mark this new phase of his business life, Stickley also changed the spelling of his name to Gustav. He had shaped his career and called into being a new man—a self-made one at that: Gustav Stickley. His career became a constant struggle to keep that new creation continually new. It required a total attention to innovation, to whatever would pass as new and modern, as liberating and avant-garde. It also required continual growth, fueled by more and more capital.

Stickley wanted designs that would be recognizably American. He chose the name "United Crafts," perhaps, in this regard, to echo the phrase "the United States." Through new furniture designs, Stickley clearly signaled his revolt against America's shoddy, hastily produced, European imitations. He compared contemporary furnishings to the royal appointments of seventeenth- and eighteenth-century courts. He described such furniture in the strongest terms: "Shapes of exaggerated slenderness; sofas and chairs adapted from the furnishings of palaces; stuffs more or less cheaply reproducing, by means of machine processes and commercial dyes, the fabrics once designed and woven by artist-workmen for the delight of a parasitic class: these are the objects which make their foreign, intrusive presence felt today in a large proportion of American middle-class homes."[12] All his life, Stickley railed against elaborate American imitations of foreign furniture, arguing that when designers properly integrated form with function, Americans would find the furniture familiar and hence comfortable. For Stickley, functional furniture, freed of ornament and gee-gaw, could be described in no other word but *simple*.

Simplicity alone, Stickley argued, would free American furniture from dependence on foreign designs. Through the ideal of simplicity, Stickley believed, he could design furniture in the "form which would naturally suggest itself to the workman," thereby eliminating what he called "styles" and achieving instead "style," or the incorporation of the "structural element" into the object itself. For Stickley, styles meant novelty and restriction, a wrong-headed desire to evoke the past. An adherence to simplicity, on the other hand, "denotes the growth of the aesthetic faculty."

This structural style was not original to Stickley. Horatio Greenough argued it in the nineteenth century, Frank Lloyd Wright in the early part of the twentieth. But Stickley's prose made every idea sound as if he had just invented it. So, for

Magazine stand of fumed oak (42″ high, 22″ wide, 13″ deep). Circa 1909.

Library table of fumed oak, with iron hardware
(30″ high, 20″ wide, 30″ long). Circa 1912.

example, for Stickley the structural style would signal the arrival of "an organic period," a time when America's leaders in government and science will be working "not for effect, or . . . toward pre-arranged definite, and limited results. But rather, the politician, the scientist, the designer, must truly represent the force of the period, its creations like those of nature itself."[13] The idea of designs modeled on nature's principles of organic growth was also obviously not Stickley's. In the nineteenth century, Morris argued for organic designs, and so did others; for instance, Christopher Dresser in England described in a number of books the application of natural law to structural design. In this country, once more we need look no further than Frank Lloyd Wright, whose organic designs pulled together aesthetic theories from artists such as Dresser, Owen Jones, and Viollet-le-Duc. The object of the structural style for Stickley was to create furniture that expressed its function frankly and in the materials properly suited for that expression. So, the designer did not begin the task by searching out historical models, for only when a piece of furniture was honestly bound to its prescribed task could beauty result.

Stickley translated such philosophical concerns into practical guidelines for effectively working in wood. First, the structural lines of the cabinet must be proudly displayed, for "such lines in cabinet-making declare the purpose and use of the object which they form." And it was the lines, expressed through the joinery and in other details of construction, which provided decoration. Second,

Stickley's cabinetmakers exploited the grain of wood to accentuate the conformation of the cabinet and to emphasize its vertical and horizontal lines.

Stickley began formulating his ideals and goals—both political and aesthetic—for the United Crafts while he was producing the furniture. Each month a new idea would appear in his magazine, or a modification of an old one, a borrowing from William Morris, an inspiration from Ruskin. In December 1901, Stickley reflected on the United Crafts, summarizing its spirit:

> *The United Crafts in their work for the betterment of household art, place before their associates and workmen a constantly ascending ideal. They do this in the belief that a generous dissatisfaction in the present invariably assures success in the future. They foster, in every way possible, the enthusiasm of the craftsman, in order that the work of his brain and hands may bear the mark of his personality, and that the man*

Clothes press of fumed oak, copper and glass. Circa 1906.

himself may never degenerate into the tool, or machine. Individualism is the watch-word of the new century. Originality is perceived and appreciated by the people to a degree never before reached. Art, which must express the thought and follow the im-pulse of the times, is casting off the slavery of the imitation, and the crafts, those "lesser arts of life," respond to the intellectual movement by producing objects of ev-eryday utility which frankly state their purpose, and do not falsify themselves by sug-gestions of customs long since obsolete.[14]

Strangely enough, these philosophical statements seem to have helped Stickley's sales. They certainly didn't hurt. Stickley's first year in business was a significant one. For example, he quickly and broadly expanded operations at United Crafts. The loose association of cabinetmakers, metalworkers, and leather workers that he formed in 1901 had expanded by July 1902 into these specialties: cabinet and clock makers, leather dressers, workers in metal, designers and mak-ers of apparatus for electric and other lighting systems, bookbinders, printers, and publishers of his magazine, *The Craftsman*. By this time readers could also write to the factory at Eastwood, New York, for information, designs, or catalogs. The successful pattern for the remainder of his career was established with United Crafts: to add new furniture to his catalogs, new departments to his magazine, and new specialties to his factories. For instance, beginning in October 1902, so as to significantly mark the first birthday of *The Craftsman*, Stickley enlarged the size of his magazine: pages became larger, issues longer, "which will permit," he said, "the addition of several new departments necessary to the function of a complete organ and exponent of the arts and crafts making for the ennobling, the comfort, and the pleasure of life." But the crowning achievement was unwrapped at the end of the year, his Christmas present to his workers: in December 1902 he opened the United Crafts Hall in the Crouse Stables.

The Hall, which could hold several hundred people, would be a place for Stickley's workers to hear musical concerts, listen to important lectures on the arts and crafts, or merely hold an occasional party. Stickley intended the Hall to be a working example of his Arts and Crafts philosophy. Surrounded by beauty and quality, people's ideas would be lifted, their lives ennobled, and their religious convictions affirmed. From the description in *The Craftsman*, one has difficulty telling whether the Hall was in fact a delight to be in, or if Stickley's words were so carefully and deliberately chosen as to make us believe it was:

Its effect is roomy and inviting: an effect in part due to a grave harmony of color and to the low ceiling which apparently increases the area. The ceiling shows open timbers and is supported by squared pillars of fine-fibred brown oak in natural finish. These pillars are clasped at three-fourths their height by wrought iron bands from which spring brackets carrying electric lanterns. At one end of the hall rises a low stage, ele-vated two steps above the floor; and again, at the back of the stage, appears a tall chim-ney-piece with a deeply-overhanging hood. On either side is a window glazed with small diamond-shaped panes, the central one of which bears the device of the United Crafts: a joiner's compass accompanied by the legend in Dutch, Als ik kan (If I Can). The windows are provided with cushioned seats and the stage is further furnished with movable settles, tables bearing lamps in Grueby faience, and a fine grand piano. The side walls of the auditorium are wainscoted in a wood finished like the pillars, and are hung with burlaps of a soft, deep green, which forms an admirable background for sketches and photographs, large collections of which are left for long periods to the United Crafts by the Scribner and Century Companies. The wall opposite the stage is pierced by a series of windows, also with cushioned seats, and the floor-space is occupied, not crowded, by the simple, hospitable settles and chairs made in the workshops of the organization.[15]

On December 1, 1902, Stickley staged the first lecture in the Hall: Germaine Martin gave a talk, "The Gothic Churches of France." More events quickly followed. Stickley loved music, particularly opera, and thought his workers should too. So on December 13, he invited all of his workers and their families to a musical recital performed by the Mandolin Club of Syracuse University. Clearly, Stickley saw himself as more than a businessman; he also saw himself as an educator. His subject was the Arts and Crafts Movement. This new furniture, philosophy, and lifestyle—this revolution—might be difficult for some people to accept, but Stickley patiently educated them.

However, immediate success weakened Stickley's revolutionary ardor. His reformist rhetoric gave way to the practicality of commercial solutions. A true revolutionary would have been pleased that his designs were being reproduced and made widely available. But Stickley became terribly concerned about other manufacturers copying his designs. He appended this note to his 1902 United Crafts catalog: "Owing to the fact that household furnishings purporting to be made by the United Crafts have been offered for sale in various places throughout the country, it seemed advisable to adopt a trademark by which our productions may be identified." Stickley already had a trademark, the motto *Als Ik Kan*, "If I Can," which he borrowed from the painter Jan van Eyck. *Als Ik Kan* was also a version of William Morris's *Si Je Puis*, who, in turn, had borrowed it from Sarah Bernhardt. And from the moment Stickley produced his first piece of furniture, he stamped that motto in Dutch indelibly in bright, obtrusive red ink within a joiner's compass on every piece. Imitators seemed to worry Stickley from the outset.

Stickley skillfully explained various aspects of his motto, *Als Ik Kan*, every month in the first ten issues of *The Craftsman*. Stickley craved power and pursued it all his working life. He asked his readers to give themselves over to him, to rely on him, for he not only knew what was best, but he could accomplish it as well. He possessed the power. He alluded at times to the medieval definition of *craft*: strength and power. And he arrived at the same meanings for the word *can*. Here is Stickley in June 1902:

Liquor cabinet of fumed oak, with iron hardware; top surface copper lined
(closed: 36″ high; open: 40″ high. 24″ wide, 17½″ deep). Circa 1907.

Als Ik Kan. If I Can. If we look in the dictionary at can *we find it derived from the Old English* cunnen, *to know, to know how, to be able. We can trace the family resemblance to the Anglo-Saxon* cunnan, *the Danish* kunnen, *Icelandic* kunna, *German* konnen, *Gothic* kunnan, *and English* ken, *to know.*

    From the Anglo-Saxon cunnan *came our word* cunning, *now used in an ignoble sense, but whose original meaning was knowing, skillful. In Exodus we read of one of the tribe of Dan, "an engraver and a cunning workman." It is curious and interesting to notice the fact that everywhere the word seems to carry the double meaning of knowledge and power. This voices a universal instinct. He who knows, can. Carlyle says in* Hero Worship *"King is kon ning, kan ning, man that knows or cans." But we say "We are tired of kings, we suffer them no more." We shall say it no longer if our eyes are opened and we see the true kings, men who know the best and can do it.*

    "If I Can"—deliver lectures, write articles, educate boys, publish a magazine, manufacture household furnishings, build houses—then I know, and hence I am powerful. Stickley's shop mark designated him as king.

    Medieval craftsmen adopted shop marks as a way of setting one guild apart from another. For Stickley, the mark served as a kind of spiritual stigma, and the United Crafts a religious enclave:

A MISSIONARY ZEAL

All strongly banded associations jealously guard some visible sign which may keep the principles for which they stand ever before them; while, at the same time, the sign, by its mystery, serves to awaken the interest of those outside the body.[16]

Stickley also signed his last name across the bottom of the joiner's compass. Later, he used decals and, for a time, he burned his logo into the wood. Some pieces even carried a paper label, pasted on the bottom of chair seats; on the undersides of tables, the backs of bookcases, and so on. His red trademark and signature can be found in the drawers of desks and tables, on the rear stretchers of chair legs, the backs of cabinets, the bottoms of umbrella stands, the undersides of tables. He also added his signature to most of his metal work. As if all these marks of identification were not sufficient, Stickley added one more, in the 1912 catalog: "A further mark of identification is THE CRAFTSMAN LEATHER TAG attached by raffia to every piece." He made it near impossible to mistake a piece of Gustav Stickley furniture.

Stickley's attention to identifying marks does seem excessive. But he was angry at his imitators, principally at his two brothers, Leopold and Julius George, who, other than Gustav, were the most well known of the Stickleys. In 1900, recognizing the sales potential of Gustav's new furniture, Leopold and Julius George left their brother for Fayetteville, New York, to manufacture their own furniture. Two years later, on September 8, 1902, Leopold wrote to the Gustave Stickley Company on his company letterhead, which read *The Onandaga Cabinet Shops, L. and J. G. Stickley, Fayetteville, New York:* "Please accept my resignation as a stockholder in 'The Gustave Stickley Co.,' to take effect at once. Kindly acknowledge and oblige. Yours truly, Leopold Stickley."[16] Perhaps Leopold remained a stockholder in his older brother's company from 1900 to 1902 in order to receive the dividends, for he needed to finance his own company. In 1902, however, Leopold's resignation became a necessity, for at about that time the firm name became L. and J. G. Stickley, and the two brothers started to produce copies of Gustav's furniture. They signed their furniture "L. and J. G. Stickley," and used the trade name "Handcraft," echoing Gustav's word "Craftsman." They also made a deliberate graphic connection with their older brother's furniture by printing the word *Handcraft* in red across a red carpenter's clamp, which resembled Gustav Stickley's red joiner's compass. (Sometimes they signed their furniture "The Work of L. and J. G. Stickley," or tacked a brass identification plate to the piece.) They used decals, like Gustav, and sometimes they, too, branded their logo into the wood. L. and J. G. Stickley's workmanship, their choice of woods, details, and care of construction in the majority of pieces were inferior to Gustav's. Their best pieces, however, were every bit as well produced as Gustav's. But his brothers had clearly stolen their designs from the furniture produced by Gustav at the United Crafts.

A COMPLEX FATE

As Gustav Stickley began to establish a solid connection between the name "Stickley" and quality furniture, his other brothers, besides Leopold and Julius George, capitalized on that connection. George and Albert manufactured copies of Gustav's Mission designs in Grand Rapids, after 1901, under the names Stickley Brothers and Quaint Furniture. They were not as well known, however, as L. and J. G., and their furniture was somewhat inferior to that of L. and J. G. Generally, their furniture is heavier and clumsier than Gustav's and shows little restraint: metalwork is ornate and machine made, chairs and cabinets insinuate with oversize proportions and inappropriate cutout designs. Charles Stickley, who started his business with Schuyler Brandt, manufactured Mission furniture and at times produced a few handsome pieces—some very large, regal arm chairs with spindle backs and sides; massive sideboards with large metal strapping. But generally Charles Stickley's furniture, comprised mainly of rockers and side chairs, cannot stand up to the quality of his older brother's. He usually burned his signature into the wood. He was not a leader in furniture design, and perhaps Gustav remained friends with him his entire life, for he did not present a threat to Gustav Stickley's career.

Leopold and Julius George's success, however, dogged Stickley's career, and he answered back by calling them "unscrupulous imitators of Craftsman literature in style and form."[18] Much later, when Stickley's furniture became more popular and hence more imitated, he wrote:

> From its success in 1900, the popularity achieved by Craftsman furniture was the signal to an army of imitators who saw in it what they considered a money-maker. These manufacturers at once began to turn out large quantities of furniture which was designed in what seemed to them the same style. . . . This imitation has grown instead of decreased with the passage of time. . . . Restrained by law from the use of my registered name, Craftsman, these manufacturers get as near to it as they can and variously style their products "Mission," "HandCraft," "Arts and Crafts," "Crafts-Style," "Roy-croft," and "Quaint." To add to the confusion, some of some of the most persistent of these imitators bear the same name as myself and what is called "Stickley furniture" is frequently, through misrepresentation on the part of the salesmen and others, sold as "Craftsman furniture or just the same thing."[19]

Besides adopting a trade name, using a shop mark, and signing his name on the furniture, Stickley also obtained patents for some of his furniture designs. For him, the United States Patent Office granted authority and, hence, power. He used that office very early to protect himself from his brothers. And though he proposed no mechanical innovations, by September 1901 he received patents for three designs: a Morris chair body, a library table, and a round table. He also registered his shop mark and the word *Craftsman* with the Patent Office. Thus, he said, "authenticity is assured, comparisons of progress are made possible, and every fidelity of information is afforded the one who shall acquire the piece."

Stickley's obsession with "authenticity" suddenly placed the design of chairs and tables in the category of inventions. Morris chairs had been around since the nineteenth century, though no one had received a patent for one. Stickley took the time and trouble to apply. Apparently, it was important to establish himself as the original, or the innovator, the one who did it first and best.

Stickley's desire to see himself as an inventor was appropriate for the period. From 1858, the year of Stickley's birth, to 1900, the year he showed his furniture, patents were issued for the electric light, sewing machine, phonograph, steam engine, internal combustion engine, electric engine, telegraph, telephone, typewriter, linotype, and trans-Atlantic cable. An invention was almost a necessity for one to be recognized in the twentieth century.

And Gustav Stickley got what he had worked for: recognition. By 1903 he had established his United Crafts so solidly that he had already staged two design competitions, the first in October 1902 and the second in December of the same year. The United Crafts Design Competition, Number One, called for a design for a library, sufficiently detailed to indicate door and window openings, together with bookcases, tables, and desks. In *The Craftsman* (vol. 3, no. 1, p. vi), Stickley announced:

> *While the editors have no desire of imposing any limit as to style or period, or to hamper the competitors in any way by the making of suggestions, they nevertheless wish it clearly understood that serious attention will be given to the type of work advocated by The United Crafts in the pages of this magazine, as well as the examples appearing in the various European papers which are published under the auspices of exponents of the Arts and Crafts Movement.*

Third prize was $25, second prize $50, and first prize $100.

The United Crafts Design Competition, Number Two, offered the same prizes for designs for the decorative treatment of the mural panel in the United Crafts lecture hall. Stickley suggested as subjects for his competition incidents from the lives of the great medieval craftsmen of France, Germany, or the Low Countries, or scenes from William Morris's life or from the lives of his followers. *The Craftsman* never announced the winner for either competition, and the magazine dropped the idea. The scheme, perhaps, did not draw enough entrants; Stickley needed something that would attract more publicity.

In January 1903, Stickley again visited with Arts and Crafts manufacturers in England and Europe, this time to get ideas for an Arts and Crafts exhibition in America to be sponsored by the United Crafts. He spent a good deal of time with Barry Parker, who remained his friend throughout his life, and who wrote on architectural design for *The Craftsman* for more than ten years. He also met with Voysey once again. Clearly, architecture attracted Stickley, and he took time to compare the two men:

He [Voysey] differs from Mr. Parker in that the latter seeks in all the furniture and interiors which he plans to express the ideas and tastes of the owners, while Mr. Voysey is more apt to express his own highly cultured and original ideas, both as an artist and artisan. He has, in fact, accomplished a style of his own in England. . . . Being first of all an architect, Mr. Voysey is naturally a designer of practical furniture.[20]

Stickley desperately wanted to emulate Voysey's "highly cultured and original ideas," but was torn all his life by what would prove commercially successful. The United Crafts Exhibition reflects those conflicting demands on Stickley.

On his return from Europe, Stickley proudly announced the Arts and Crafts Exhibition to be held March 23 to April 4, 1903, under the auspices of the United Crafts, at the United Crafts Building in Syracuse, New York: "It will be the first exhibition of the kind ever held in Central New York. The enterprise is attracting wide attention . . . the exhibits will be classified under the divisions of ceramics, glass, metal work, leather work, textiles, photographs, book-binding, and printing."[21] From Syracuse it would travel to Rochester. Operations such as Hull House, the Kalo Metal Shop (Chicago), Grueby Pottery, Rookwood Pottery Studios (Ohio), Newcomb College Pottery (New Orleans), Merrimac Pottery (Massa-

Three-door bookcase of fumed oak, with copper hardware
(55″ high, 72″ wide, 12½″ deep). Circa 1901.

chusetts), Volkmar Pottery (New York), the Busck Metal Shops (New York), and Robert Jarvie, a metalsmith (Chicago) were all represented. In addition, Stickley brought back from his trip examples of European Arts and Crafts furniture and metalwork from France and England to show at the Exhibition.[22] He featured pieces of Voysey's furniture in the Exhibition, and showed one of them, an inlaid cabinet, in *The Craftsman*. The cabinet, made of white holly, was finished with a surface polish so fine, evidently, that it resembled enamel. Stickley held it up as a wonderful example of design and workmanship. The exhibit not only contained samples of fine artwork, but featured artists, scholars, and craftsmen, who delivered papers. Stickley's Arts and Crafts Exhibition represented the most extensive display of the Movement ever presented in America. The foreword to the catalog reads like a manifesto for the Arts and Crafts Movement in its formative years:

> *The Arts and Crafts Exhibition opening under the auspices of the United Crafts is an effort to further the interests, artistic, economic and social, of the section in which it is held. The excellent results obtained by similar means in certain of the Eastern and Western States suggested to the projectors of the present Exhibition the rich possibilities of profit and pleasure which might accrue to our community through the assemblage of things wrought by the human hand as expressive of modern ideals of form, color and style. They have therefore sought to illustrate the new movement in the lesser arts; to show the progress which has been made, within a short period, toward the most desirable union in one person of the artist and workman: a result reached in the Middle Ages (when art and work were forms of religion), then lost for centuries, and now, apparently soon to be re-established.*
>
> *In each of the various classes of exhibits, it is encouraging to note the skill and the talent displayed by American workmen: faculties which, until recently, were believed to be the prerogatives of foreign craftsmen, who had in their favor tradition, heredity and environment. But a visit to the galleries of this Arts and Crafts Exhibition will prove to the observer that the American is possessed of a color-sense rivaling that of the French and the Japanese; a respect for form that rejects the fantastic; an originality and adaptability that are peculiar to him alone among modern workers.*
>
> *The principles of the new art that is developing among us will be recognized as prophetic of a long and vigorous existence. They are, briefly stated: the prominence of the structural idea . . . second, the absence of applied ornament . . . third is the strict fitting of all work to the medium in which it is executed; the development of all possibilities of color, texture, and substance. . . .*
>
> *Classes of objects having been selected and approved according to the law set by the prototype of craftsman, William Morris, who counseled wisely: "Have nothing in your houses which you do not know to be useful, or believe to be beautiful."*
>
> *The impulse thus begun toward the luxury of taste as distinguished from the luxury of costliness, will doubtless advance beyond our conceptions of today, creating sound economic and social conditions, leaving in its name — "THE HANDICRAFT MOVEMENT" — the power of the most delicate, obedient and effective instrument ever created.*[23]

Library table of fumed oak (29" high, 30" wide, 48" long). Circa 1909.

The Exhibition represents not only a significant and singular presentation of the Arts and Crafts Movement in America, but stands also as a tribute to the persuasive skill of Gustav Stickley. Stickley, after only three short years in business, had brought together artists and craftsmen from across the country. He was able to accomplish this in part because he could promise them publicity through his own magazine and, in a real sense, ensure the success of the Exhibition while encouraging the careers of the exhibitors. In the process, of course, he was subtly declaring himself the éminence grise of the Movement, the figure around whom people were eager to congregate. No one remembered that three years earlier Stickley had little knowledge of furniture design and knew nothing about publishing. Here was yet another example of Stickley ingeniously using alternative routes for advertising his home furnishings. The cooperative exhibit that he had arranged with Grueby Faience in 1901 he had now promoted into something much grander. But the Exhibition was not wholly self-serving: it showed that cooperative effort on a grand scale could be accomplished in the arts, and it demonstrated the variety of artistic work being produced in various parts of the country. Most important, if anyone doubted, Gustav Stickley had established himself, not only as the major force behind the Arts and Crafts Movement in America. He had done something more remarkable: with the help of one or two others, he had called the

42

American Arts and Crafts Movement into being. And for more than a decade, he would determine its direction.

In terms of sheer sales, Mission furniture was surely one of the most popular styles of furniture ever produced in the United States. Besides Gustav himself, his five brothers also manufactured Mission furniture. Other companies knocked off Stickley designs and produced cheaper models. Sears, Roebuck and Company eventually manufactured a complete line priced for the working person. People built the furniture themselves from *Popular Mechanics* plans; students constructed pieces in manual arts classes.

Throughout the years, though, Gustav Stickley's designs remained in the category of elegant and refined furniture. Crafted with such great care, most of his furniture could be afforded only by the wealthy. Mission furniture could thus be found in a wide range of settings, from small pieces in a simple farmhouse in Des Moines, Iowa, to grander pieces in the governor's mansion in Kennebunk, Maine. A good number of country inns, restaurants, and colleges also decorated with Mission furniture. And while the furniture was familiar to many Americans, the origin of the name "Mission" remained unknown. In fact, its exotic, mysterious origin helped to keep sales lively.

Sears, Roebuck and Company had no doubt about the source of the name. Its 1908 catalog stated, "Mission derived its name from original pieces found in an

Sidebard of fumed oak, with copper hardware (42″ high, 54″ wide, 22″ deep). Circa 1904.

old Spanish Mission in Southern California." But not everyone bought that story. A guild of furniture manufacturers in Grand Rapids, Michigan, offered a different account of the furniture's lineage, one that surrounded the old oak with even more mystery and antiquity:

> *Mission is really rather a type than a style. Its origins, as the name implies, is the early Spanish California Missions of the Jesuits. An old chair and settee from an ancient house secured by a collector of odd and antique furniture furnished the inspiration for the American adaptation of the style.*[24]

The guild never named the ancient house, nor the collector.

George Wharton James, writing in 1905, had already taken issue with those who thought Mission furniture derived from the Missions of California:

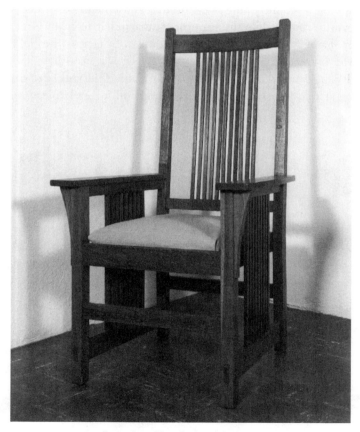

Spindle armchair of fumed oak, with leather cushion
(48½" high, 27½" wide, 20½" deep). Circa 1905.

Within the past few years, the term "Mission Furniture" has become current. But it has been accepted too freely, and without having been subjected to proper investigation. If by the use of that name the idea is conveyed that it is modeled after the furniture made and used in the old California Missions it is clearly unjustified, since the Spanish fathers who established the California Missions failed to create a style of furniture as distinctive as their architects.[25]

Thomas Pelzel, an art historian, believes that *Mission* meant purpose; here was furniture designed primarily to be used.[26] Stickley himself offered a more commercial and what turns out to be a more historically accurate explanation of the origins of Mission furniture:

A number of years ago a manufacturer made two very clumsy chairs, the legs of which were merely three-inch posts, the backs straight, and the whole construction crude to a degree. They were shown at a spring exposition of furniture, where they attracted a good deal of attention as a novelty. It was just at this time that the California Missions were exciting much attention, and a clever Chicago dealer, seeing the advertising value that lay in the idea, bought both pieces and advertised them as having been found in the California Missions.

Another dealer, who possesses a genius for inventing or choosing exactly the right name for a thing, saw these chairs and was inspired with the idea that it would be a good thing to make a small line of this furniture and name it "Mission" furniture. The illusion was carried out by the fact that he put a Maltese Cross wherever it would go, between the rails of the back and down at the sides; in fact, it was woven into the construction so that it was the prominent feature and naturally increased the belief in the ecclesiastical origin of the chair. The mingling of novelty and romance instantly pleased the public, and the vogue of "Mission" furniture was assured.[27]

Stickley's account can be documented. In fact, contemporary magazines filled in the details. The March 1915 issue of *Good Furniture*, for instance, named the designer:

The idea for the style of furniture was suggested to Joseph P. McHugh by a single chair, sent from California to New York in 1894. This chair had been designed by a California architect for a small Mission church, and its character was inspired by the sturdy and simple style of the early Spanish missions. Its quaint outline and interesting honest and primitive construction indicated the possibility of a complete scheme of sturdy, handmade furniture.

Mr. McHugh, aided by the exceptionally able and ingenious designer, developed, from the first original chair, over a hundred varied pieces, covering every kind of furniture commonly in use. The designer, Walter J. H. Dudley, was gifted with technical skill amounting to genius, and this, combined with his unusual artistic appreciation, made acceptable and usable forms from the necessarily crude prototype without losing any of the strength of the original idea.[28]

Dinner gong of fumed oak, with hammered copper striking plate
(37″ high, 24″ wide; gong: 18″ diameter). Circa 1901.

Left: coal bucket of hammered copper (16″ high, and 11½″ diameter at base);
right: umbrella stand of hammered copper (24″ high, and 12″ diameter at top).
Both circa 1905.

More than fifty years after this article, Robert Judson Clark, an art historian from Princeton University who launched the first significant exhibition of Arts and Crafts material in the United States, uncovered more details about the passage of this new Mission design from coast to coast. That journey back and forth across the country may in part account for the enormous popularity of Mission furniture. The furniture designs themselves provided for a unique aesthetic conversation:

> *A chair of native ash with two horizontal slats between bulky posts, a duplicate of those made in the mid-1890s for the rustic sanctuary of the Swedenborgian Church in San Francisco, was sent to Joseph P. McHugh in New York, who began to produce a line of furniture based on this prototype. The San Francisco building, erected in 1894, had been inspired by an Italian country church; but it was often referred to as a "mission church in California," and the suggested reference of Franciscan fathers making the benches for their adobe missions made McHugh's sales brisk. Thus his production came to be known as "mission furniture," as did the work of countless followers, including Stickley, in the next decade.[29]*

Five McHugh chair designs were shown in the 1900 issue of the *Ladies Home Journal*, and by 1904 Joseph McHugh and Company was selling furniture in what it called the McHugh-Mission style.

The other dealer Stickley mentioned, who placed a "Maltese cross wherever it would go," probably referred to Elbert Hubbard. Hubbard had been a highly successful salesman and later a junior partner in his brother-in-law's soap business, the J. D. Larkin Soap Company, in Buffalo, New York. He gave it all up in 1893. Around 1894 Hubbard, or "the Fra," as he liked to be called, began printing little books in East Aurora, New York, and he soon expanded his printing business to include leather working and bookbinding. A consummate entrepreneur, he quickly saw the commercial possibilities of Mission furniture. Sometime around 1896, Hubbard began making furniture modeled on Mission designs.

He called his community of artists and craftspeople the Roycrofters, a word derived, Hubbard loved to announce, from *roi croft*, "royal craftsman" or the "king's craftsman." (The name also referred, to those in the know, to two English brothers, Samuel and Thomas Roycroft, who printed and produced books in the seventeenth century.) Hubbard's mark was not a Maltese cross, as Stickley indicated, but an orb and cross surrounding a capital *R*, which Hubbard burned into every piece of his furniture. Stickley probably called Hubbard's shop mark a Maltese cross to be flip: the two men had egos much too large to allow them to be friends. Hubbard demanded in his catalog that his furniture not be called "Mission," because "ours is Roycroft—made by us according to our idea." And so, Hubbard suggested to his customers, proudly give this response to anyone who asks: "My house is furnished in Roycroftie."

A COMPLEX FATE

Stickley, too, continually took care to clearly and deliberately dissociate his furniture from "so-called Dutch, Tyrolean peasant, and Mission styles." For Stickley, Mission furniture represented crude and bulky boxes, assembled with shoddy craftsmanship and finished to look old. Stickley described his own pieces as simple, straight-lined, handcrafted, and beautifully hand finished. He intended each piece of furniture from the United Crafts to be unusually heavy, so that it could not be moved about the house at a whim. Stickley believed that the values built into his furniture would permeate the lives of those who used it. Thus, furniture solidly and permanently set in place would promote solidity, permanence, and security. He went so far as to argue that couples who surrounded themselves with Mission furniture would have a better chance of having successful marriages. Finally, and perhaps most important, Stickley's furniture fit in with a basic philosophic movement of the period. Free of any decoration, the furniture would underscore the early twentieth-century desire for simplicity and moderation in everyday life.

The 1902 United Crafts catalog included an eclectic variety of objects, including forty-two models of Craftsman furniture, plus one piece, a hall settle with cabinet cover, that could be purchased by special order only. The catalog listed pieces of furniture designed for use in clubhouses and business offices: large tables, desks, and chairs. It also announced a line of billiard and pool tables. Stickley constructed each piece of native American white oak, which he called "the most human of woods, that is, the most amenable to the educative process: The literal drawing out of all that constitutes its value."[30] Oak represented the people's wood—common, inexpensive, and thus suited to Stickley's idea of a "democratic art."

What an elusive term—"democratic art." For Stickley, it seemed to mean furniture that would be available to the masses. Only when people filled their home life with beauty, he believed, could their lives be ennobled. Thus ennobled, they could move more easily into the world of spirituality. Stickley believed that people deserved his new furniture, for his customers constituted, in his eyes, the strength and soul of America:

> But those in whose interest I make my plea for a democratic household art, constitute the majority of our American people. They are the busy workers, "troubled about many things": professional people; men and women of business; toilers who reach out after objects of beauty and refinement, as if they were the flowers of "Paradise Lost." They are the real Americans, deserving the dignity of this name, since they must always provide the brain and sinew of the nation. They are the great middle class, possessed of moderate culture and moderate material resources, modest in schemes and action, average in all but virtues. Called upon to meet stern issues, they have remaining little leisure in which to study problems of other and milder nature. But as offering such great and constant service, these same middle classes should be the objects of solicitude in all that makes for their comfort, their pleasure and mental develop-

ment. For them art should not be allowed to remain as a subject of consideration for critics. It should be brought to their homes and become for them a part and parcel of their daily lives. A simple, democratic art should provide them with material surroundings conducive to plain living and high thinking, to the development of a sense of order, symmetry and proportion.[31]

Stickley may have intended his furniture for the middle class, but he ran up against the same problem William Morris faced. As Stickley tasted success, he gradually priced his furniture further and further out of their reach. For one thing, he employed techniques of construction that proved costly. For another, he opted to use a good deal of quartersawn oak, an admittedly more wasteful use of the tree. (Boards cut from a log that was first cut lengthwise, into quarters, to display the cross-grain of the wood). Stickley used the more expensive cut not only to increase the strength of each board and to prevent checking and warping, but also to exploit the wood's medullary rays—the glasslike fibers that run across the grain and bind the perpendicular fibers together. This practice resulted in more interesting grain patterns, which Stickley exploited for contrast with the plain sawn boards in the legs, stretchers, and slats of dining room chairs, cabinet doors, drawers, and tabletops.

Quartersawn oak cost more for another reason: it required lengthy and complicated drying procedures. As Stickley developed more experience with cabinetmaking, he worked out elaborate steps for drying his oak. His attention to such details reflects his overall attention to all the fine points of construction:

The drying of woods is not a thing to be attempted unadvisedly or indiscreetly. It demands knowledge, care, experience and constant watching. If the outside of lumber is dried too rapidly it produces what is known as "case-hardening." This is the solidification of the outside so that the moisture of the inside is confined. This causes the checking (splitting at the ends) and warping of the wood.

Quarter sawn oak is the hardest of all woods to dry, and requires the longest time. The reason for this is that the flat surfaces of the ray flakes being as impenetrable as glass prevent the moisture from escaping through them, and therefore it has to come out at the ends and sides. It is obvious how carefully and thoroughly this must be done, and that only men of large experience and trustworthiness can be placed in charge of such responsible work.

To ensure thoroughness all quarter sawn oak is carefully inspected again, after it leaves the dry-kiln, not only to see that it is ready for use, but also for the purpose of selecting the pieces best adapted to certain work, and that match well in color and grain. Woods with beautiful or special markings are set aside for extra fine work, and more ordinary pieces are used for the more ordinary work.

Then saw, chisel, planer and other tools do their work, and, in due time, after the scraper and smoother has done his part, the chair, or table, or other article is ready for the final coloring process . . . which heightens, beautifies and renders permanent the texture and traceries bestowed by Nature.[32]

Only these careful drying techniques enabled Stickley to achieve his characteristic deep-colored finishes. No one else during the period seemed to achieve those same colors. An original Stickley finish offers as sure a way of identifying one of his pieces as his signature.

Believing that the inherent beauty of furniture finally revealed itself through color, Stickley spent considerable time hand finishing each piece of his furniture. He produced his earliest pieces—those shown at Grand Rapids—in "gun-metal gray and Tyrolean green," but over time he finished more of them in brown, until gray and green disappeared entirely from the catalogs. Stickley vehemently refused to use commercially prepared stains to achieve his particular brown; he adopted instead a process called fuming, whereby ammonia fumes released inside a specially built tent reacted with the tannic acid in the oak to create what Stickley described as a "rich nut-brown color." Only fuming, Stickley maintained, could produce that particular depth of color, especially in the quartersawn boards: "[Fuming] acts upon the glossy hard rays as well as the softer parts of the wood, coloring all together in an even tone, so that the figure is marked only by its difference in texture. The result is not so good when stains are used instead of fuming, as staining leaves the soft part of the wood dark and the markings light and prominent."[32] If the finish turned out uneven in places, then Stickley recommended a touch-up with Vandyke brown or lampblack. And though most people believe that Stickley used no final covering, he does mention a final coat of lacquer (actually one-third white shellac and two-thirds German lacquer). Stickley also manufactured his own paste wax.

Coloring techniques held a special interest for Stickley; all his life he experimented with various chemicals for fuming, lacquers for finishing, and waxes for maintaining his furniture. He held endless discussions with the men in the finishing department about perfecting a particular shade of brown. Virtually all of his catalogs contained a section on Craftsman finishes, and he devoted many articles in his magazine to the fuming of various woods.

Fuming was not unique to Stickley. Furniture makers had already used the technique in England in the nineteenth century. But Stickley, with his ministerial prose style, could make it sound like his very own process: "The action of fuming and other chemical processes . . . might be compared to the experiences and trials of an individual, [for fuming] discloses unsuspected qualities of beauty previously lying concealed within its heart."[34]

Stickley's prose here is typical of his tendency to describe things either simplistically or so poetically that they often sounded unbelievable. But Stickley's furniture may owe part of its success to his prose. And writings by other designers of the period do not sound much different. Articles by Frank Lloyd Wright read at times like the sermons of an evangelical preacher, and Elbert Hubbard wrote with even more fervor. People were willing to be convinced of the philosophical importance of Mission furniture, its aesthetic virtues, and its moral implications, for they were already convinced of the moral implications of just about everything else.

The 1890s in America was a time of extraordinary expansion. The frontiers had closed, so Americans began exporting a way of life to the rest of the world to keep it morally and ethically secure: foreign politics was all a part of a serious mission. One of America's missions, for instance, according to certain economic proponents, was to promote world trade. The more religious described the task differently:

> *American overseas expansion was . . . a kind of spiritual* mission *to regenerate the torpid and inferior races of the world. . . . Prominent Protestant churchmen ratio- nalized our expansionist activities as a kind of Christian crusade—the bringing of the gospel to unenlightened nations in the manner of the sixteenth-century policy of Fe y Or. The alacrity with which* missionaries *followed the flag into all parts of Asia and Oceania and the generosity with which Church members and Sunday School children responded to appeals for* missionary *contributions testified to the popularity of the imperialistic policy as a spiritual mission [emphasis added.].*[35]

Lamp table of fumed oak (29″ high, 30″ deep). Circa 1904.
On top of table, Dirk Van Erp lamp of hammered copper.

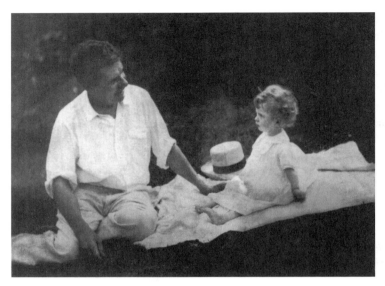

Gustav Stickley with his granddaughter.

Missionary zeal continued to mark the entire Progressive Era. Henry May, in his classic work on the years 1912 to 1917 in America, characterizes that era as "the time when people wanted to make a number of sharp changes because they were so confident in the basic rightness of things. . . . It may also be defined as the time in which the leaders of the people believed in their own *mission* and also in

Settle of fumed oak (30″ high, 56″ long, 22″ deep). Circa 1904.

democracy, and in which they were able to get the support, most of the time, of a majority of active citizens. It may be defined still better as the time when eternal morality and progress seemed to be joined together" [emphasis added].[36] Religion had insinuated itself into politics, business, and, less obviously, art; the idea of "a mission" insinuated itself into the general political and aesthetic consciousness at the turn of the century and became one of the unstated credos of the Arts and Crafts Movement.

There existed, then, a quasi-religious force pushing Mission furniture—furniture that, for some reason, had been resurrected from some old California mission or from an actual San Francisco church. Leaders in the movement reinforced that feeling. Elbert Hubbard, who ran the Roycrofters, acted, dressed, and spoke like a preacher; he preferred to be addressed as Fra Elbertus. He published *An American Bible*, which purported to offer "a selection of practical truth concerning everyday life from the writings of Franklin, Jefferson, Paine, Lincoln, Ingersoll, Walt Whitman, Emerson, and Elbert Hubbard."[37] He had sold more than one hundred thousand copies by 1919. The most popular of his little religious tracts, *A Message to Garcia*, reached several million copies in print by 1919.

Though he was less garish about his religion, Stickley saw his furniture and philosophy, as Hubbard did, as a salvation for America. The men Stickley acknowledged as immediate professional and moral influences all studied for the clergy, received Holy Orders, or preached as men of the cloth: William Morris, Edward Carpenter, and Charles Wagner. More important, the English roots of the American Arts and Crafts Movement found their nourishment deep in the theol-

"Crib" settle of fumed oak (69″ high, 39″ wide, 33½″ deep). Circa 1904.

ogy of John Ruskin and Thomas Carlyle. Stickley attempted to transplant their spirituality and to build his furniture out of their strong and central moral convictions. Object as he might, the public referred to Stickley's furniture not as Craftsman, as he wished, but as Mission. It was only natural for people to call the furniture Mission, for the idea of having a mission was an integral part of their lives.

The furniture supposedly built in the early California missions was big and heavy, box-shaped and primitive. Most of the United Crafts furniture in the first catalog in 1901 and in the first several issues of *The Craftsman* also appeared bulky, almost clumsy. The editor of the *Beaconfield*, a newspaper in Boston, wrote to Stickley about a United Crafts billiard table, for example, describing it as an object "with six enormous, square, uncompromising bulks of timber for legs, and which looked almost equal to supporting the weight of an iron-clad."[38] The furniture Stickley showed at Grand Rapids in 1900, however, was not as large and clumsy as that in his first catalog. In fact, he showed a hall bench at Grand Rapids that appears fairly light in design and a rocker with the same light proportions. These Grand Rapids pieces also lacked the severe, straight lines of most of Stickley's later benches and rockers. Stickley quickly emphasized the heavier pieces for commercial reasons: they had designed in them the unspoken values of solidity, stability, and durability.

Margaret Edgewood, writing in the most influential of the commercial magazines, *House Beautiful*, commented on Stickley's furniture: "The large pieces of furniture are the best examples of the new school. They are severely plain. The tables are built on the Belgian method of slot and bolt, and this gives to them a great solidity of appearance."[39] Stickley must have taken those remarks to heart; after all, *House Beautiful* did call itself "The American Authority on Household Art." Stickley immediately dropped the lighter hall bench and rocker from his catalog. He even dropped the name "hall bench" in favor of the Teutonic word, "settle," a term suggestive not only of a medieval past, but also of a solid construction.

The United Crafts settle he showed in his first catalog rested on six huge legs, connected to side planks by elongated mortise and tenon joints. This settle was not large—it measured six feet long and thirty inches wide; Stickley showed a settle with larger dimensions in later catalogs—but its proportions made the piece seem huge. Box-like and heavy, two extra legs supported the center of the settle, which it did not need for structural support. Stickley added them to create a feeling of massiveness. In addition, overstuffed seat cushions accentuated its appearance of largeness.

In the second issue of *The Craftsman* (November 1901), Stickley showed a picture of a United Crafts chair called "The Eastwood," which even Stickley referred to as "large." Its measurements made it practically a three-foot cube: thirty-seven inches high, thirty-four inches wide, and thirty-three inches deep. With leather cushions, it sold for $52.50, almost the same price as his small sideboard. The

Watercolor rendering of the armchair that eventually became the Eastwood.

chair does not appear to be built for grace or style, but rather for comfort and stability. The Eastwood is also notable because it provides an example of Stickley's design procedure.

Although Stickley argued for the union in one person of designer and workman—a principle he picked up from his readings on the medieval guild system—that union never existed in his factory. First of all, he organized his factory into carefully specialized functions—cutting, assembling, finishing, tanning, dyeing, and so on—performed by trained craftsmen. Stickley himself would conceptualize a new piece of furniture by starting with a picture of it in his mind. Then he would describe that picture to an artist, who would sketch the idea for him. Page 55, for example, shows a pen and watercolor rendering of the armchair that eventually became the Eastwood. The sketch indicates no exact dimensions but rather locates pegs and captures the general proportions of the chair. Later, a cabinetmaker, using the drawing as a guide, would work out the proper dimensions and construct the chair. Some alterations made their way into the final version of the Eastwood, changes that would either add more strength or radically alter the appearance.

A COMPLEX FATE

So, according to one daughter, Stickley himself never actually set his pencil to paper.[40] Stickley would examine the final product, and perhaps offer further suggestions, until the piece could be added to the catalog. The process, she explains, took months. Sometimes it didn't work: Stickley's designs might take too wild or extravagant a turn. In the end, someone in the leather shop would design the cushions for the chair, and other craftsmen constructed and finished them.

While the design for the Eastwood may have taken considerable time to produce, the United Crafts most assuredly operated as a factory. And while the United Crafts may not have been an assembly-line affair, carpenters did cut out blanks on power saws for all the furniture produced there. Finishing men skillfully hand assembled and finished each piece. Stickley believed, like Frank Lloyd Wright and others, that the machine could be "put to all its legitimate uses as an aid to, and a preparation for, the work of the hand, and the result [would] be quite as vital and satisfying as the best work of the hand alone."[41] Stickley never mentioned the other, more practical reason for mechanizing his plant: With machines, he could produce a large amount of furniture with greater efficiency.

For a complete understanding of the United Crafts, it is important to examine not only how the craftsmen produced furniture, but what they produced as well. The United Crafts offered, for example, a wide variety of chairs. Early armchairs and rockers were particularly interesting for the accentuated curves on the top slats and the thinly padded seats available in fine Spanish leather, treated in "browns of various tones, deep water green, and a red approaching the ruby shade, which is known as Elizabethan or Tudor."[42] Stickley used laced edges on his early large chair cushions. A customer could also order lighter dining room and side chairs with rush or reed seats, materials that Stickley believed created the proper contrast in texture and color with his fumed oak:

> The artistic quality of the rush or reed has been generally ignored by the cabinet-maker. The strength and durability of its fibres have largely caused its employment. But it lends itself easily to aesthetic color and textile schemes. Made soft and pliable, and retaining its natural vegetations, it gives a whole gamut of greens, with occasional rusty glints punctuating what otherwise were a too spiritless mass of color. It is then often combined with the mellow tones of "fumed oak," as we find it in certain chairs and seats recently produced in the workshops of the United Crafts. The combination cannot be otherwise than a perfect one, as it is based upon Nature as displayed in the Autumn woods.[43]

But of all the early designs from the United Crafts, the sideboards were the most dramatic, mainly because of their imposing proportions. One immediately notices the hardware: large metal straps and large, stylized metal plates behind the doorknobs. Even the rivets that hold the metal trim in place assume an obvious and dramatic role. Severe, ninety-degree slots are cut dramatically into slab sides to accommodate the legs, and tops lie there, thick, square, and sharp, devoid of any elevating curves. Some sideboards were large enough to require six legs.

By 1903, however, Stickley began to be criticized for the heaviness of his furniture. On March 10, 1903, for example, a reader named I.N. Rainsbottom had already written his first shrewdly analytical letter to *The Craftsman*, expressing his displeasure with the overwhelming massiveness of the furniture:

> *I am glad to see that the movement has taken such hold here; but, since my arrival, a few months ago, I cannot help noticing with some surprise the elephantine proportions, exaggerated crudity and rectangularity, the ponderous and frigid austerity, the almost aggressive plainness, not to say ugliness, in fact, of some of the articraftural furniture of which I have seen pictures, so different from the lightness and grade one always associates with American productions.*
>
> *Granted that simplicity is a condition of the mind, rather than any specific outward manifestation, true simplicity cannot be necessarily divorced from grade and beauty of form, such as one finds in the old Elizabethan and Jacobean periods, and later in the classic and beautiful forms of Sheraton, Chippendale and Adams, compared with which the square ponderosity of some of the designs I speak of suggest that a railroad-wreck-equipment, a crane, would be needed for the spring cleaning of a house furnished in that style; unless perchance it might prove easier to move the house than the furniture. These signs of the times cannot imply a reversion to log houses, saw-horse furniture, and home-spun.*
>
> *I speak with much diffidence, not being an artist . . . but it seems to me that an otherwise admirable movement may run some risk of being misunderstood and perhaps burlesqued through being confounded with a wholly unnecessary severity or sheer ugliness: a consummation, I think, devoutly to be deplored. "A thing of beauty is a joy forever," and we need all the joy there is.*

Stickley responded to the criticism in the same issue in calm, programmatic language, carefully pointing out the political implications of his designs:

> *Your strictures have in them an element of truth. But in justification of what you characterize as the "aggressively plain, elephantine style" there is, also, much to be said. All revolutions, political, social and aesthetic, are violent. Reformatory measures to be lasting, must be strong, even extreme.*
>
> *In reverting to the primitive ideas of articles of household furniture we find simple and even crude lines. These, in accordance with sound, artistic principles, we have preserved; since in architecture—the first of the building arts—the constructive features must be plainly visible and declare the purpose and use of the work. Furthermore, ornament must not be applied. It must result from such modifications of the structural features as do not impair their validity. Applied ornament is a parasite and never fails to absorb the strength of the organism upon which it feeds; as is witnessed by the history of the Decorated Gothic in both France and England, which succumbed beneath the luxuriance of floriated design.*

> *It is true that our severe and simple style now errs on the side of crudeness. But it suggests vital force and progress. It is yet in its formative period, and, in time, its asperities will be softened. Still, all modifications should proceed slowly and a middle course is always safest.*

Stickley apparently took the Rainsbottom letter seriously, or perhaps he received more criticism. For in December 1903, Stickley published an article in defense of his furniture in *House Beautiful*. Quoting from Rainsbottom's letter, and repeating some of the same lines he used in answering Rainsbottom, Stickley promised a change in the furniture:

> *This revulsion to severe simplicity in cabinet-making has been criticized as pointing to a reversion to log houses and homespun, to a crudity of life incompatible with our actual ideas of culture. The criticism is based upon appearance rather than fact. It is true that our severe and simple style now errs upon the side of crudeness. Yet this very crudity, absolutely structural, is a proof of vital power, and is in itself a promise of progress, since chaos, that is, formlessness, precedes, never follows, crudeness, and since decadence is the natural sequence of over-refinement. Coming after the historic styles, the simple and structural arrests and commands attention, as it could not do did it resemble its predecessors, or seek to compromise with them. But it is yet in its formative period, possessing a debatable quality comparable to the appearance of a youth who, lacking the symmetry of the mature man, attracts by reason of irregularities, which are nothing else than undeveloped beauties.*[44]

By December, Stickley could write with force and confidence about "undeveloped beauties," for he had already hired a new and brilliant designer named Harvey Ellis, who would bring subtle but important changes to Stickley's furniture in the next few years.

When Ellis came to the United Crafts in 1903, he had just turned fifty-one, "preserved in alcohol," Ellis bragged, "for twenty years."[45] Striking in appearance, Ellis sported slicked-down hair parted in the middle, a big bushy moustache, high starched collar, tie, and always a long, thin cigarette. His face was hard and chiseled, cut in half by a sharp nose, and accentuated by sad, dreamy eyes. Claude Fayette Bragdon, a New York architect and critic who wrote for *The Craftsman* and a friend of Ellis's, fondly referred to Ellis as "the beloved vagabond." He recalls Ellis's last days: "He had the dress, bearing and manners of a gentleman; there was a certain quiet dignity about him, and I think it was never more present, nor better became him, than in that crowded public ward of a city hospital to which (before his friends rallied to his aid) he had been taken, mortally stricken."[46]

Unlike Stickley, Ellis actively shunned recognition and notoriety. He used false names, gave incorrect addresses, disappeared for long stretches of time, and when confronted with his accomplishments, strongly denied them. His signature appears on none of his furniture at the United Crafts, and "out of a working life of twenty-six years, his own name as architect appears on his published drawings only during a two-year period."[47] William Gray Purcell, who wrote architectural reviews for *The Craftsman*, offered this lofty homage to Harvey Ellis: "Facing you—see a very great architect—before LHS [Louis Sullivan], before Wright—paying no fealty to any—in my view greater than [Henry H.] Richardson—you have a man to appraise who stands on his own feet. No man's name should be mentioned on any page about him."[48] In 1981, after trying to track down everything about Ellis I could possibly find, I reached this conclusion: "His accomplishments were indeed significant and wide ranging: his early renderings were pinned up beside the drafting tables of young architects in Sullivan's office; his later designs influenced some of the architects of the Prairie School; he brilliantly translated English Arts and Crafts and Scottish art nouveau motifs into an American idiom. Even before Wright or the Greene brothers, Ellis utilized exotic Japanese prints to inform his growing concern for simplicity. When he worked for Gustav Stickley, one of America's finest and most important furniture makers, he transformed stark, medieval chairs and cabinets into wonderfully graceful architectural objects. Finally, he designed one of the first skyscrapers in America.[49]

By contemporary accounts, Ellis was disorganized, forgetful, and an absolute genius. After working as a draftsman, Ellis had opened an architectural office with his brother Charles in the 1880s and designed banks, churches, huge mansions, and comfortable houses, mainly in the Midwest, particularly in Minnesota.[50] The best-preserved Ellis building in the Midwest, according to Roger Kennedy, is the Mabel Tainter Memorial in Menominee, Wisconsin, which consists of a theater, a library, and town offices. Although it has been difficult to uncover much specific information about Ellis's past, Kennedy reports that "tradition among St. Louis draftsmen confirms stylistic evidence that Ellis made a trip to the southwest during this period—probably in 1890—for there then appeared in his work a simplifying, refining impulse. Surfaces were cleaned of decoration or heavy masonry."[51] Ellis worked in a style that tended toward horizontal balance, approaching the work later associated with Frank Lloyd Wright. In architecture, he aimed for one thing: simplicity. And during the last years of the nineteenth century, when Ellis became involved in painting, Japanese wood-block prints exerted a strong influence on his sense of composition. Here again, his work moved toward a simple, direct line. Ellis brought this developing attitude, both in architecture and painting, to the United Crafts.

Once there, Ellis quickly introduced a line of lighter, delicately inlaid furniture. Since Stickley himself had earlier taken a strong stance against nonstructural ornament, he must have been, at least temporarily, thoroughly impressed with Ellis to allow him his decorative experiments. If Ellis had lived longer, perhaps the line would have continued. Stickley reproduced several of Ellis's furniture designs in a January 1904 *Craftsman* article titled "Structure and Ornament in the Craftsman Workshops." The inlay work on the table and chair shows an obvious concern for lighter, European Art Nouveau designs. Stickley praised these inlay designs, made of pewter, copper, and colored woods:

> *[The inlay] appears to proceed from within outward. It bears no trace of having been applied. It consists of fine markings, discs, and other figures of pewter and copper, which, like the stems of plants and obscure, simplified floral forms, seem to pierce the surface of the wood from beneath, as the edges of planks and the round ends of tree trunks continued in semblance to pierce the Greek frieze, even after the translation of the original timbers into marble.[52]*

Suddenly, then, after arguing for simplicity, for plain, unadorned furniture, Stickley made an elegant case for the organic integrity of these inlay designs.

Rocker of fumed oak, with inlay of copper, pewter and darker woods
(42½" high, 17" wide, 19¾" deep). Circa 1903.

A MISSIONARY ZEAL

Writing table of fumed oak, inlay of copper, pewter and various woods
(30" high, 29¾" wide, 18" deep). Circa 1903.

He had to. People demanded a more softened, lighter style of furniture, and in general Ellis designed a more graceful and elegant kind of furniture than the United Crafts. He achieved a vertical lift and airiness in his dining chairs, for example, through exaggerated curves on the apron, the tall stiles, and the addition of a top slat, and reinforced that vertical lift through the addition of those remarkably graceful inlay patterns. Ellis also achieved delicacy in what had traditionally been a fairly heavy object, the library table, by slicing the top very thin and dropping the stretchers close to the floor to promote a large, unobstructed airy feeling. Taking its orientation from the inlay pattern, the eye travels upward, from the base of the table to the top. In contrast, the library table prior to Ellis's arrival sits with a dramatic heaviness, the top and legs bulky and thick. Stickley's version appeared rough and rugged looking; Ellis's more genteel table more closely resembled English Arts and Crafts furniture in its broad legs, gently curving top, and base supports.

If Stickley's designs spoke of geometry, Ellis's recalled architecture. One would not expect to find Ellis's furniture in a mountain cabin retreat, a hunting lodge, or even some game room. He designed with more elegance for a more refined audience.

Although Ellis worked at the United Crafts for only one year, his influence persisted for as long as Stickley manufactured furniture. His design elements were clearly present in the later pieces: in the gently curving aprons on cabinets and on the stretchers of chairs, in the gently bowed legs of certain chests of drawers and in the lightness of the fall-front desks. Since Stickley lacked the skill as a designer to do it himself, he used Ellis to "soften the asperities" of his furniture.

Stickley hired Ellis in 1903 when he was down and out, alcoholic and ill. The year before, Ellis had left the architectural firm he had started with his brother in Rochester, New York. He had then separated from his wife and had fallen into an alcoholic stupor: "Ellis was ready to be rescued when Stickley invited him, early in 1903, to his United Crafts operations in Syracuse."[53] In great part, Stickley took care of him. Mrs. Wiles (a daughter of Stickley's) maintains that her father enjoyed a close working relationship with Ellis, closer than he had with any other artists in the factory, for Ellis understood Stickley's designs better than anyone else; he understood what Stickley wanted to accomplish. "Ellis worked with father's ideas," she said, "encouraged and refined them, until they met with father's pleasure and approval. Ellis was extremely important in father's career."[54] Shortly after Ellis came to the United Crafts, he made a bed for Stickley beautifully inlaid with brass and copper, which Stickley later took to his home in New Jersey. Ellis intended it as a token of their friendship. From every indication, Stickley and Ellis hit it off well.

Beginning in July 1903, Ellis initiated a series in *The Craftsman* that showed plans for house designs compatible with the philosophy of the Arts and Crafts Movement. The series, called "The Craftsman Home Series," became so popular it continued to run throughout the life of the magazine. In addition to providing house plans and room sketches and writing articles about architecture for *The Craftsman*, Ellis inspired a special department in the magazine. In November 1903, Stickley announced the formation of the Homebuilder's Club. An advertisement for the club appeared in *House Beautiful* in December 1903, and in it Ellis displayed a rendering of a house interior, complete with his designs for stained glass, table scarves, rugs, wall sconces, and furniture—virtually everything in the room.

In the midst of all this activity, Ellis unexpectedly died on January 2, 1904, perhaps after a drinking bout on New Year's Eve. Stickley wrote a surprisingly dispassionate obituary for his friend:

> *In the death of Harvey Ellis, which occurred on January 2,* The Craftsman *lost a valued contributor to its department of architecture. Mr. Ellis was a man of unusual gifts; possessing an accurate and exquisite sense of color, a great facility in design and a sound judgment of effect. These qualities were evidenced in his slightest sketches, causing them to be kept as treasures by those fortunate enough to acquire them.*
>
> *As a teacher, Mr. Ellis was very successful, while many of his fellow students, among whom are several eminent painters of the country, have acknowledged their debt to him lying in the counsels and criticisms which he gave them.*
>
> *As an architect, Mr. Ellis showed style and distinction: his ability having received public recognition through the award of the first prize in the design competition for the tomb of General Grant.*

A Missionary Zeal

Mr. Ellis was, further, a connoisseur of Japanese art, the principles of which he assimilated and practised. Altogether, he is to be regarded as one who possessed the sacred fire of genius.

Although Stickley felt saddened by the death of Harvey Ellis, he also seemed rejuvenated by it. No one could any longer credit Ellis for the new designs. January 1904 became, in many ways, a turning point in Gustav Stickley's career. For one thing, the idea of profit sharing had lost its appeal for Stickley. Because his furniture was selling so well, he no longer desired, perhaps, to give away part of his profits—even a small part. So in 1904 he dropped the idea of the medieval guild known as the United Crafts and moved to a more conventional, commercial, and sophisticated enterprise. He expanded his operations and changed the name to the Craftsman Workshops.

Stickley acted like a man reborn. Just three months after Ellis's death, he took a vacation and traveled to Colorado and California. During this same time, he changed the spelling of his name, as I have already mentioned, from Gustave to Gustav. And he altered the signature on his furniture. Under the joiner's compass,

Curved arm Morris chair of fumed oak (height of back from floor, 40″; height of seat from floor, 16″; seat: 22″ x 23″). Circa 1909.

63

Stickley began to sign his entire name rather than affixing the name of his business. With the conversion of his business from a guild to a workshop, he started to treat his furniture as if each piece were a canvas that he had painted. His prose also took on a new tone during this period—more serious and elevated—as he began to talk about himself as an artist. In his editorials, now titled "Chips from the Craftsman Workshops," Stickley wrote about himself by creating a new persona he called the Craftsman. In one of these editorials he explained the need for the new signature. The article reveals in its content and its length the new phase Stickley had entered:

> *The Craftsman sat in his workshop, unmindful of everything about him. The fresh beauty of the youthful year, the discomfort of the first heats he passed unnoticed, living for the moment only in his work. Before him lay a design showing few lines and rapid execution. It was his first conception of an object which, later, he was to realize in solid form. He was aglow, mind and body; his pulses beating, his brain quickened by the joy and pride of having created something. In this special labor he had as yet experienced nothing to cool his ardor. The always unforeseen, inevitable disappointment coming from the impossibility to adjust the ideal to the real, had not occurred. The thing upon which all his mental powers were concentrated, appeared to him adorable and perfect. He was not silently apologizing to the world for its faults, as he would be later, when he should see it developed from the design which was its embryo, and standing in three dimensions before him.*
>
> *And because his pride, his joy, his love were temporarily so acute, his sense of ownership was strengthened. A few moments later, his mood changed, as a bolt strikes from the blue. A feeling of pain, as intense as his former happiness, a sense of suffering wrong verging upon the consciousness of servitude, siezed him. He grasped his design, as if to save it from a hostile hand, and while feeding his eyes upon what he regarded as its perfections, his frame contracted with anger. A thought destructive of calm swept through his mind, as a sudden violent storm blackens and destroys the beauty of a summer day.*
>
> *In imagination he saw the object which he had already conceived by the effort of his knowledge and experience, finished and complete, going out from his workshop to be forever lost to his parentage. He was denied the privilege of the artist who signs the work which he produces. His own sign manual, the mark of his tool which he wielded with absolute conscientiousness and accuracy, counted him for nothing. The line dividing the fine from the industrial arts, appeared to him as expanded to a profound abyss into which precious values were dropped from the weak grasp of the hopeless.*
>
> *He saw the artist protected and the craftsman ignored. He saw his own creation ill-treated at the hands of other workmen less skillful and less honest than himself; its excellence half-understood by them and debased by servile copying: that euphism [sic] for robbery. At length, his fertile fancy showed him the factories of the country yielding imitations of his cherished object, multiplied to infinity and deformed to the point of positive ugliness and vulgarity, like those malformations, those structural vagaries of nature which caused him to shudder as he met them in his walks and journey.*

Library table of fumed oak, with leather top decorated with iron brads (30" high, 48" wide). Circa 1902.

Magazine stand of fumed oak (40" high, 14" wide, 10" deep). Circa 1905.

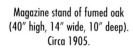

Three-fold screen of fumed oak, burlap, and linen (58" high, 54" wide). Circa 1905.

Two-door bookcase of fumed oak, with copper hardware (56" high, 48" wide, 13" deep). Circa 1905–1912.

Chest of drawers of fumed oak, with iron hardware (42½″ high, 36″ wide, 20″ deep). Circa 1903.

Sideboard of fumed oak, with iron hardware (49″ high, 60¼″ wide, 21″ deep). Circa 1905/08. Alongside it, a desk chair of fumed oak, with leather seat (height of back from floor 40″, height of seat from floor, 18″). Circa 1905.

Hexagonal library table of fumed oak, with leather top (30" high, 48" at smallest point, 55" at widest).
Circa 1902–1903.

Library table of fumed oak, with copper hardware (30" high, 30" wide, 42" long). Circa 1909.

Copper pull from library table above.

Stickley signature on
chair leg. Circa 1903.

Cabinet of fumed oak
(46″ high, 20″ wide, 18″ deep).
Circa 1905.

Detail of mortise and tenon joint
on library table. Circa 1909.

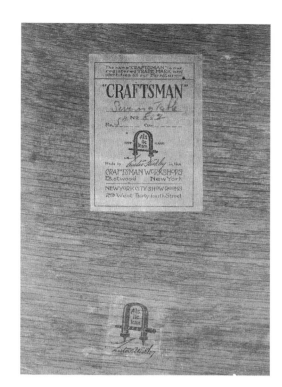

Paper label and decal.
Circa 1908–1912.

Ladies' desk of fumed oak, with copper hardware (46" high, 32" wide, 12" deep). Circa 1904.

Chair of fumed oak, with inlay of
copper, pewter, and light wood
(43½" high, 24½" wide, 19" deep).
Circa 1903–1904.

Spindle library table of fumed oak (29" high, 30" wide, 48" long). Circa 1907.

Together with the spreading development, the Craftsman also saw clearly the result of the evil. The caricatures of his cherished creation, things "common and unclean," palpable falsehoods and mockeries, brought discredit upon their model and original. Like unworthy children, they involved their parent in their own disgrace . . .

Arrived at this point of his revery, the Craftsman lost momentarily the steps of his argument in the maze of his emotions. . . . And now he abandoned himself to discouragement. Since he saw the use and end of honest production defeated, he approached the decision of no longer continuing to produce. He would not falsify, in order to earn easily that he might idle afterward. He could not create without the spur of enthusiasm, nor yet could he suffer his creations to meet with indignities offered them by his unworthy colleagues. . . . He began minutely to note the tools upon his working bench, as another, plunged in equal despair, but differently circumstanced, might have traced out the interlacing lines of a Moorish pattern on wall or rug.

The sight of external objects brought distraction and then developed a thought in the mind of the despairing workman. The design of his new object which he had raised his hand to destroy, he smoothed into place upon his drawing board. The presence of the traditional tools upon his bench brought to him pictures of other times and memories of happier conditions. He turned in thought to the period when "art was still religion" and craftsmanship was the lay sister of art; when there was little question of lower or higher, provided that the thing wrought by the tool for the daily domestic service of man, like the cup or the chair, received the impress of the genius of the workman to the same degree as did the things wrought by the brush, or the chisel, solely to gratify the aesthetic sense.

Following this argument in substance, the Craftsman could not avoid the conclusion that, to judge from historical precedent, which is another name for fact, his functions and destiny were equal, parallel and united to those of the artist.

The consciousness of this great truth suggested to him the advantage to be taken of his legitimate and strong position. Amid obstacles and difficulties, he saw clearly the way to relieve his own despair, to force the respect of the people and thereby to regain his historical position, to improve economic conditions in the republic of which he could not but recognize himself as one of the most useful citizens, finally to contribute to the spread of the gospel of beauty, which is also the gospel of content and of temporal happiness.

In pursuance of his new resolutions, the Craftsman grasped with eagerness a sheet of paper upon which he traced a signature, symbolic and characteristic, which he would impress upon each one of his subsequent creations. Similar signatures, he reasoned, had been the deep-lying causes of the economic prosperity and political importance of a government such as Florence, and of municipalities such as those of Flanders. The devices of the old guilds and of their master-workmen were responsible in their time for the map of Europe. Why then, reasoned the Craftsman, could not the modern representative of these oaths of honesty and good faith become strong agents in maintaining the internal peace of the newer America? The good accomplished by the Clothdressers' Company for Florence might certainly be repeated in a modern sense for a broader fatherland.

Again hopeful to the point of inspiration, the Craftsman resolved to assume for himself, to advocate for his colleagues, a representative sign to be impressed upon each one of the objects formed by his hands, as a token of his own responsibility, as a right to which he was entitled by reason of his attainments, as a public safeguard, and finally as an incentive and spur to generous, honest action, thrown out like an exhortation or battle cry, to influence and encourage whomever it might.[55]

Stickley had not merely created a literary character; he had in a real sense given himself a new identity. He created the benevolent, friendly, and knowing character of the Craftsman, so that he could talk about himself, this new literary creation, without shame. The Craftsman ruminates in his study, designs in his workshop, writes in his office; he loves people, beauty, good design, peace, and simplicity. He runs a business but does not gouge his customers. He edits a magazine but keeps his mind open to include as many points of view as possible. He stands for the rights of women and the practical and wholesome education of children. Nowhere does Stickley announce, I am the Craftsman. But there is little doubt he called himself into being as a character, reshaped by the pen. Like Samuel Clemens, he created himself anew, established himself as a character—an American character who loomed larger than life.

This new persona, the masterful artist, created, of course, fine pieces of furniture. Art historians and cultural historians, however, would not call them masterpieces. By elevating himself, Stickley had moved beyond the confines of the Arts and Crafts Movement. He became a movement all to himself. To make the break more apparent, shortly after Stickley renamed his business the Craftsman Workshops in 1904, he began to refer to his furniture as Craftsman furniture and to the movement as the Craftsman Movement. He made his position well known through his magazine, *The Craftsman.*

5

THE CRAFTSMAN MAGAZINE

AFTER LAUNCHING THE UNITED CRAFTS, Stickley faced the challenge of both distributing his new furnishings to the vast American market and disseminating his philosophy. He came up with a brilliant marketing strategy—he would create his own magazine in which to argue for his Arts and Crafts philosophy and by which to create a wider market for his furniture. Just after the turn of the century Americans were concerned with literacy; more people than ever were reading, but they were not ready for anything tough or erudite. They wanted to feel smart but not frustrated. Magazines provided the perfect reading material.

In Stickley's case, the idea of a magazine worked extraordinarily well. *The Craftsman* received immediate and widespread approval. A contemporary magazine, *Boston Ideas*, praised Stickley's venture: "*The Craftsman* is strikingly attractive, vitally interesting, and potentially valuable, in helping to solve the modern labor-problem" (December 14, 1901). The influential *Chicago Tribune* commented, "It is a handsomely printed and illustrated monthly which should be welcomed by everyone interested in the artistic advancement of the country" (January 13, 1902). The *Piedmont* (West Virginia) *Herald* said: "A master hand seems to be at the helm of the publication. This is seen alike in choice of subjects and in manner of ilustration" (January 17, 1902); and *Book and Newsdealer* stated: "Should the publication not gain fame and fortune for its promoters it will not be for lack of intrinsic and extrinsic value" (December 1901). By 1912, Stickley's reputation had spread so far that he could claim an international following. The Union de la Presse Périodique Belge praised *The Craftsman* in the highest terms: "After careful comparison of the most important magazines in all countries, we have decided to give the Palm to *The Craftsman*, an American publication of which the elegance, dignity and beauty have impressed us ever since our first opportunity of seeing it."

Although the idea of *The Craftsman* may have been Stickley's, the inspiration behind the magazine, according to Mrs. Wiles, Stickley's eldest daughter, actually came from Irene Sargent, a professor of art history and romance languages at the University of Syracuse.[1] While teaching, Irene Sargent lived full time at the Yates Hotel in Syracuse, where Stickley stayed when he commuted from Auburn State Prison. According to Mrs. Wiles, Irene Sargent enjoyed a reputation in Syracuse as a "grand old lady with a good deal of knowledge." And she impressed Gustav with her intelligence; he told his granddaughter to take Professor Sargent's Introduction to Art History class. She was popular and tough, thorough and learned.

Her students made these comments about her:

> *She insisted on being called Doctor or Madame, never Miss. We freshmen were terribly in awe of her, believing of her, both truth and legend.*
>
> *We usually referred to her as "Doc Sargent" among ourselves, but sometimes used the title "Empress Irene," after the Byzantine ruler of that name.*
>
> *She always looked the same—dark blue suit, dark blue shirt waist, and dark blue hat with a broad brim.*
>
> *She believed that architecture is the greatest of the arts. The architecture students were her pets. She told them, "Never work for money. Work for the love of your art." She began many of her lectures, "Gentlemen and architects . . ." To her the names were synonymous.*
>
> *She was one of the seven most brilliant women in the world. It was rumored that she had willed her brain to the Yale Medical School. Another rumor was that she had promised her brain to Harvard and was living off the proceeds. That was why (we thought) she could afford to take a taxi back and forth from the Yates Hotel, where she lived, to Crouse College every day.*[2]

Irene Sargent started her brilliant teaching career in 1895, when she was already forty-three years old, not unlike Stickley, who made his career move at age forty. Once her father had the idea for the magazine, Mrs. Wiles maintains that Irene Sargent gave it its shape. She decided what articles to include; edited them; selected the illustrations, the photographs, or stencil designs; and she laid out the magazine. In addition, she not only edited Stickley's prose in the beginning, but also, according to John Crosky Freeman, taught him enough basic French for his trip to Europe in 1903 and instructed him in Art Nouveau and other contemporary art movements thriving in Europe. Stickley relied heavily on Sargent to publish *The Craftsman*, as he relied on the designers in his factory, particularly Harvey Ellis, when he wanted to redesign his furniture.

The first issue of *The Craftsman*, printed in Eastwood, New York, appeared October 1, 1901; it sold for 20 cents a copy, or $2 for a year's subscription. *The Craftsman* could also be purchased directly from the United Crafts or from newsdealers. At the time, Stickley, described the magazine thus: "[It] advocates reform which improves the economic position of the workman, and increases the comfort of the American home by reacting against the love of display and the desire to rival and imitate, which are the two most powerful disintegrating forces now at work in the social system."[3] Stickley devoted this first issue to William Morris, and Irene Sargent wrote all five articles. She also wrote all eight articles for the second issue, which was devoted to John Ruskin, and all four articles for the third issue, on the medieval guild system. For the rest of volume 1, or the next three issues, she translated the twenty-eighth Idyl of Theocritus of Syracuse and wrote a piece about Robert Owen and factory reform, a long and detailed article on the Gothic Revival, and a review of a series of lectures on architecture by Barry Parker and Raymond Unwin.

Versatile and energetic, while she "edited" *The Craftsman* from October 1901 to September 1905, Sargent wrote a total of eighty-four articles.[4] She wrote with familiarity on ceramics, sculpture, books, French art, German art, Russian art, and Indian basketry; she reviewed the work of Réné Lalique, Merrimac Pottery, and Newcomb College Pottery; she analyzed opera and mural painting; and she discussed the architectural merits of the Mission of San Francisco Xavier in Tucson, Arizona, and Trinity Church in Boston. Toward the end of her stay at the magazine, Stickley sent her to Europe to write about the latest developments in the Arts and Crafts Movement. She seemed to represent for Stickley what it meant to be a woman in early twentieth-century America.

Irene Sargent skillfully designed the magazine, paying special attention to the covers. The cover of the first issue, printed on heavy, dull brown paper, showed a simple illustration of wildflowers, with the floral motif continued on the title page. The magazine measured 5¼ by 9½ inches, a smaller format than, say, *House Beautiful*, small enough, in fact, to lie open on the arm of a Morris chair.[5] Over the years, the covers underwent many changes. The most elaborate designs were those created by Ellis in 1903—gracefully stylized and delicately colored flowers. Beginning in 1908 cover designs consisted of block prints of flowers or fruits, in deep reds or blues or shades of green and yellow, on heavy brown paper. Each cover bore the initials of the artist, most of whose names have been lost.

The first issue carried this epigraph: "William Morris, Some Thoughts upon His Life: Work and Influence." Not only were all the articles about Morris, but Stickley also borrowed Morris's gothic typeface and artwork and liberally sprinkled quotations from Morris throughout the issue. Concerning his decision to focus on Morris, Stickley wrote, "As I set myself to prepare the initial number, it seemed most fitting to me that this should be devoted to William Morris, whose example of courage in radical and lonely experiment had sustained me through the trials of my lonely undertaking. Therefore, this number appeared as practically a monograph dealing with the patron saint of 'integral education' from the different points of view of art, socialism, business affairs and friendship. By this publication

I sought to honor an abstract principle in which I was interested to the limit of my energies and resources, as well as to pay homage to one of the strongest Anglo-Saxon heroes of the nineteenth century."[6]

But this first issue of *The Craftsman* was more than a mere encomium of Stickley's "patron saint." It doubled in effect as a catalog of furniture from the United Crafts. Although Stickley unashamedly proclaimed, "Through these articles it was hoped to combat the spirit of commercialism which is the worst peril of our prosperous new century,"[7] it quickly became obvious that behind *The Craftsman* lurked a practical commercial goal. The magazine provided an immediate way to publicize and sell Craftsman furnishings and to disseminate Stickley's philosophy. The first issue contained seven pages illustrating thirteen different pieces of furniture, in addition to five photographs or sketches of house interiors that also featured furniture from the United Crafts. In all, Stickley showed some two dozen different designs. The January 1902 United Crafts catalog contained only a dozen more designs. The last page of the first issue even carried a short advertising note, in obtrusive red ink: "The examples of cabinetmaking shown in this magazine are from the workshops of the United Crafts, Eastwood, New York." In later issues, Stickley would show recent Craftsman furniture designs and print articles such as "A Visit to the Workshops of the United Crafts at Eastwood, New York," in which his philosophy would be made clear.

Stickley's philosophy worked its way into the hearts of reviewers. For example, the *Lincoln* (Nebraska) *Courier* effused over the first issue in 1901: "The desks, chairs, and sofas and tables are parts of squares. The lines are strong, clean and, above all, secure. The sub-conscious influence of furniture and the familiar objects of the home upon a child is being pointed out by students of child-culture. . . . It is apparent that furniture which teaches a lesson of sincerity, strength and simplicity plays no unimportant part in the formation of standards of character value."[8] To equate wood fiber with moral fiber seems outlandish today. But Stickley knew his audience: His prose fed directly into the spirit of early twentieth-century America.

Stickley's magazine reached Charles and Henry Greene, two major architects working on the West Coast during the Arts and Crafts period. Randell Makinson, writing about the furniture of the Greenes, points out that "the publication which had the most dramatic impact on the Greenes was the first issue of Gustav Stickley's *The Craftsman*, which arrived in October 1901. That first issue must have exhilarated the Greenes for here was a man not only writing of a new Craftsman philosophy in America but also producing furniture of the highest quality and workmanship."[9] Makinson goes on to say the Greenes furnished rooms in the James Culbertson House (early 1902 in Pasadena) with Stickley furniture they had probably seen in the October and November 1901 issues of *The Craftsman*. He concludes, "Stickley's influence upon the Greenes went far beyond the mere use of his 'United Crafts' furniture, and can be clearly seen in the interiors and furniture designs of the Greenes' work between 1902 and 1904."[10] Judging from their work, the Greenes must have been thoroughly impressed not only with the first two issues of Stickley's magazine, but with the subsequent ones as well.

Stickley recognized the sudden importance of his magazine. The first anniversary number of *The Craftsman*, in October 1902, opened on a note of sheer optimism. Stickley even wrote a special foreword:

> *The publishers of* The Craftsman *in sending out the first anniversary number of their periodical, feel that they have real cause for encouragement in their enterprise. One year since, they offered as their initial number a monograph upon William Morris, the great model of the free workman: a man who in life and in art represents the principles to which* The Craftsman *and the association of which it is the organ stand fully pledged. With the course of the year 1901–2, the magazine developed beyond expectation, while it remained entirely faithful to the spirit which prompted the utterances of the first foreword. Writers of reputation, foreign as well as American, lent their pens and their influence to the establishment and strengthening of the new periodical, until it gained the right of existence among its fellows and the hope of usefulness and survival in the future. Now, entering upon the second year of its existence, it appears in a permanently enlarged form, which will permit the addition of several new departments necessary to the function of a complete organ and exponent of the arts and crafts making for the ennobling, the comfort and the pleasure of life. Among the more important of these departments will be one of criticism and review dealing with new accomplishments and movements interesting to the art-artisan and the friend of social progress. A second department will be founded in the desire to give technical and thoroughly practical instruction in the methods and processes employed in those activities which William Morris styled "the lesser arts of life"; that is, the construction and beautifying of the objects which constitute the belongings of a home: these methods and processes involving the arts of the joiner, the smith and the leatherworker, as well as the science of the chemist exerted in the more simple and popular forms. By this increase of interests it is felt that appeal will be made to a wider circle of readers than can possibly be reached by the thought which remains passive and refuses to deal with active and practical concerns.*[11]

By 1903, Stickley seemed to rely less heavily on Irene Sargent for his articles. She still contributed a piece or two, but so did numerous other people, including some important names from the Arts and Crafts Movement such as Barry Parker (architect and furniture designer), Amalie Busck (metalworker), and Charles Wagner (social activist and pastor). The magazine also began to feature special notices and reviews of Arts and Crafts exhibitions held across the country. It increased its price to 25 cents an issue, $3 for a year-long subscription. Having outgrown Eastwood, *The Craftsman* now had its own separate quarters in Syracuse.

In volume 3, Stickley added yet another feature. He included a novella, *The Fatal Hand*, "in translation from the original, which was taken from *Le Magasin*

Pittoresque, a French periodical whose anonymous stories and articles are written by the best authors of the time."[12] The translator was the indefatigable Irene Sargent. From that moment on, according to Stickley, fiction would become an occasional feature of The Craftsman.

By the end of volume 3, Stickley felt assured of his success, and he began to add to the magazine his own interests and concerns, which, of course, necessitated expanding *The Craftsman*. He added departments that explored the connections between manual training and citizenship and provided literary sketches of contemporary figures who exemplified the simple life. One department, "The Open Door," resembled an early version of *Consumer Reports*; it reviewed commercially manufactured home materials and accessories for durability, beauty, service, effectiveness, honesty of advertising, and price. At the end of 1903, at the instigation of Harvey Ellis, Stickley instituted Craftsman Home Plans, and departments related to architecture began to emerge in *The Craftsman*. Magazine covers started to appear with intricate illustrations, some designed by Ellis, and the magazine, for the first time, carried paid advertisements.

In 1904, in the middle of expanding his Craftsman Workshops, Stickley also enlarged *The Craftsman*. The typeface became larger and easier to read, the paper thicker and of better quality. The format had increased in size, and by October 1904 issues averaged 130 pages, well over the previous year's average of 100 pages. Toward the end of the year, Louis Sullivan, whom Stickley would later entice into writing for *The Craftsman*, wrote a letter to Stickley praising the magazine: "I like the spirit you are infusing into *The Craftsman*. It comes at a critical time . . . I hope that you realize how noble a system of design might be founded upon the superb underlying qualities of the American people."[13] The October 1904 issue carried an optimistic, buoyant article by Stickley titled "Thoughts Occasioned by an Anniversary: A Plea for Democratic Art." In the article, Stickley talks about his initial interest in furniture, then in accessories for the home, and how finally he came to publish the magazine. He concluded his article with this statement: "I should personally suggest that for the single word 'beauty,' there should be substituted 'the beauty of simplicity.' " That idea would remain the basic philosophy of the magazine for its entire life. Perhaps the notion of simplicity, as expressed in a kind of self-reliance, forced Stickley's separation from Irene Sargent, for by 1905 Irene Sargent stopped contributing altogether. Like Stickley's name change, perhaps getting rid of Irene Sargent was a way of saying: This magazine is my own! This business belongs to me.

Stickley's philosophy of simplicity was shaped in part through his early reading of William Morris. But other writers reinforced it, in particular, Charles Wagner, an Alsatian of German origin, who attended both French and German universities and eventually became a Lutheran pastor in Paris. Wagner and Paul Desjardins had been leaders in a late nineteenth-century social reform group known as the Union for Moral Action, a moderate organization. Wagner's philosophy, best illustrated in his book, *The Simple Life,* had been favorably reviewed in the second volume of *The Craftsman.*

For Wagner, superfluity of any sort reduced the possibilities for happiness. Externals of whatever kind mattered little. Paramount was what a person did with his or her life:

> *A man is simple when his chief care is the wish to be what he ought to be; that is: honestly and naturally human. We may compare existence to raw material. What it is, matters less than what is made of it, as the value of a work of art lies in the flowering of a workman's skill. True life is possible in social conditions the most diverse, and with natural gifts the most unequal. It is not fortune, or personal advantage, but our turning them to account, that constitutes the value of life. Fame adds no more than does length of days: Quality is the thing.*[14]

Wagner's line—"quality is the thing"—strongly marked Stickley's career and the furniture he produced. But Stickley was especially taken with Wagner's notion of a movement toward a simpler life, an idea upon which Stickley founded his own movement. Wagner argued in *The Simple Life* that

> *all of men's agitations for greater justice and more light have also been movements toward a simpler life; and the simplicity of olden times, in manners, art and ideas, still keeps its incomparable value, only because it achieved the setting forth in high relief of certain essential sentiments and certain permanent truths. It is a simplicity to cherish and reverence; but he little comprehends it who thinks its peculiar virtue lies in its outward manifestation. In brief, it is impossible for us to be simple in the forms our fathers used; we may remain simple, or return to simplicity in their spirit.*[15]

Stickley continually searched out people who interested him or who, for a time, might help him. He had already found Irene Sargent and Harvey Ellis, for example, and now sought out Charles Wagner. In 1903, Stickley took another European trip, during which he probably met Wagner, most likely while visiting Samuel Bing in Paris. He invited Wagner to lecture in Syracuse, and on October 11, 1904, Wagner came to the Craftsman Hall to deliver a speech entitled "My Books and My Occasions for Writing Them." By Wagner's own account, the plain, solid architecture and simple appointments of the Craftsman Hall impressed him, and he described Stickley's cabinetwork as "truthfulness translated into material objects." Wagner stayed with the Stickley family and spent long hours before the fireplace chatting about his philosophy. Wagner, pleased that he had answered Stickley's invitation, had found in his host an American who put into practice, both in his workshops and in his own house, the ideals of the simple life.

At the beginning of his formal lecture at the hall, Wagner commented on Stickley and his work: "Now we are here in the Craftsman's Meeting Room. This

Craftsman is an artist. I will tell you how I understand what it is to be an artist. This room is full of simplicity and beauty; its lines are strong and rugged. There is one idea here expressed, and that one idea gives beauty and is in itself beauty."[16] Wagner then moved to the theme of his book:

> All that is beautiful in Nature is simple. Nothing is greater than simplicity and one may have it free. I plead for simplicity in the household. We are often slaves to our furniture, to our books, to our curtains, to our rugs, to our ornaments. Our garments are often the sign of slavery . . .
>
> It is all simplicity. The most beautiful songs are those of the people in which the soul of man shines through in the simplest words and in the simplest form. The highest eloquence in every period of humanity is the simple, spontaneous, emotional expression of what lies in the heart. A man unable to make gestures and having a broken voice, if only he be a good man, has but to say one word, and this word is immortal. Often has humanity been helped for centuries by such a word. It is the character that speaks. A simple word, with one or two simple men behind it, will give spiritual life to millions.[17]

After his lecture, Wagner retired to Stickley's home. George Wharton James, whom Stickley appointed as Wagner's official escort, records the event in detail:

> With entire ingenuousness M. Wagner looked about him in the large room which he first entered. He remarked upon the architecture and furnishings, similar to those of the Craftsman Meeting Room, and then, seeing an inviting, roomy arm chair, he approached it, examined its structure and cushions, and, with a gesture of approval, seated himself, relaxing his frame and closing his eyes. In this attitude, he remained for several minutes, and when he again spoke, it was to say: "I am quiet and happy. This chair is no temporary resting place. I feel as if I had secured a permanent situation." Then, glancing at the smooth surface of the arm, upon which the grain showed its beautiful markings, he exclaimed: "I love the direct wood. Here is something wrought by the hand of Nature herself. The tree knows the secret of growing old gracefully. Wood is like a child, because its best qualities are apparent. It makes no pretenses and carries no deceit. It is like a child, too, because it may be spoiled by varnish—which is another name for false education. If a surface polish be given to either, it will not mature agreeably. In the case of the child, the contact of the world will produce defacement and scars; in the case of the wood, the hand laid upon it will leave disfiguring marks. But this chair is hospitable and humane. It is willing to support your weight; your hands might be soiled and perspiring from labor, but it would, like a gracious friend, fail to observe them. It would receive no impression from them. It is one of those enduring things which deserve to be heirlooms; to be a center around which family memories cluster; to become dear to successive generations, like the homestead and the legends of domestic honor."[18]

The following morning, Stickley asked Wagner to deliver a few brief words to some classes at Syracuse High School, where Stickley's daughters attended.

George Wharton James and Stickley accompanied Wagner. No details of the talk remain, but returning home from the school, Wagner reportedly turned to Stickley and commented, "And you, Mr. Stickley, when the day comes, will teach us to build with your simple, direct, honest lines. For it seems to me that you have done and are doing for the house and home of man, all that I am trying to do for man himself. We both have difficult, sometimes even stubborn material with which to deal, but may God bless our tasks."[19] Wagner's comments must have pleased Stickley. They certainly pleased James, who said he would "ever remember the author of *The Simple Life*."

George Wharton James became the fourth person essential to the development of Stickley's Arts and Crafts reputation. Irene Sargent had given shape to and provided direction for the early issues of *The Craftsman*. Harvey Ellis had redirected the design of the furniture. Charles Wagner had reinforced Stickley's philosophy of simplicity and broadcast Stickley's name throughout Europe. Now James not only would provide a certain depth to that developing philosophy of simplicity, but would also make it particularly American. So Stickley hired James as associate editor in 1904. Stickley described him thus: "Mr. James is widely known in the United States as a lecturer and writer on 'Americana.' He is the author of the standard book on 'Indian Basketry,' and of deservedly popular works treating the 'Grand Canyon,' the scenery and architecture of the Southwest and California, and the 'Indians of the Painted Desert.' " Over the course of his lifetime, James wrote forty books on "romance, history, botany, birds, science and scenic wonders of California and the Southwest." [20]

Though he only stayed one year at *The Craftsman*, from 1904 to 1905, James wrote seventeen articles ranging from "William Morris the Man" to pieces on the Spanish and Franciscan missions and the Indians of the missions. He wrote a series on aboriginal American homes; articles of appreciation on Browning, Wagner, and Morris; general articles on primitive instruments; and technical ones such as "The Influence of the Mission Style upon Civic Architecture of Modern California."

James had imbibed too much of the Indian spirit to stay for long in New York. In late 1905 or early 1906, he left the city to take up residence in Pasadena—then a so-called garden community set between the desert and the ocean—on the side of the Arroyo Seco, where a small community of artists and musicians had begun to gather just after the turn of the century. In 1909, James tried to do in Pasadena what Stickley had done in Syracuse; he edited and published his own magazine, modeled on *The Craftsman*, called *The Arroyo Craftsman*. *The Arroyo Craftsman* was the organ of the Arroyo Guild of Fellow Craftsmen, an association modeled on the Craftsman Workshops and located south of James's home on the arroyo. The magazine's subtitle, "A Quarterly Magazine of Simple Living, High Thinking, Pure Democracy, Genuine Art, Honest Craftsmanship, Natural Inspiration, and

Exalted Aspiration," included all of Stickley's concerns, while its motto, "We Can," took Stickley's "If I Can" one step further. Although James intended to issue his magazine quarterly, he managed to publish only one issue, in October 1909, eight years to the day after Stickley's first issue. James simply lacked the charisma, drive, energy, persistence, and determination of Gustav Stickley.

Besides Charles Wagner and George Wharton James, Stickley's greatest contemporary philosophical inspiration was Edward Carpenter, a progressive British author and poet, an outspoken socialist, and a man who became known, oddly enough, as the popularizer of the sandal. Carpenter fell under the influence of Morris, Tolstoy, and particularly Walt Whitman, who described Carpenter as "a man of means on whom his estate sits lightly; is intensely interested in the radical problems; is of a religious nature—not formally so, but in atmosphere." Carpenter lived a radical and simple life, openly sharing his house with another man, George Merrill, a worker from Sheffield. But Stickley became interested in Carpenter principally through his book *England's Ideal*, which argued for that now familiar goal, the simple life. Stickley sensed that Carpenter could add practical elements to his own philosophy. After all, Carpenter lived his life according to the principle of simplicity. Stickley commissioned John Spargo, a socialist writer, to prepare a short biographical sketch of Carpenter for the October 1906 issue of *The Craftsman*.

Born in 1844 in Brighton to wealthy parents, Carpenter received his education at Cambridge and in 1868 took Holy Orders. In 1874, however, he left the church, crediting Whitman's *Leaves of Grass* with having profoundly influenced his decision. He wrote to Whitman on the eve of his departure: "Now I am going away to lecture to workingmen and women in the North. They at least desire to lay hold of something with a real grasp. And I can give something of mathematics and science. It may be of no use, but I shall see."[21]

Within seven years his lectures had developed into the University Extension Movement, a program of classes taught outside the university for working people. After visiting Whitman in America on two occasions—in 1877 and 1884—he left the movement to write books on socialism and simple living, in a small cottage he built himself in the English woods. He also took up market gardening and, in 1886, "moved by his yearning for greater simplicity in dress, he began to make sandals for himself and friends from a pattern-pair received from India, and this industry has grown into a considerable business, being now carried on by his friend, Mr. Adams, of Holmesfield, near Sheffield."[22]

What Stickley learned of Edward Carpenter's life fascinated him. In 1905, Stickley started printing pieces by Carpenter, including a long excerpt from the chapter "The Simplification of Life" out of *England's Ideal*. In September 1906, *The Craftsman* favorably reviewed Carpenter's book on Walt Whitman.[23] Stickley continued to read Carpenter and, in February 1908, ran a one-page excerpt of

Carpenter's titled "What the Return to Nature Really Means," a short time before Stickley himself began to write articles on the same subject.

Stickley wanted firsthand information about Carpenter, but by this time he was too busy with his Craftsman enterprises to travel to England. Besides, Carpenter lived in seclusion a good deal of the time or traveled around Europe—no one knew where. Stickley had many friends in London who tried to find Carpenter for him, but to no avail. Stickley, however, usually got what he wanted; in this case, he sent Irwin MacDonald, one of *The Craftsman's* frequent contributors of biographical sketches, to visit Carpenter at his cottage in the village of Millthorpe. When Carpenter asked MacDonald why he had come, MacDonald says he gave this answer, embellished, no doubt, for the *Craftsman* article: "I came chiefly because the editor of *The Craftsman* told me to come. You see, your books have been something of a help and an inspiration to him in the work he is trying to do himself, and he wanted to know just what kind of man you were when one saw and talked with you in your own home.' His look of embarrassed diffidence deeped a little. 'That was very kind of him,' he said. 'Give him my regards and tell him I should like much to meet him personally.' "[24]

That was enough for Stickley. He now offered his own lavish appraisal of Edward Carpenter:

> *From generation to generation every nation has the privilege of nourishing men and women (but a few) who think and live thus sincerely and beautifully, and who so far as possible strive to impress upon their own generation the need of such sincerity and beauty in daily life. One of the rarest and most honest of these sincere personalities in modern life is Edward Carpenter, an Englishman who, though born to wealth and station, has stripped his life of superfluous social paraphernalia and stepped out of the clumsy burden of tradition, up (not down) to the life of the simple, common people, earning his living and that of his family as a cobbler (and a good one, too) and living in a peaceful fashion in a home planned and largely constructed by himself. His life and his work are with the people. He knows their point of view, he writes for them, lectures for them, and though a leader in modern thought in England and a man of genius, he is one with his daily associates in purpose and general scheme of existence. In all his present writings the common man and his relation to civilization, is Mr. Carpenter's theme, and he deals with the great problems of sociology in plain practical terms and with a straightforward thought born of that surest knowledge possible, experience.*
>
> *From the beginning of the endeavor of* The Craftsman *to aid in the interests of better art, better work and a better and more reasonable way of living, the work of Edward Carpenter has been an inspiration and an ideal, born out of that sympathy of purpose which makes men of whatever nation brothers and comrades. We have from time to time in the magazine quoted from Mr. Carpenter's books at length, feeling that he was expressing our own ideal as no words of ours could, and particularly have we felt a oneness of purpose with him in his book* England's Ideal, *in which he publishes a chapter on the "Simplification of Life," which with its honesty, sincerity,*

its high courage and rare judgment should make clear the pathway for all of those among us who are honestly interested in readjusting life on a plane of greater usefulness and higher beauty.[25]

A relationship thus blossomed.

At the heart of Carpenter's philosophy lay a question: "If you do not want to be a vampire and a parasite upon others, the great question of practical life which everyone has to face, is how to carry it on with as little labor and effort as possible."[26] Carpenter needed, then, to describe the excess and triviality that filled people's lives and to point out the benefits of simplifying the details and labors of those lives. Curtains, hangings, cloths, and covers, those fixtures not absolutely essential for one's life, should be disposed of, for they only gather dust and create stiffness in the house. "I like a room which looks its best when the sun streams into it through wide open doors and windows," Carpenter maintained, and if a room could not stand that test, he urged people to change it. Eliminate ornament, and adopt the rule of necessity in everything: dress, daily habits, labor, food, and furnishings.

Carpenter realized that these changes would be difficult for people to make, for civilization had progressed to the point that people's habits had ossified. Salvation could be achieved only by starting over, by taking up "the thread of history at a past point." If the soul of humankind was to survive, people would have to make such changes. The simple life could be accomplished most easily in the country, because there, changes could be effected most easily and they could be felt most intensely. In addition, the essentials existed close at hand: blue sky, green trees, rich earth. But he warned against a return to nature that functioned as "a mere cover for formless sentiment"; people must be sincere if they expected the movement to take firm root. He exhorted: "Simplify your lives that you may be sound and strong in mind and body. Simplify your lives that you may obtain peace! Simplify your lives that you may be pure! Simplify your lives that your mothers and sisters may be redeemed from drudgery to become your comrades! Simplify your lives that you may be free and that you may know at last the joy of right living."[27]

Over the years, Stickley printed numerous articles that promoted Carpenter's far-reaching philosophy of simplicity. Articles on the Hopi, reed and willow baskets, Navaho rugs and pottery, Hiroshige prints, Korean and Japanese art, Oriental gardens, and European peasant art and architecture were all written with the idea of simplicity in mind. Some of the house plans reproduced in *The Craftsman* grew simpler and simpler until one of the ideal houses became the log cabin.

The Craftsman magazine itself was characterized less by simplicity than comprehensiveness. It applied its philosophy not only to the decorative arts, but also to architecture, poetry, drama, politics, music, economics, history, conservation, gardening, city planning, and education. As readers riffled through its pages, they might find an article by Jacob Riis, a New York muckraking reporter and author who worked for police reform, or one by William Gray Purcell and George Grant Elmslie, both influential architects in the Prairie School tradition. Natalie Curtis, a musician and lecturer on music, wrote articles such as "Folk Music of America," "The Negro's Contribution to Music," and "The Value of Music School Settlements in Cities," while conductor Leopold Stokowski urged audiences to become better listeners. Naturalist John Burroughs showed up in Stickley's magazine, described by his own son, Julian. John Gutzon Borglum, who sculpted Mount Rushmore, wrote about his experiences, Jane Addams about hers in social reform. Rabindranath Tagore, the Indian novelist and poet who won the Nobel prize in literature, presented an article with the intriguing title "The Bee-hive: Feminism Contrasted with the Zenana." Stickley expected his readers to know that the zenana referred to that part of the house where only Indian women could enter. But then Stickley expected his readers to be ready for everything: he pursuaded more than five hundred authors to write for his magazine, and some of them wrote five or six articles.

These authors explored each of the decorative arts and uncovered the beauty of each in exacting, loving detail. Amalie Busck, founder of the Busck Studios in New York, described the intricacies of beaten metal and repoussé, invoking William Morris as her guide: "We must diligently cultivate in ourselves the sense of beauty, skill of hand, and niceness of observation, without which only a makeshift effort can be got." Charles F. Binns, who directed the prominent New York State College of Ceramics at Alfred University, argued for the importance of ceramics in a series of articles: "Clay in the Potter's Hand," "Education in Clay," "In Defense of Fire," "The Art of Fire," and "The Future of Ceramics in America." Helen Rickey Albee, a pioneer in the Arts and Crafts Movement and founder of the Abnakee Rug Industry in 1897, reconstructed Abnakee's struggle to become the first rural industry in America to make rugs. Stickley omitted no major artist in the movement. René Lalique, Louis C. Tiffany, William Grueby, Robert Jarvie, Artus and Anne Van Briggle, Adelaide Alsop Robineau—all had their work displayed in the magazine.

As for Stickley himself, he did not confine himself to his most familiar topic, furniture making. *The Craftsman* contained more than two hundred articles by (or ghostwritten for) Gustav Stickley on a wide range of subjects. He explored every area in which he had even a marginal interest, and his interests seemed limitless. His articles ranged from "The Relation of Dancing to a Commercial Age" to "The Home of the Future" to "The American Woman's Taste in Dress" to "A Practical Application of All the Theories of Home Building Advocated in This Magazine." He could be optimistic ("The Rapid Growth of the Garden City

Movement, Which Promises to Reorganize Social Conditions All Over the World") or scornful ("The American Boast: How It Has Helped to Increase the Cost of Living"). He wrote about the family ("The Ethics of Home Furnishings"), about domestic issues generally ("The Lesson of the Beef Famine"), and about national issues ("The National Spirit of Speculation: Are Not Our Financial and Corporate Morals Merely the Outgrowth of the Moral Sense of the American People?"). He believed strongly in the average citizen's ability to share in the enormous wealth of the country: "The Power of the Small Investor: Wisdom of the Policy Pursued by Some Railroads in Encouraging Purchase of Their Stock by People Living Among Their Lines." He took on big business, however, in articles such as "Trusts" and "The Strength of the Trusts Lies in the Weakness of the People." But no matter what the subject, he always talked reform: "Postal Service Extension: What Postal Savings Banks and a Cheap and Efficient Parcel Post Would Mean to Farmer and Wage Earner" and "Woodrow Wilson: One of the Men Needed by the People." Stickley indulged even his most arcane obsessions. Questions of hygiene, for example, continually occupied him: "Sensible and Hygienic House Plans Are One Significant Result of the Present Campaign Against Disease." And he paid particular attention to current trends in fashion: "Fashion and the Development of Women" and "Is a Nation's Character Revealed in Its Dress?"

Not all of Stickley's articles can be classified as serious or technical. One of his most enjoyable pieces, a long discussion titled "The Colorado Desert and California" (June 1904), detailed the places he had visited in the spring of 1904. On that trip, as Stickley pointed out, he conceived of an idea that he never managed to convert into a reality. Stickley's brief reverie provides a glimpse, however, into his visionary side:

> *At Palm Springs station, five miles away, the wind was still high; but as we neared the valley-oasis, great buttresses of the mountain range stretched out their walls to offer protection against the elements. Orange, lemon, fig, almond and apricot trees were in full bloom; the air, of a caressing softness, was laden with mingled perfumes; the eye was intoxicated with the beauty of the sky, foliage and flowers, and the outside world seemed a troubled dream.*
>
> *That evening, resting in a tent cottage belonging to the hotel of Dr. Wallwood Murray, I remembered those other delightful alberghi, scattered laong the bay of Naples, which so often bear the name Quisisana—(Here one is restored to health.) Then, my thoughts reverted to a scheme long cherished in my fancy, but for which I had vainly tried to find a suitable place of execution. My scheme was the establishment of a community in which men and women would work out together the problems of a useful, moderately laborious life, which should assure health, provide against the corroding action of care, and afford sufficient leisure for the pursuance of means of culture and recreation.*

Though Stickley wrote frequently and at great length about the possibility of a romantic community, he also made certain that *The Craftsman* contained practical information. He offered detailed instructions on how to weave, hammer copper, tool leather, bind books, and embroider curtains, but he focused on popularizing his philosophy by printing a series of thirty articles titled "Home Training in Cabinet Work," the first of which appeared in March 1905. In this series, Stickley provided plans, lumber lists, and step-by-step directions for building Craftsman furniture. He encouraged people to build his furniture in their workshops at home and in classes at school as part of his desire to create democratic art and to train young people in the manual arts. He offered plans for dining chairs, tables, Morris chairs, cabinets, dressers, library tables, children's furniture—virtually every standard piece of furniture that Stickley featured in his catalogs—and he periodically reproduced photographs of furniture made according to his plans. His "Home Training" series gave rise to a series of *Popular Mechanics* books on building Mission furniture, the most notable of which was *Henry Haven Windsor's Mission Furniture: How to Make It*, which came out in three volumes—1909, 1910, and 1912—because of its popularity. Stickley also offered instructions on how to finish various woods, reserving his most elaborate instructions for white oak.

At times *The Craftsman* seemed so practical it resembled a farmer's almanac. One could find timely advice on where to buy the best stove or refrigerator, how to increase the yield of fruit trees, the health hazards of wall-to-wall carpeting, and the pleasures of outdoor living. Stickley wanted *The Craftsman* to be more than an esoteric journal devoted to some antiquarian aesthetic. He wanted a magazine that would embrace, as he said, "all of life," and he consciously and vigorously worked toward that ideal.

By 1905 the prestigious *New York Tribune* noticed how far the magazine had advanced from its early, insular concerns with Morris, Ruskin, Carlyle, and the English artists: "There has lately been a distinct advance evident in this magazine, which is losing more and more its character of a trade paper picked out with essays on the arts of other days, and is taking its place as a lively exponent of the *modern* arts and crafts movement" [emphasis added][28] By the "*modern* arts and crafts movement" the *Tribune* probably meant the Craftsman Movement, Stickley's name for his philosophy, which encompassed every aspect of life in twentieth-century America.

Not everyone, however, responded favorably. For some, Stickley had taken on too much. One reader, for example, complained to Stickley in 1905 that *The Craftsman* included too much extraneous information; articles on civic and political leaders had no place in an Arts and Crafts magazine. "In short," this reader said, "I believe in sticking to one's text . . . I make this suggestion not so much as a personal preference, but as my conviction after thirty years in the publishing business. I have made my best success when I have 'stuck to my text'—the closer the better. This principle applies to modern magazine making, in my opinion, and while I do not claim to be infallible I feel sure enough of my judgment to warrant me in inviting your attention to the matter." Never given to one-line answers, Stickley responded at length. That response brings into focus an important aspect of his personality. While he argued over and over again for the simple life, he could never be content with simple solutions, and no one could call Gustav Stickley a simple, plain man. But he never apologized for his inconsistencies or made excuses for his idiosyncrasies, as his response to the concerned reader makes abundantly clear:

> The Craftsman *is distinctly a magazine with a purpose. It stands for a great move-ment, real, positive and progressive, although its membership is unenrolled and un-counted. It seeks to represent, in a practical and efficient way, the portion of our population that believes in making life worth living. There is a difference between living and mere existence.* The Craftsman *believes that man is more than his work, that life is more than raiment, and that happiness can better be found when men and women live simply than when they yield to the exacting demands of our complex civ-ilization, or seek to follow the dictates of fashion.*
>
> . . . The Craftsman *believes that the simple is more likely to be right and good than the complex. It believes that a frank recognition and adaptation of every object to its required purpose is better than artificiality and pretense. It believes that these last promote unrest, unhappiness, and degeneracy. And it believes that these principles apply alike to men and things.*
>
> . . . *To please our readers is a good thing, but to help and inspire them is better, and it is this better thing that gives its scope and purpose to the policy of* The Craftsman.[29]

Overexpansiveness was not the only criticism leveled at the magazine. By 1906, Stickley's initial commitment to what he called socialism had waned consid-erably, but he still offended some people by adopting a strong political stance and arguing for revolution.

Stickley's political philosophy surfaced more strongly when in 1905 he dropped a department from the magazine called "Chips from the Craftsman Workshops," chatty talks with the wise and friendly cabinetmaker, in favor of his new editorial column, "Als Ik Kan," which centered on modern subjects such as political and personal power. In the majority of these columns, Stickley went well beyond the usual concerns of the Arts and Crafts Movement; he commented on corporate wealth and political corruption, as well as the corruption of the arts through wealth and the destruction of democratic art through commercialism. As "the simple life" lost ground in a world growing more and more complex, Stickley found it necessary to emphasize it: beginning with volume 8, 1905, he changed the full title of his magazine to *The Craftsman, An Illustrated Monthly Magazine for the*

Simplification of Life. From this point on, Stickley became more politically outspoken in his editorial columns.

His political forthrightness culminated in 1906, when he published Leo Tolstoy's "A Great Iniquity: Extracts from the Famous Letter on Land Ownership in Russia." The letter had never appeared in its entirety in this country until the Public Publishing Company of Chicago had printed the letter in a pamphlet; Stickley believed that Tolstoy deserved a wider audience. Some of his readers strongly disagreed; and they complained to *The Craftsman.* But, as usual, Stickley bounced back with a bold response: "We are just as much interested in sociology, in politics, in education, in healthy outdoor living, in revolution and in dress reform . . . life itself is our only concern, and art is only one way of getting at and expressing life."[30]

By this time, the kind of "life" Stickley had in mind began to take definite shape. One indication was yet another change in the magazine's title. One year after the first change, Stickley renamed it *The Craftsman, An Illustrated Monthly Magazine in the Interest of Better Art, Better Work, and a Better and More Reasonable Way of Living,* a curiously long name for a simple idea. The "simplification of life," perhaps clear enough in the beginning, had now become too vague and general, for Stickley knew better the areas in which he had an abiding interest. Here, Edward Carpenter provided the direction. When Stickley reproduced Carpenter's "The Simplification of Life," in *Craftsman Homes,* he wrote, "From the beginning of the endeavor of THE CRAFTSMAN to aid *in the interests of better art, better work, and a better and more reasonable way of living,* Edward Carpenter has been an inspiration and an ideal, born out of that sympathy of purpose which makes men of whatever nation brothers and comrades [emphasis added]."[31] The new title helped rest the magazine squarely on Carpenter's philosophical ideals: to move people back to nature and to combine handicrafts with farming. This sharpened focus began to affect the look of the magazine as well.

In 1907, Stickley once more changed the magazine's graphics. He selected a smaller typeface so he could squeeze more words onto each page, and he made the artwork more stylized and more consciously part of the Arts and Crafts aesthetic. He greatly enlarged his handicrafts department, providing more practical instructions for home building of Craftsman furniture and accessories. He announced his new goal in a comprehensive list: "We propose to take up work in wood, metal and leather, needle work, weaving, stenciling, block printing, book binding, pottery and kindred crafts, as well as a thorough course in designing, wood finishing, and house decoration."[32] In addition, he began to devote a good deal of his articles to farming. In 1908, Stickley wrote a general article describing America's renewed interest in agriculture, titled "Railroads as Aids to Farmers: How the Need for More Traffic Has Led Them to Help in the Revival of Agriculture." Stickley then broadened his argument, from "Small Farming and Profitable Handicrafts: A

General Outline of the Practical Features of the Plan" to "Why Back to the Farm?" and "Small Farms: A Solution for the Evils of Overcrowded Cities and Unnatural Living." Finally, he presented a pair of articles that provided a moral base for his agricultural concerns: "The Value of a Country Education" and "The Value of the Small Farmer."

From 1909 on, a focus on living fully surfaced as an essential feature of the magazine. Stickley supplemented articles on handicrafts with pieces on farming and natural living: the value of walking and driving in the woods; biographies of naturalists John Muir and John Burroughs; the importance of native American Indian life; healthy Russian peasants; and gardening. *The Craftsman* thrived during the years 1909 to 1912 on this modified approach. In the November 1909 issue, Stickley reported a 15 percent increase in the number of paid advertisers and the magazine's "first 'spread' . . . a four-page advertisement . . . in red and black." For the first time, Stickley also referred to the position of advertising manager, held by Frank Nye.

All these changes seemed to boost sales, for in 1909 *The Craftsman* reached its peak: 60,000 readers. The average size of the magazine had also increased to 175 pages. *The Craftsman*, popular and influential, remained healthy for the rest of its life. At the back of his 1912 furniture catalog, for instance, Stickley reported "a gain of 51 per cent in subscriptions during January 1912, as compared with January 1911, a further gain of 101 per cent, in February 1912, over February of last year, and still greater progress this March." Gustav Stickley's enterprises, it seemed, could go on forever.

In 1915, Stickley proudly advertised, as a premium to subscribers, a collection of readings in eight separate categories that his magazine had covered over the years. He presented it in the form of another impressive list: American Architecture and Homebuilding, Furniture and Furnishings, American Gardens, Modern American Art, American Crafts, Photographic Art the World Over, Bird Life in America, and New Ideas. *The Craftsman* had helped found, give shape to, and popularize Gustav Stickley's Craftsman Movement. Based on the experience of the magazine, this department store of ideas circulated to homes across America, Gustav Stickley could triumphantly proclaim, "There seems to be no limit whatever to the things which the Craftsman Movement can accomplish."

6

GUSTAV STICKLEY AS ARCHITECT

OF THE MANY SUBJECTS STICKLEY EMBRACED in his rapidly expanding Craftsman Movement, none mattered more to him than architecture. It was even more important to him than furniture making: architecture produced objects much more expensive, and much more visible, than mere tables and chairs. Although Stickley received no formal training as an architect, by 1903—the year Ellis joined the United Crafts—he began listing himself as an architect in the Syracuse, New York, telephone directory. Architecture had always transfixed him. Ruskin had been keenly interested in Gothic architecture, helping to raise architecture to a position of prominence in the English Arts and Crafts Movement. And it was, after all, William Morris's profound interest in preserving Gothic and Romanesque architecture that had initially catapulted Stickley into the movement. Ellis, too, had designed buildings.

For Stickley, "the great aspirations of the times" found expression through architecture. When Stickley described the construction of one of his cabinets, he deliberately equated it with the design of buildings: "In the lesser as well as the greater building art, the structural lines should be obtrusive rather than obscured. Such lines in cabinet-making declare the purpose and use of the object which they form, and are, in their way, as important as the contours which announce a church, an opera-house, or a business structure."[1] Beyond that, architecture expressed the grandest ideas in the most permanent way; it spoke to the world as no other art form could. Even in the supposedly liberated Arts and Crafts Movement in England, women could move into needlework, metalwork, even furniture design, but architecture—the man's profession—admitted few women.[2] That is true of the profession even today. Throughout time, architecture has been the private reserve of men. In 1903, Stickley listed himself as an architect because he aspired to be one and desired to be thought of as one.

A COMPLEX FATE

Stickley's concerns centered more on general theories about building materials, finishes, details of interiors and exteriors, and styles of living than on the dynamics of space. He also focused on the influence that the home exerted on people's moral development, as the following description of the necessity for Craftsman Homes clearly demonstrates:

> *That the influence of the home is of the first importance in the shaping of character is a fact too well understood and too generally admitted to be offered here as a new idea. . . . The people whose lives are lived simply and wholesomely, in the open, and who have in a high degree the sense of the sacredness of the home, are the people who have made the greatest strides in the development of the race. . . . We [at the Craftsman Workshops] regard it as at least a step in the direction of bringing about better conditions when we try to plan and build houses which will simplify the work of home life and add to its wholesome joy and comfort.*[3]

The description smacks of Stickley's own brand of elitism. There were, of course, people living simply and wholesomely who did not make "the greatest strides in the development of the race." And, certainly, scores of poor people in America did not have the luxury of living "in the open," as Stickley puts it, but still believed in the sacredness of the home.

As with his furniture designs, Stickley turned evangelical about his architectural plans. He wished not merely to provide simple, well-designed houses, but to change people's living habits, to move them from superfluity to simplicity. He urged them to leave luxury and opulence for what he called "kinship with nature." In this regard, Harvey Ellis influenced the naive Stickley.

When Ellis arrived at the United Crafts in 1903, he had already had his own architectural office with his brother and had designed and built some large buildings in the Midwest. Some credited him with erecting the Midwest's first skyscraper. At any rate, he brought drafting and architectural know-how to Stickley's enterprises. Naturally, Stickley began to emphasize architecture in *The Craftsman*. In May 1903, he reproduced the plans for a house he had designed with E. G. W. Dietrich, a New York architect. Stickley briefly described this five-bedroom, two-story, fieldstone house, suggested the proper interior details and furniture, and appended this offer: "To all subscribers of *The Craftsman* any processes or details incident to the building, finishing, or decoration of the 'Craftsman House' will be willingly given, through the Correspondence Department of the Magazine, or more directly by private letter." Stickley thus coined the name "Craftsman house," which would come to stand less and less for a particular style of house and increasingly for a particular style of living and philosophy of life, based on a "kinship with nature."

That philosophy became more apparent in the next several issues of *The Craftsman*, with Harvey Ellis leading the way. Ellis's first house design appeared in the July 1903 issue of *The Craftsman*. Ellis proposed in his design "to erect a house for an average family, on a city or suburban lot of fifty feet front and not less than one hundred twenty-five feet deep." The house, which would cost $4,000 to construct, would be "convenient, harmonious, and related in all its parts. A structure fit and, therefore, a work of art; for nowhere is the axiom 'fitness is beauty' so obvious as in a domestic structure." Stickley used this philosophy to inform all of his house designs.

Ellis's designs and description in the July 1903 issue cover eight pages and include floor plans plus four sketches of the exterior and interior of the house. He proposed the proper color scheme for the inside and outside of the house, the ideal wood finishes, the best materials suited to the particular location and style, the philosophical justification for placing one room next to the other—almost everything one could possibly conceive of in building a house. Ellis designed from an absolutely fresh beginning: "Let us abandon as much as may be, and try, if possible, to think of no house as ever having been designed before."

By the end of 1903, Irene Sargent had recognized Ellis's unusual architectural talents. She gave him the lead article in December of that year, titled "An Urban House: Number Three in the Craftsman Series." But more than that, Stickley saw the possibilities in Ellis's brand of architectural series. Stickley would, in fact, reproduce plans for Craftsman houses for the rest of the life of his magazine.

Ellis probably also inspired another department related to architecture in *The Craftsman*. In November 1903, Stickley announced the formation of the Homebuilders' Club and placed an ad for it in the prestigious *House Beautiful* in December 1903. The announcement in *The Craftsman* featured a sketch of a dining room for which Ellis had designed the stained glass, table scarves, rugs, curtains, furniture—everything in the room. The sketch showed the hallmarks of Ellis's style: gentle curves on the furniture, graceful designs on the table scarves, and the vertical lift on the backs of the chairs. The Homebuilders' Club would supply, free of charge, the plans for a bungalow, farmhouse, detached city house, or a small artisan's house. The prospective builder simply had to provide an estimated budget; the locality, including peculiar climatic conditions; and the materials desired. The Homebuilders' Club then planned the total environment—down to the appropriate trees and shrubs. Stickley, who had been in business only a couple of years, began reaching out to customers with the long arm of the Craftsman operations to mold and shape their everyday lives.

And the customers stood ready. The response to his Craftsman House Series caused Stickley to write: "*The Craftsman* is daily receiving letters from readers who are striving to simplify their lives by ridding themselves of the meaningless in their surroundings. It is gratifying, in an age of accumulation and display, to receive assurance that here and there in our land men and women are trying to make houses that are a simple expression of their individuality."[4] With his charismatic personality, Stickley attracted talented artists to carry out his grand ideas. In furniture, he drew designers around him to execute his particular philosophy of design so effectively that he quickly produced a complete line of furniture; for *The Craftsman*, Irene Sargent, his managing editor, translated his vague, initial interest into a full-fledged magazine that quickly became highly popular. In architecture, he relied heavily on Harvey Ellis. Stickley never seemed to stumble (or he never let on that he did). He saw opportunities where others saw only problems. Even when his star, Harvey Ellis, died, Stickley took no time to mourn, as if his philosophy were too large to be sidetracked on account of any one artist. After Ellis's death, Stickley quickly hired a staff of architects to create another new department, Home Designing and Building, further expanding the magazine. He formalized his plans for a Craftsman house series and announced that each month during 1904 he would publish the "design of a detached residence of which the cost should range between two and fifteen thousand dollars." Each set of plans included a description of building materials, as well as construction costs.

Stickley launched the Craftsman Mail Service, which provided free to members of the Homebuilder's Club complete plans for projects in needlework, leather, metal—in fact, all of the arts and crafts necessary for home decoration. The Mail Service would answer questions about decorating and furnishing homes, as well as provide an ancillary service that offered landscape gardening ideas. He next created a department in the magazine called Landscape Gardening, and for a nominal fee, a Home-Finding Service. These services resulted only in increased circulation and sales.

Stickley's treatment of architecture in *The Craftsman* was, as usual, comprehensive. He printed articles on Japanese, English, and Gothic architecture; on the architecture of the West Coast, the Southwest, and the East; on bungalow courts, skyscrapers, missions, cottages, farmhouses, wooden buildings, and cement and concrete buildings; on office buildings and bank buildings. He also included information on more arcane subjects such as log cabins, American aboriginal dwellings, Russian peasant housing, Costa Rica's native architecture, and the Swiss chalet. *The Craftsman* featured articles by or about Myron and Franklin Hunt, William Purcell and George Elmslie, Claude Bragdon, Frank Brown, Barry Parker and Raymond Unwin, and Irving Gill. Almost every conceivable aspect of home building, furnishing, and care received attention in *The Craftsman*.

Coupling Harvey Ellis's architectural expertise with his own shrewd business sense, Stickley almost immediately convinced people—scores of them—to build his houses. He received letters from readers all over the country who had built their houses according to Craftsman plans, and he reproduced the pictures they sent into his magazine. A huge extended family of readers who shared Stickley's philosophy and ideals began to develop across the country.

GUSTAV STICKLEY AS ARCHITECT

House Beautiful started to print articles about and show photographs of these new houses, in places as far apart and as different as New York and Wyoming. These one-story, single-family homes with large front porches and sleeping dormers, wrapped in shingles or lap siding, went under the name "bungalow." *Bungalow* derives from a Hindu word, *bangla*, which means "in the Bengali style." Mary Ann Smith gives a truncated history of the bungalow:

> *In the nineteenth century and perhaps earlier, the word had been used to refer to a gabled native hut. The native Indian bungalow was gradually modified for use by Europeans in India. Verandas or porches were common. The Indian bungalow, gener-ally one story high on a very low foundation, had a large living-dining room and small bedrooms. During the nineteenth century, the Anglo-Indian bungalow was thought of as a temporary or vacation house for the hot season. The bungalow type had all the basic elements which eventually became part of the American bungalow in the early twentieth century. Although the means of transmitting the Indian bungalow house type are unclear, many bungalows were being constructed in California by the early 1900s, probably because the open plan, porches, and closeness to the ground suited the California climate so well. Bungalows were also considered to be inexpen-sive to construct, an added advantage of the house type.*[5]

Stickley helped popularize the bungalow. Shortly after he started printing plans for his houses, a number of pamphlets on the California bungalow began to appear, most notably Henry Wilson's *The Bungalow Book*, printed in Los Angeles in 1908. By 1909, the California bungalow style had grown so popular that the November issue of *The Craftsman* carried advertisements for Henry Wilson's *Bungalow Magazine*, the *Bungalowcraft Company Book*, and *House Builders*, a collec-tion of 100 plans for bungalows. In 1910, a Los Angeles investment company is-sued a booklet called *Practical Bungalows of Southern California;* it sold for 50 cents. Clearly, the time had arrived for Stickley to capitalize on his own house plans.

In 1909, Stickley edited, published, and distributed a collection of his house plans under the title *Craftsman Homes.* Bound in linen, it sold for $2. In addition to the illustrated descriptions of a large number of houses, the volume featured practical articles on making Craftsman furniture, refinishing woods, and decorat-ing interiors. And, of course, here was another opportunity for Stickley to push his line of furniture, needlework, and metalwork. The *New York Times* and the *International Studio* both reviewed the book favorably. According to his own ad-vertisement for *Craftsman Homes* in *The Craftsman*, Stickley intended the book as a collection of "helpful suggestions to prospective home builders and to those al-ready possessed of a home who wish to increase its beauty by simple and astute means. It contains plans for houses costing $500 to $1500 which, it is obvious from the detailed descriptions, represent the best ideas in American domestic architecture."

A Complex Fate

In *Craftsman Homes*, Stickley offered what he considered to be the best of the houses designed at the Craftsman Workshops and published in *The Craftsman* from 1904 to 1909. He collected them in part to show the development of Craftsman ideas about home building, decoration, and furnishing and to make clear the principles of the Craftsman House: "Simplicity, durability, fitness for the life that is to be lived in the house and harmony with its natural surroundings. Given these things, the beauty and comfort of the home environment develop as naturally as a flowering plant from the root."

Craftsman Homes contained plans ranging from cottages and bungalows costing a few hundred dollars to large, expensive houses, but it emphasized the smaller, simpler homes. All of Stickley's designs, whether constructed of wood, cement, brick or stone, large or small, he called Craftsman, because they shared certain qualities:

> *They are all designed with regard to the kind of durability that will ensure freedom from the necessity of frequent repairs; to the greatest economy of space and freedom in the interior of the house by doing away with unnecessary partitions and the avoidance of any kind of crowding. For interest, beauty, and the effect of home comfort and welcome, we depend on the liberal use of wood finished in such a way that all its friendliness is revealed; upon warmth, richness, and variety in the color scheme of its walls, rugs and draperies, and upon the charm of structural features such as chimney pieces, window seats, stair cases, fireside nooks, and built-in furnishings of all kinds, our object being to have each room so interesting in itself that it seems complete before a single piece of furniture is put into it.[6]*

Stickley's objective of a totality of design was a continuation of Harvey Ellis's philosophy. Stickley never mentioned Ellis's name in *Craftsman Homes*, however, even though he reproduced four of Ellis's drawings in the book. In one of those sketches—originally published in *The Craftsman*—Ellis's signature mysteriously disappeared. Stickley had erased him!

Stickley also borrowed Ellis's ideas about floor plans, best seen in Stickley's emphasis on a large living room and an adjoining, slightly smaller dining room. And though Frank Lloyd Wright had talked much earlier about the hearth as the center of the home, Stickley treated that idea as if it were his own:

> *We have made the general living rooms as large as possible and too much separated one from the other. It seems much more friendly, home-like and comfortable to have one big living room into which one steps directly from the entrance door . . . and to have this living room the place where all the business and pleasure of common family life may be carried on. And we like it to have pleasant nooks and corners which give a comfortable sense of semi-privacy and yet are not in any way shut off from the larger life of the room.*

Such an arrangement has always seemed to us symbolic of the ideal conditions of social life. The big hospitable fireplace is almost a necessity, for the hearthstone is always the center of a true home life, and the very spirit of home seems to be lacking when a register or radiator tries ineffectually to take the place of a glowing grate or a crackling leaping fire of logs.

Equally symbolic is our purpose in making the dining room either almost or wholly a part of the living room, for to us it is a constant expression of the fine spirit of hospitality to have the dining room, in a way, open to all comers. Furthermore, such an arrangement is a strong and subtle influence in the direction of simpler living because entertainment under such conditions naturally grows less elaborate and more friendly—less alien to the regular life of the family and less a matter of social formality.[7]

In *Craftsman Homes* Stickley selected articles and house plans that for the most part emphasized plain country living. He chose suggestive chapter titles: "A Comfortable and Convenient House for the Suburbs or Country," "A Roomy Inviting Farmhouse, Designed for Pleasant Home Life in the Country," "A Log House That Will Serve Either as a Summer Camp or a Country Home." Of the thirty-six house designs in *Craftsman Homes*, twenty-one of them were cottages, farmhouses, log cabins, or country homes.

Stickley provided his readers with this back-to-earth philosophy in the lead article for his *Craftsman Homes*, an article already printed in *The Craftsman*. It was entitled "The Simplification of Life: A Chapter from Edward Carpenter's Book Called 'England's Ideal' ":

Such right living and clear thinking cannot find abiding place except among those whose lives bring them back close to Nature's ways, those who are content to be clad simply and comfortably, to accept from life only just compensation for useful toil, who prefer to live much in the open, finding in the opportunity for labor the right to live; those who desire to rest from toil in homes built to meet their individual needs of rest and peace and joy, homes which realize a personal standard of comfort and beauty; those who demand honesty in all expression from all friends, and who give in return sincerity and unselfishness, those who are fearless in sorrow, yet demand joy; those who rank work and rest as equal means of progress—in such lives only may we find the true regeneration of any nation, for only in such simplicity and sincerity can a nation develop a condition of permanent and properly equalized welfare.[8]

Stickley now incorporated Edward Carpenter's philosophy of simplicity into his central architectural vision: entire families would move out of the city to take up life in the country, raising crops for their consumption, producing and selling handicrafts to pay for their supplemental foodstuffs, and living in simple houses. To bring this romantic vision to his twentieth-century audience, Stickley proposed yet another magazine, *The Yeoman*, devoted to all things agricultural.

The Stickley home at the proposed site of Craftsman Farms, Morris Plains, New Jersey.

Stickley came up with so many ideas, some were bound never to come to fruition; *The Yeoman* never saw the light of day. Stickley instead concerned himself more and more with architecture.

So while Stickley assigned Carpenter a position of importance in *Craftsman Homes*, he focused the rest of the book narrowly on architecture. The first article featured a house built in the California Mission style, the first house designed by the Craftsman Workshops. Stickley initially published this plan in *The Craftsman* in January 1904 to inaugurate the newly formed Homebuilders' Club. This house contained three design elements characteristic of all of Stickley's Craftsman houses: simplicity of building materials, construction features that serve as decoration, and a subtle and harmonious play of house color with the natural surroundings. Stickley reinforced that harmony through the idea of the "invisible" foundation, with grass and shrubbery that seem to cling to the house. Stickley wanted to create the effect that the house was solidly planted on the ground, rather than floating above it on a quarry stone or boulder foundation. Craftsman houses were usually built without cellars, to further enhance the illusion of a house growing naturally out of the earth.

Most Craftsman houses followed a standard floor plan—a dining room and living room connected by a large reception hall, and a kitchen connected to the dining room by a serving room. The second floor normally contained several bedrooms and a bathroom. The interior attempted to achieve the "maximum effect of beauty and comfort from materials which are few in number and comfortably inexpensive." So Stickley recommended that Craftsman interiors be finished in wood and that the living room be fitted with recessed window seats, overhead beams, and a high wainscot built with recesses to hold hammered metal vases or pottery. Hanging Craftsman lighting fixtures—typically of hammered copper—provided warm, diffused illumination. Living rooms generally had fireplaces made of quarry stone or boulders or perhaps faced with art pottery tiles in earth tones. The hardwood floors may have been covered with Oriental or American Indian rugs or, later, handwoven Craftsman rugs that Stickley had ordered from Scotland.

An interesting Craftsman house feature was the large entry hall that led to the stairway providing access to both the living and dining rooms. Stickley believed the entry hall should convey the same inviting feeling as any other room and should be completely furnished, for this room gave visitors the first impression of the house: "It is the preface to all the rest and in a well planned house it strikes the keynote of the whole scheme of interior decoration. Above all things, the hall ought to convey the suggestion of welcome and repose."[9] In large houses Stickley recommended that the entry hall be used like the great hall of a castle, the room in which the social life of the house takes place—ideally it served both as a dining room and a living room. If the large room needed to be divided, then a Craftsman screen might be employed. In small houses, he suggested omitting the reception hall and replacing it with a small entrance hall. In any event, strict attention should be paid to details of wood, furniture, and color scheme.

The recessed porch also played a prominent role in every Craftsman house and became most popular in southern California, where the climate encouraged outdoor living. Sometimes Stickley showed these porches enclosed with glass for use in the winter. Since these porches were recessed, the walls of the house afforded protection against wind and hot sun. Whenever possible, Craftsman houses were built facing south, so that the sun swept across the front porch and so that people sitting on the porch might avoid looking directly in the glare of the setting sun.

Stickley described his new offspring, Craftsman houses, with great care and remarkable facility. He rhapsodized about how it felt to relax in one of his houses, talked about its unique way of filtering sunlight through various patterns and textures of wood, and pointed to its special intimacy. What made his descriptions remarkable was the fact that he had never built one of these houses. He based his praise solely on information he received from his architects who had designed them and on responses from readers who had built them. He used that kind of evidence like a novelist and created the fiction, in his magazine, of a busy building program. In fact, it was not until 1908 that he decided to build one. Of course, he announced his building venture in the grandest, most eloquent terms: he made his house the star in the latest chapter in a story that might be titled "The Adventures of the Craftsman Workshops."

In 1908, Stickley purchased a 600-acre estate in Morris Plains, New Jersey, which he called Craftsman Farms and on which he hoped to place his own three-story house.[10] On the rest of the property he would situate a school "for the definite working out of the theory [he had] so long held of reviving practical and profitable handicrafts in connection with small farming carried out by modern methods of intensive agriculture."

Stickley first published the plan for his house in *The Craftsman* in October 1908, and also gave it a prominent place in *Craftsman Homes.* Stickley offered what appeared to be a strikingly candid statement about designing his own house: "I can think of no creative work that is so absolutely delightful as this creation of a home to live in for the rest of one's life. I have always felt that this might be so and have said and written it many times, but now the realization of the truth of it comes home to me with a force that is entirely new, for this is the first house I have ever built for my own use, from the ground up to the last detail of the completed structure."[11] Stickley fudges slightly by saying this is the first house "for my own use"; in truth, it was the first house he had any hand in building.

The plans for Craftsman Farms loom large in the history of Stickley's career, for they represented, as Stickley later boasted, "the most complete example in existence of the Craftsman idea." For his "most complete example," Stickley had chosen one of the most beautiful sites in the state. Here is Stickley's description of his property:

> It has heavily wooded hills, little wandering brooks, low-lying meadows and plenty of garden and orchard land; and the house will be built on a natural terrace or plateau halfway up the highest hill. The building faces toward the south, overlooking the partially cleared hillside, which turns down to the orchard and meadows at the foot and which needs very little cultivation to develop into a beautiful sloping greensward with here and there a clump of trees or a mass of shrubbery. Beyond this and over the tops of the low-lying hills around one looks straight out to the line of the Orange Mountains in the misty blue distance. Back of the house the thick woods, which will remain almost untouched, cover the hill to the summit. . . . The combination of sheltering swale or meadowland gives interesting variety in the immediate surroundings, while the view of the whole country from the hilltop through the gaps in the surrounding hills does away with any sense of being shut in.[12]

In an earlier age the world would have taken him for a landed aristocrat, a gentleman of real estate. He owned a piece of the earth. The effect was not lost on him. In one of Stickley's few terse statements—about anything—he referred to Craftsman Farms this way: "This is my Garden of Eden. This is the realization of

The Stickley home at the proposed site of Craftsman Farms, Morris Plains, New Jersey.

the dreams that I had when I worked as a lad." Ironically, where Stickley had the most on the line—his house and school, the idealization of his vision—he stumbled. Craftsman Farms fell far short of the Garden of Eden, for Stickley never built his dream house and his idea for a school of farming and handicrafts never came to pass. In the fall of 1908, however, Stickley writes as if his dream house will shortly come true.

STICKLEY HAD THREE REQUIREMENTS for the design of his house. First, it must be suited to his style of life. Second, the house must harmonize with its dramatic environment. And, third, Stickley wanted to build, as far as possible, solely with native materials found near the site. So the foundation and the lower walls of the building were to be fabricated out of split fieldstone and boulders from the nearby hillsides. Timbers were to be cut from chestnut trees growing on the land, which needed to be thinned anyway, "and the lines, proportions and color of the building . . . designed with a special view to the contour of the ground upon which it stands and the background of trees which rises behind it."[13]

Stickley demanded that the land be graded as little as possible, to maintain its natural contours against the stone walls of the first story. He decided to construct the upper walls out of plaster and half-timbers. Even the plaster was given special attention; Stickley proposed a pebble-dash finish in a dull brownish green, brushed off afterward to give a final irregular tone. The walls themselves would serve as a tribute to the industrious life of the countryside: each large panel of wet plaster would contain a picture tile "symbolizing the different farm and village industries—for example," he said, "one will show the blacksmith at his forge: another a woman spinning flax; others will depict the sower, the plowman, and such typical figures of farm life. These tiles will be very dull and rough in finish and colored with dark reds, greens, blues, dull yellows, and other colors which harmonize with the tints of wood and stone."[14]

It is worth reflecting on the scope of Stickley's failed project. He had planned a house on the grandest scale, almost six thousand square feet, with six bedrooms, two sun-rooms, a workroom, and a large billiard room. Heating and laundry facilities were so elaborate they required a separate building. Food storage too got the special Stickley touch: he planned to sink stone storage vaults for fruits and vegetables deep into the side of a hill. Even with built-in furniture, the house would have demanded an enormous amount of furnishings. His design provided for more than the bare necessities, and the price finally soared well beyond the grasp of anyone but the most wealthy. It seemed to rise, in fact, past the grasp of Stickley himself.

It seems ironic, then, for Stickley to have held this particular view: "I have also held that beauty in the home is not necessarily the result of pretentious architecture or elaborate furnishings, but should rather be a quality that belongs naturally to the simplest dwelling or the plainest article intended for daily use, and that, therefore, it is as much within the reach of the man who has but little money to spend as it is within the reach of the millionaire who can command the resources of the world."[15]

This house plan, unlike most of Stickley's Craftsman house designs, contained no front porch. Instead, an unusual pergola broke the severity of the front lines. The pergola would be constructed of cedar timbers left in their natural shape and color, with a floor (almost level with the ground) of dull red vitrified brick laid in a herringbone pattern. In place of porches, Stickley designed two sun-rooms that ran across the front of the first and second floors; these rooms would be enclosed in glass that could be easily removed in the summer, and each would have its own fireplace for use in the winter.

Even with New Jersey's sometimes cold winters, outdoor living was a top priority for Stickley. Outside each bedroom he designed a small balcony that formed an outdoor nook for sitting and reading. At the back of the house a large balcony could be left open or covered with an awning for summer sleeping. But the most interesting "country" feature was the addition of an outdoor dining room, with a rough stone fireplace, extending out from the east side of the house; it consisted of a long, twenty-four-by-twenty-foot pergola of cedar timbers, with a wide-eaved roof of tiles like that of the main house, as an "expression of an individual fancy for an outdoor dining room and a sort of camp cooking place." For the floor, he decided to move vitreous brick into a herringbone pattern, as in the front pergola.

Some Craftsman houses had chimneys that appeared to grow from large piles of haphazardly arranged boulders, gradually thinning to the top. Stickley planned one of those chimneys for his indoor-outdoor dining room. And from the inside, he said, "the fireplace is seen to be recessed in such a way that it forms a little three-sided room, the sides of which are taken up by cupboards intended to hold provisions and cooking utensils, and the whole end of which is given to the large fireplace, flanked on either side by an oven built into the chimney. One of these was designed for baking bread and the other for roasting meats and the like. The fireplace itself is fitted with hobs, a crane and a contrivance for broiling and general cooking."[16]

From Stickley's description, the interior of his house would have been spectacular. The entire lower floor, with the exception of the kitchen, was designed to be, in effect, one large room with a series of nooks, finished in chestnut fumed to a soft tone of brown. He decided to case overhead beams and girders with chestnut and finish them off in the same soft brown. "So open is the arrangement," Stickley proudly declared, "that one standing in the sun-room can look straight through the house into the woodland at the back."[17]

The walls, for half their height, he wainscoted with narrow panels and broad stiles, an unusual and attractive effect, because, as Stickley pointed out, it reversed the usual proportions of room walls. Above the wainscoting he placed several groups of casement windows, and between those groups of windows, panels of leather finished in soft brown. One might feel overwhelmed by such a profusion of wood, or at least of dark browns. But, of course, Stickley had anticipated the criticism:

> *This impression is done away with by the glow of color and the friendliness of the soft, dull surface of the wood, which retains all its woody quality under a finish that leaves it lustrous without any hard glitter such as comes from the use of varnish. So marked is this radiation of color from the wood that a room finished in this way seems to be always filled with a mellow autumnal light, irrespective of the degree of light outside. In this case, the sunniness of the color effect is heightened by the dull, soft yellow of the plain plaster frieze, and by the warm ivory tone of the plaster panels that appear between the beams. A liberal use of the yellow, olive-green, dull brick red and old blue is made in the rugs, hangings and other furnishings, and the highlights given by the copper lighting fixtures, door escutcheons, and other metal work combine with these in a play of color that is never obtrusive and yet, against the background of wood, is as rich and radiant as a forest in autumn.*[18]

Stickley planned for built-in window seats, sideboards, and cupboards with hammered metal trim. Hanging Craftsman fixtures made of hammered copper provided soft illumination in each room. Stickley even designed a piano for the living room, below a long, narrow window of leaded glass that would contain Stickley's joiner's compass and the motto, Als Ik Kan. He used quartersawn oak in all the floors, which he intended to fume to a deep brown. Stickley paid almost as much attention to details and craftsmanship as those master craftsmen and architects Charles and Henry Greene.

A COMPLEX FATE

BUT STICKLEY NEVER BUILT HIS HOUSE. In the December 1908 issue of *The Craftsman*, Stickley announced that Craftsman Farms needed a clubhouse much more than it needed his own house. It may have been a question of finances, though Stickley would never admit to such a pedestrian reason. He did say, however, that the clubhouse would be built out of cedar logs since mature cedars already dominated the grounds, making log construction inexpensive. Ground would be broken in the spring of 1909. Mary Ann Smith describes the clubhouse:

> *The proposed clubhouse . . . was to have a porch across the front and a wide dormer to illuminate the second-story rooms. The gable ends were to have a log half-timbered structure similar to the house earlier proposed for the same site. The first floor plan was divided into three long sections: the porch, reception room, and kitchen-sitting room. Each section was articulated on the ends of the house by the round log ends of exterior walls and the center room, and two additional bathrooms. The basement was to contain a smoking room and men's rest room. Thus there was a three-part horizontal division of the clubhouse—for women, joint activities, and men—as well as the three-part floor plan division.*[19]

With some major alterations—basically a scaling back of size—this would become Stickley's own residence on the Morris Plains estate.

According to Stickley's personal ledger, he planned to move his family into the log house as a temporary measure until he could build his dream house.[20] So in July 1910, the family moved from Syracuse to Morris Plains and took up residence in the log house. This marks the first time that Stickley even appeared to compromise on any issue. He must have felt at least a tinge of disappointment, and his family, after being primed for something grand, must have shared the feeling. The layout of the log house would have required some getting used to as well, since it did not lend itself to a feeling of familial closeness, despite Stickley's strong belief in the effects of space on morals and values.

Stickley, however, never expressed a word of regret. Constant references to his original house plans appeared in *The Craftsman*, but Stickley himself never mentioned them. As late as October 1913, *The Craftsman* still referred to the house as a possibility: ". . . the permanent house of Mr. Stickley being placed eventually on a hillside standing somewhat higher than the present building."[21] Stickley expressed no disappointment, it would appear, for good reason. In 1905, the Crouse Stables sold, and Stickley moved the offices and showrooms of the Craftsman Workshops to the heart of the action—29 West Thirty-Fourth Street, in New York City. The factory remained in Eastwood. While Stickley's family also remained behind, in Morris Plains, Stickley himself rented an apartment in Manhattan.[22] Living in Manhattan, Stickley felt no particular regret about not building his dream house. Indeed, according to his eldest daughter, Stickley lived the high life in the city, so much so that the family complained about his extended periods of absence. With his wife and children ensconced in Morris Plains, Stickley could more easily pursue the image of himself, with a minimum of worry and guilt, that he had called into being back in the early days of the United Crafts.

At any rate, in 1909, Stickley made a major decision. He diverted his money, his time, and his attention to his New York offices and showrooms and left the countrified log-house living to his wife and children. From his New York building, he could point to Morris Plains and boast of that simple dwelling, the clubhouse, as a living testimony to his philosophy of simple living in the country. Such contradictions mattered little to Stickley; he knew he could explain them with one or two tricks of prose. Besides, as one of Stickley's heroes, Walt Whitman, had instructed, he had never been embarrassed about or apologized for anything in his life.

The log house then was the perfect structure for the kind of living Stickley had in mind. First of all, the log house functioned as the heart of Craftsman Farms. Second, Stickley believed that as a vital part of America's early history the log house strongly suggested the American character. But for Stickley, not just any old log house would suffice. The log house at Craftsman Farms, as Stickley called it, was "the log cabin idealized." In an article in *The Craftsman* entitled "The New Log House at Craftsman Farms: An Architectural Development of the Log Cabin," Natalie Curtis described in detail its romantic architectural appeal, as well as its simple, rustic beauty:

> First, there is the bare beauty of the logs themselves with their long lines and firm curves. Then there is the open charm of the structural features which are not hidden under plaster and ornament, but are clearly revealed—a charm felt in Japanese architecture which is as Cram has said, "The perfect style in wood as Gothic is the perfect style in stone." The Japanese principle: "The wood shall be unadorned to show how beautiful is that of which the house is made" is true of the Craftsman development of the log house. For in most of our modern houses "ornament" by its very prodigality becomes cheap and "tawdry" and by contrast the quiet rhythmic monotone of the wall of logs fills one with the rustic peace of a secluded nook in the woods."[23]

No amount of romanticizing, however, can change the fact that the Craftsman Farms log house stood at the opposite extreme from the house that Stickley had designed and envisioned for himself. In its final form, the clubhouse was a simple, two-story house, the lower floor of which consisted of a general assembly room, a smaller sitting room, and a kitchen. The upper floor held three guest rooms, a private bedroom, a small sitting room, a dressing room, and two bathrooms, obviously designed to serve guests when they visited the farm. The clubhouse was simple not only in layout but also in appearance. A long, sweeping, low-pitched room was broken by a shallow dormer. Plaster covered the ends of the dormer, as well as the upper walls, and plaster paneling divided the groups of casement windows. In these plaster panels Stickley managed to salvage the idea for picture tiles that he had planned for his own house.

The details of the clubhouse, the only building Stickley designed, give insight into his architectural interests. The house was wholly constructed of chestnut logs, peeled and stained a dull brown. Where the logs came together, carpenters sawed them flat and caulked any cracks with pitch and oakum. Stickley pointed with special pride to the corbeling of the projecting logs at the corners of the house; on one side they supported the overhang of the slate roof, and on the other they supported the weight of the second story that projected above the porch. Stickley designed two fireplaces, one at each end of the large assembly room. Each fireplace he fitted with a hammered copper hood, one dramatically displaying a line from Chaucer, "The lyf so short, the craft so long to lerne," a line that Stickley intended, it would seem, to support his expansionist spirit. These hoods were used not merely to decorate the hearth or to help draw the fire but also to conceal an ingenious device for heating the entire house:

Interior view of living room at Stickley's home in Morris Plains.
The fireplace hood carries a line from Geoffrey Chaucer: "The lyf so short, the craft so long to lerne."

A broad band of metal goes all around the fireplace opening. This band, or rather frame, is four inches wide and is made to fit into the opening exactly. The hood is riveted to the frame and the whole thing may be taken out at any time when it is necessary to clean or repair the hot-water pipes placed in such a way that they will get the full benefit of the heat that rises from the fireplace. Pipes from this heater will run down back of the metal frame and below the floor to radiators placed in other rooms, thus insuring a general diffusion of heat every time the fire is lighted.[24]

Stickley concluded his discussion of the clubhouse with this note: "This club house will be open to all the workers, students and guests at Craftsman Farms and also to invited guests of the place. We intend to make it a central gathering place where it is hoped that many a pleasant entertainment will be held. Additional accommodations will be furnished by the log cottages that will be scattered over the hillside in the neighborhood of the club house."[25]

His building experience at Morris Plains taught him important lessons. He not only enjoyed erecting his own building, but recognized the business potential in home construction. The demand for Craftsman Homes was growing so rapidly that Stickley started yet another branch of his business enterprise in 1909, called the Craftsman Home Building Company; the following year the company constructed a number of houses around the New York area. But in forming his business, Stickley made a startling disclosure. In January 1909, after working on his own house at Morris Plains, Stickley confessed that he had never really built one of these houses:

However well founded may be a given theory of house planning, there is nothing like practical experience in building to show both its excellence and its defects. And if the designer be wise, every house that he builds adds to his stock of knowledge regarding the thousand and one details that go to make up the atmosphere of comfort and livableness that so essentially belongs to the right kind of home.

We had designed many Craftsman houses before we began actually to build them. These earlier plans carried our ideas into effect so far as we could tell on paper, but the plans themselves were given into the hands of local architects and builders, and in nearly all cases modified to suit the tastes and requirements of the owner, so that the experience gained through building was not ours.

About a year ago, however, we began ourselves to superintend the building of a certain Craftsman house, and since then we have been able to put out what we regard as better plans than were ever achieved through purely theoretical work.[26]

Through sleight of hand, Stickley managed to turn his inexperience in architecture to his own advantage. Look, he said, now I can plan better houses because I've actually built some! Few people would have been able to carry off such a display of linguistic backing-and-filling, but Stickley had nerve, and people responded to the sincere tone of his rhetoric.

A COMPLEX FATE

In March 1910, perhaps after some further experience with the Craftsman Home Building Company, Stickley made another disclosure: it was impossible, he now declared, to build one of his enduring, well-crafted homes cheaply. The time when one could build such a dwelling for under $1,500, he now realized, had long since passed. To popularize his Craftsman house plans, he had merely done the most expedient thing: he had apparently chosen a figure that he thought would appeal. But in response to readers who demanded houses at inexpensive prices, Stickley unashamedly responded that if one wanted high-quality construction with careful attention to detail, then "we find it difficult to supply designs for what are ordinarily called cheap houses, because it is almost impossible for us to build even a small house that is designed along purely Craftsman lines for less than $3,000 or $5,000, and more usually the cost runs from $6,000 to $8,000."[27] Stickley had greatly underestimated the cost of building one of his houses—prices originally announced in *Craftsman Homes* ranged from $500 to $1,500—but, once again, no one could never say he felt chagrined.

ISABELLE ANSCOMBE AND CHARLOTTE GERE, in *Arts and Crafts in Britain and America*, expressed shock at Stickley's behavior. They maintained that Stickley "was forced to admit in *The Craftsman* that not only had he never built the Craftsman houses, which he had designed and published, but that he knew that their cost would be much higher than his estimates. *The Craftsman's* circulation began to drop from what had been its peak."[28] Anscombe and Gere suggested that the disclosure was Stickley's undoing, but they underestimated his amazing capacity for turning failure into success. Stickley gave no indication that he was "forced" to admit anything. He had never built a piece of his furniture or one of his Craftsman houses, and he felt no compulsion to apologize. But now that he had actually built a house, he adjusted his ideas and attitudes to the new reality. In an instant, he had become an expert on building. Far from hurting the circulation of the magazine, his candor helped build support for Craftsman houses. By 1912 the entire 20,000 press run of *Craftsman Homes* had sold out. And to meet the great demand, Stickley published in 1912 *More Craftsman Homes*.

More Craftsman Homes contained plans and illustrations for Stickley's "more recent designs in Craftsman Houses suited for building in concrete, in stone, in brick and wood." No fool, Stickley carefully pointed out in this new volume that "many of these houses have already been built and have been found satisfactory by their owners."[29] Though some plans in the book dated from 1907, most of the designs in *More Craftsman Homes* were from the years 1909 to 1911. In this second volume, Stickley avoided furniture and accessories, for his furniture had already firmly established itself; he had no new pieces to introduce. Now Stickley was eager to tap the market for building houses and wanted to spread the word about Craftsman architecture.

The second volume also contained more plans for small, rustic cabins, cottages, and bungalows. And, unsurprisingly, the book emphasized log construction. The log cabin offered a solution to the problem of cost. With the log cabin, Stickley believed he could minimize construction costs and still offer "democratic art," a point he underscored in an article titled "Architectural Development of the Log Cabin in America." He featured plans for log houses and reinforced the idea with a series of articles: "The Log House Built at Craftsman Farms"; "Small but Comfortable Log Dwelling"; "Log Cottage for Summer Camp or Permanent Country Living"; "Comfortable One-Story Bungalow of Logs"; "Permanent Summer Camp of Logs"; "Log Bungalow for Summer Use"; and "Craftsman Country Schoolhouse of Logs." The book clearly reflected Stickley's new attitude that the log cabin was "the most interesting of modern dwellings."

By 1913, Stickley had organized several architectural services for his readers in search of country living: a real estate finding service, an investment service for people in search of country and suburban homes, a landscape service, and a home-finding service for country homes. In 1914 he also published a small supplement to *The Craftsman*, *Twenty-Four Craftsman Houses with Floor Plans*, which reproduced plans from *The Craftsman* for 1912 and 1913. He had become so involved with architecture that at the end of volume 23 (1912) of the magazine, Stickley announced, "*The Craftsman* for 1913 will be a handbook of reference for the home-lover." *The Craftsman* that year presented a large number of articles on home construction, home care, repair, and the planting and care of gardens. It resembled a practical do-it-yourself encyclopedia for home owners.

Over the course of thirteen years, Stickley published in *The Craftsman* plans for more than two hundred homes that ranged in price from a low of $900 to a whopping $30,000. If an anonymous article in *The Craftsman* is accurate, a great many people built them: "The number of homes built on Craftsman lines, after Mr. Stickley's plans, runs into the thousands each year. Over twenty million dollars worth of Craftsman Homes were built last year alone, 1915, in all parts of the world, from Alaska to the Fiji Islands, thus attesting to the popularity and adaptability of his style in architecture."[30] According to Mrs. Wiles, Stickley wrote many of the anonymous articles; thus the figure $20 million may be inflated. Nevertheless, Stickley's Craftsman style influenced a good deal of the country. Even today, thousands of bungalows, country cottages, large cement houses, and rustic cabins, all in the Craftsman style, can be found in small towns in the Midwest and in large cities on either coast.

Only a few architects have ever exerted that much influence, and probably none who, like Stickley, operated without any formal training. He launched his architectural enterprise, like his other ventures, by climbing on the shoulders of another person, in this case Harvey Ellis. Later Stickley hired architects to refine and popularize those architectural ideas and, through his magazine, turned them into a movement of considerable force. To Stickley's credit, he never saw an idea in isolation. Architecture fit into a network of Craftsman expressions including the magazine, furniture, catalogs, and lectures. Stickley seemed to be encircling the country with his philosophy, leaving no one untouched by the Craftsman Movement.

7

THE PRODUCTS OF THE CRAFTSMAN WORKSHOPS

By 1905, STICKLEY HAD ABANDONED the idealism of the United Crafts for the realities of competition, and he began to capitalize on the confidence that success had brought. He started early that year by announcing the publication of a new furniture catalog from the Craftsman Workshops that contained a shocking eighty pages of information, along with illustrations of Craftsman furnishings and sections on both *The Craftsman* magazine and his most recent passion, Craftsman houses. By August of 1905, Stickley had expanded his line of furniture to include cabinets designed to order in conjunction with the Herring-Hall-Marvin Safe Company (New York). Disguised as Craftsman dowery chests, writing desks with cabinets below, wine cabinets, and tables, these metal safes reflected a change from his early philosophy of a democratic art: Stickley had attracted customers with money to spend and valuables to hide. And while he had declared in 1901 that he would make furniture only in that "most democratic of woods," oak, he now offered these safes in a much more expensive wood, mahogany. In fact, virtually every piece of furniture in the 1905 catalog could be ordered not only in oak but in mahogany as well.

In 1905, Stickley received a patent for a new, even more expensive line of furniture he called Craftsman Spindle furniture.[1] Stickley distinguished this Spindle furniture from his regular line by adding a series of thin, square spindles along the backs and sometimes the sides of the chairs, on the sides of library tables and footstools, or on the foot- and headboards of beds. With these new, more expensive furniture designs, Stickley could no longer pretend to be manufacturing "democratic art." He had moved in a different direction, one that he would pursue until his last days in business.

Stickley also reached a new level of maturity in his prose style. In January 1904, Stickley had referred to oak as "the most human of woods, that is, the most amenable to the educative process." By July 1905, again describing the special properties of wood, his prose conveys a more scientific, less romantic attitude:

> *The peculiar charm of grain and texture in woods is owing to the way the tree builds up its cellular structure. Each tree does this after its own fashion, and wood is called hard, soft, light, heavy, tough, porous, elastic, or otherwise according to these cells. All are more or less familiar with the circular rings that appear when the tree is cut down, one each year, on the outside. So it is apparent the oldest portion of the tree is on the inside. This old portion is what is known as the heartwood, and is tougher, heavier, and stronger than the younger wood or sapwood. Growths materially differ in spring and summer, and these differences are marked in the rings. In the Southern pines, for instance, the spring and summer growths are shown by solid bands.*[2]

Stickley's production had increased dramatically—he now offered more than twice the number of pieces of furniture that he had offered in 1901—and he could no longer hide the fact that he employed power tools in the production of his furniture. Echoing the sentiments of Frank Lloyd Wright's famous 1901 Hull House talk, "The Art and Craft of the Machine," Stickley argued that no one could blame the machine for the obvious lack of genuine art in contemporary America, for some very routine tasks could be better performed with mechanical assistance:

> *All other things being equal, a piece of furniture, for instance, that is entirely hand-made would be apt to have more individuality, and therefore more artistic value, than one entirely machine-made, for the reason that the artisan would naturally put more of his personality into the making of it, but, given the same personal interest of the worker in the completed article, nearly every part of it, except such as are added expressly for ornament, might be made by machine without destroying its interest and value as a work of art. For example, in the making of a chair there is no particular field for artistic expression in the boring of a round hole, or in the shaping of a mortise, that such details must necessarily be done by hand when they may be done more swiftly by machinery. But if the chair is to be valued as an individual piece of work, the man who makes it must have known the joy and enthusiasm of carrying out an idea that is his own, or with which he is in such perfect sympathy that the work becomes a delight.*[3]

In October 1905, Stickley seized upon the occasion of the magazine's anniversary to introduce a new phrase, the "Craftsman Movement." He hit on an interesting public relations move that brought a new perspective to the English phrase, "Arts and Crafts Movement," which emphasized the end products and made of the artist a ghost who hovered mysteriously in the background. Stickley explained his motives for the name:

Tile-top table of fumed oak with inset of Grueby tiles
(26″ high, 24″ wide, 20″ deep). Circa 1902.

Hall settle of fumed oak (42″ high, 48″ long, 20″ deep). Circa 1903.

Writing desk and safe of mahogany, with iron hardware (50″ high, 35″ wide, 21″ deep). Circa 1907.

This, our anniversary number, begins the fifth year of The Craftsman. *Of the progress made by the magazine within the past year, and of the efficiency of the work done in its chosen field, our friends and readers are best fitted to judge. That it is a kindly judgment they give has already been expressed to us in many ways, of which the most unmistakable are the steady growth in circulation of* The Craftsman, *and the many voluntary expressions of goodwill which every mail brings us, and which, coming as they do from all parts of the country, form the best evidence of its rapidly widening influence.*

This influence has met with a response so cordial and a cooperation so hearty on the part of those allied with us in thought and feeling that is has come to be known as "THE CRAFTSMAN MOVEMENT." Without that response and cooperation our ideas and beliefs, however earnestly and persistently advocated from our viewpoint, could never have gained the strength and scope necessary to make any lasting impression upon the thought and life of the people. The idea is universal; it needs only to be spoken to gain recognition and support from all whose minds hold any quality akin to it, for it is merely a firm belief in both the need and the possibility of a simpler and truer conception and expression of life in its everyday tasks and surroundings, and an endeavor to carry out that belief in practical form. THE CRAFTSMAN MOVEMENT not only makes the home the source and inspiration of character-building, but endeavors to instill into the hearts and minds of all a realization of the beauty, the restfulness, and the uplifting influence of simplicity.[4]

As Stickley argued for simplicity in the Craftsman Movement, his business grew more and more complex. During 1905 alone, *The Craftsman's* architectural department drafted four hundred Craftsman house plans to the specifications of the various members of the Homebuilders' Club; the demand for those plans, which ranged in building cost from $2,000 to $15,000, increased every month during that year. The Craftsman Workshops had expanded their Craftsman Associates (stores with exclusive rights to Stickley's furniture) to more than sixty, located in every major city in America, plus scores of smaller cities. *The Craftsman,* already a vital and vocal force in the Arts and Crafts Movement in America, had evolved into a full-fledged magazine of about one hundred fifty pages. And Stickley continually added new and innovative features. Beginning in October 1905, for instance, Stickley instituted a "series of colored plates of the Craftsman House designs . . . showing color schemes for interiors, and the effect of fabrics, metals and tinted plaster, combined with the varying tones given the wood trim by the Craftsman finishes." Stickley repeatedly bragged that *The Craftsman* "was well written, thoughtful, instructive material that cannot be found elsewhere" and did not hesitate to end with a commercial come-on: "He is wise who makes up his full set while the earlier volumes are still to be had."

Driven by a need for thoroughness and completeness—some might call it a megalomania—Stickley also turned his attention to his line of home accessories. By 1905 his line of needlework had mushroomed to the point that it required its own catalog, *Needle-Work from the Craftsman Workshops*, so detailed that it ran to sixty pages. Like everything else, Stickley infused it with his Craftsman philosophy:

> *That which chiefly distinguishes the Craftsman needle-work is its extreme simplicity. It is, in no sense, embroidery, as this term is usually employed, but an applique of one fabric upon another. Each piece has been designed with special reference to the end which it is intended to serve, and therefore, wherever practicable, we have used for table squares, window draperies, etc., such linens and fabrics as may be most readily laundered.*
>
> *. . . The simplest stitches, in connection with the broad leaves and petal forms of the applique, are used to express the decorative motif, which more often than not is a pretty interpretation of some simple plant form, as the honeysuckle, the wild rose, or the cowslip. Color, here, as in all design, forms an important factor. The harmonies that these stuffs afford are almost limitless and it is quite possible to select from them the exact combination needed for a particular room.*

Those interested in learning needlework could write to the Craftsman Workshops for instruction. Finished items could also be ordered from Stickley's wide list of fabrics and designs.

Stickley offered his line of needlework in an exhaustingly wide range of fabrics: Craftsman canvas, plain linens, homespun, bloom linens, figured linens, toile, lustre canvas, all-wool taffeta, figured challis, silk and mohair, willow weave, stripe velour, plain velour, Craftsman crepe, Pompeiian cloth, Gothic silk and caddis. The catalog also described the kinds of stitchery he employed in the workshops—couching, outlining, and drawn work—and then explained through detailed illustrations how women in his factories actually made the individual stitch, to "obtain the most striking results in both line and mass."[5]

Householders could choose from table scarves, luncheon sets (a centerpiece, tea cloth, and six doilies), pillows, window draperies, and bed covers, all available in appliqué motifs drawn from nature. Stickley called on his designer to offer not one or two designs, or even a half dozen; he offered an entire forest of trees, shrubs, and flowers of every possible kind: seedpods, gingko, poppy, pomegranate, orange, apple tree, pinecone, cornflower, wintergreen, checkerberry, crocus, horse chestnut, ivy leaf, teasel, wild rose, grapevine, and tulip. Different fabrics came in different colors, but Stickley generally preferred earth colors or other muted shades, such as foliage brown, pomegranate, salmon, rose pink, russet, green, gray green, and apple green. Finally, in the same catalog Stickley presented—in one design only, probably because it did not emanate from his own factory—an imported Oriental carpet woven of camel's hair in old yellow and carpeting of grass matting in a soft green.

The endless array of Craftsman needlework and fabrics boggles the imagination. Even for someone like Stickley, whose interests could be both exhaustive and exhausting, the line of needlework he produced was prodigious. He may have had not only a commercial but also a psychological reason for producing such abundant designs. The Arts and Crafts Movement in England was founded primarily—though certainly not exclusively—by William Morris, C. R. Ashbee, and W. R. Lethaby. These three men, all trained as architects, articulated the theories on which the entire movement so solidly rested. In this country, the movement had an entirely different beginning. In perhaps typical American fashion, an untrained, mostly uneducated farm boy, with a headstrong determination and heartfelt desire, translated those English theories for the American public. And because he played the role of innovator and not inventor, Stickley had to prove himself in the grandest style imaginable. So Stickley came to measure his importance in the numbers of objects he produced and the numbers of stores that carried his dizzying array of objects.

HIS APPROACH TO NEEDLEWORK was not an aberration. He gave to each of the arts and crafts the same treatment. Over the years, for instance, Stickley greatly expanded his metalwork designs. From the beginning of his United Crafts days, Stickley employed metalworkers. But the first catalog offered no metal accessories for sale; the only metalwork consisted of hinges, pulls, and escutcheons on various cabinets. The early issues of *The Craftsman* talked about the artistic

Interior of Stickley's home, Morris Plains, New Jersey.

111

Hammered iron pull.

merits of handwrought metal and featured mainly Russian artisans who worked in metal. Then, in May 1902, Stickley ran an article titled "Beaten Metal Work," by Amalie Busck, with photographs of hammered and repoussé work in copper from her Busck Studios. This article was a transition, taking readers from the work of foreign metalsmiths to that of his own metalworkers. Only two months later, Stickley announced that the United Crafts now offered for sale a series of electric and other lighting devices. Soon he was presenting a whole array of other copper and brass work, including fireplace screens, andirons, coal scuttles, wine coolers, umbrella stands, plaques, screens, and ashtrays.

In the early years, Stickley may not have produced much of the metalwork in his own workshops. Early artwork for his metalwork—photographs that would serve as illustrations in his catalogs—carried the name of a metal specialty studio, the Onandaga Metal Shops, stamped on the back of each photograph. Stickley bought accessories from Onandaga that he sold as Craftsman. But by 1905, in predictable fashion, Stickley's own workshops hammered out every single piece. He even received a patent for a square nail—sometimes made of iron and sometimes copper—that he used to finish the corners of stretched leather on chair seats and footstools. These nails gave each piece a more complete and more medieval appearance. And in 1905, Stickley issued yet another catalog, this one devoted to all things metal and entitled *Hand Wrought Metal Work.*[6]

Stickley gave his metalwork the same care and attention that characterized his woodwork. Anyone who has pulled open a drawer or a door on a Stickley cabinet or desk knows the heft and feel produced by the great care that went into each piece of his hardware. Indeed, the most immediately tangible proof of the quality of his metalwork, for most people, came in the form of metal pulls on his cabinets and drawers or metal straps on his sideboards. Though Stickley made some handles for his earliest furniture out of pewter, he moved quickly to iron or copper.[7] Handwrought and hand-finished in the Craftsman Workshops, each piece of metal had an incredibly rich, dark patina. The iron was finished in what Stickley called "armor bright," and the copper was darkened by "an old process of firing that gives a surface that mellows with age and exposure."

Medieval craftsman had developed that "old process." In fact, metalwork occupied a privileged place in the pantheon of medieval crafts. For one thing, metalsmithing tapped into the mystical powers of the universe by combining all of the four elements: raw metal came from the earth; fire made it malleable; to make the fire burn hotter, a bellows blew air into the flames; and, finally, the finished piece was submerged in water. A successful metalsmith not only forged metal, but he also forged a union of extremes—red-hot metal with ice-cold water. Only through such a collision of opposites could the metal reach an even temper, that is, acquire the ability to bend without breaking or fissuring.

Gustav Stickley's attention to details of all kinds paid off. Stickley had moved in five short years from obscurity to a position of national attention. He had shaped the Arts and Crafts Movement to such a degree that he could rename it the Craftsman Movement—after himself. Possessed of astonishing charisma and drive, Stickley was early twentieth-century America's consummate entrepreneur/craftsman: no one else was hammering metal, building furniture, offering a staggering array of needlework, editing and publishing a national magazine, and designing and building homes on his grand scale. Stickley managed not only to encompass the movement but also to give it shape and direction. The sheer task of organizing the entire range of activities would have exhausted most people, but it appeared to thrill and exhilarate Stickley.

By November of his decisive year of expansion, 1905, Stickley announced that, as a consequence of the rapid growth of the Craftsman Movement, he would move his executive and editorial offices to larger quarters—29 West 34th Street, a few doors east of Broadway, in New York City. The move to Manhattan meant a great deal to Stickley. For one thing, it signaled enormous financial success and announced that Stickley commanded more than just a furniture business. New York, after all, served as the principal financial and mercantile hub of the country (its closest rival was Chicago). To occupy several floors in a Manhattan office building meant that Stickley had managed to create an enterprise, a small manufacturing empire. One can drive from Syracuse to New York City in a short time, but in terms of power and prestige light years separate the two.

In characteristic fashion, Stickley argued that he had to move to New York for practical, altruistic reasons. The commercial reasons for his move lay well buried in his prose:

A Complex Fate

It has seemed to us that we should enlarge our field of usefulness and be better able to serve our friends and readers by opening in New York a place, central in location and easy of access, which should be in itself a practical exposition, not only of our own ideas and principles, but of others naturally allied to them.

This will enable us to show The Craftsman idea of rooms fitted exactly for the work that is to be done in them, where the surroundings of the worker shall be comfortable and beautiful in their practical simplicity.

An entire floor will be devoted to the Exposition and for the reception of all who are interested in The Craftsman Movement.

The intention is to make it a complete example of Craftsman ideas, a place where anyone who wishes to know about our work, or other features connected with Home-building and Furnishing may come and confer with us.

The large and interesting collection of original designs of Craftsman Houses, with colored perspective illustrations, both exterior and interior, will be shown, together with samples of The Craftsman Wood Finishes, Wall Coverings, Fabrics and other accessories.

Further than this, friends of The Craftsman, *who are temporarily in New York, are cordially invited to make this department a resting place, where they meet their own friends in a familiar way. Out of town people, who visit the city occasionally, may have their mail sent in* The Craftsman's *care to be held until called for.*

The entire floor will be a typical Craftsman interior, furnished according to Craftsman principles of space, freedom and restfulness.[8]

New York City held a fascination for Stickley for other reasons. He saw himself less and less as a simple furniture designer and more and more as a cultural figure, a man of ideas. A Manhattan address meant not only that he had "made it" on a grand scale but also that he had joined the avant-garde: whatever could be considered new and different in the arts debuted in New York City and only gradually filtered out to the center of the country. Stickley could pursue his image as an innovator and originator more easily in New York than in Eastwood or Syracuse, or Morris Plains. Stickley, who five short years before had exhorted his public with back-to-the-country rhetoric, now settled into a new life in the heart of Manhattan.

New York proved a receptive audience to Stickley and his ideas. Sir Caspar Clark, who had recently assumed directorship of the Metropolitan Museum of Art, had been director of the South Kensington Museum (now the Victoria and Albert), which had promoted the handicrafts of the Arts and Crafts Movement. The Metropolitan would certainly welcome Arts and Crafts ideas, and that museum set an artistic standard for the city and thus for a good deal of the country.

Finally, and of some consequence, in Manhattan Stickley could indulge his own ethnicity. By 1900, of all the foreign-born residents of Manhattan, more than one-quarter were German. More than two-thirds of the entire population of New

York City that year had parents born in a foreign country—the majority of them in Germany. By 1910 more Germans lived in New York City than in any city in Germany except Berlin. As a New Yorker, Stickley would seem like less of an oddity. Moreover, in New York his German background spoke loudly of old-world craftsmanship. German craftsmen had carved the intricate animals on the first carousel in America, in Central Park. Those animals became an instant sensation, introducing many New Yorkers to the marvels of German woodworking. Stickley referred to his German background his entire life, and after he moved his offices to New York City, he claimed it as a mark of special distinction.

In 1906, the first year after the Craftsman Building was opened, Stickley presented his largest catalog ever—ninety-two separate furniture designs, covering every room of the house. Stickley knew, however, that a catalog, even with the best of photographs, could not show the furniture's unique finish or details of construction. In New York, Stickley could construct model rooms outfitted with a complete line of Craftsman furnishings. And since that furniture occupied the very heart of Stickley's Craftsman lifestyle, we might profitably examine the major pieces as a way of trying to understand his mind-set.

For each room of the house Stickley recommended standard pieces of furniture.[9] He saw the center of activity in the Craftsman house as the living room. Using an idea that Frank Lloyd Wright had earlier advanced, Stickley believed the living room should, as a gesture of hospitality and warmth, expand to accommodate as many guests as possible:

> *It seems to us much more friendly, homelike and comfortable to have one big living room into which one steps directly from the entrance door . . . and to have this living room the place where all the business and pleasure of the common family life may be carried on. And we like it to have pleasant nooks and corners which give a comfortable sense of semi-privacy and yet are not in any way shut off from the larger life of the room.*
>
> *Such an arrangement has always seemed to us symbolic of the ideal conditions of social life. The big hospitable fireplace is almost a necessity, for the hearth-stone is always the center of the true home life, and the very spirit of home seems to be lacking when a register or radiator tries ineffectually to take the place of a glowing fire or a crackling leaping fire of logs.*[10]

If hospitality can be conveyed through a piece of furniture, then the single item that best expressed largesse and openness throughout the Arts and Crafts period must be the Morris chair. This chair epitomized not only Stickley's Craftsman furnishings, but Mission furniture in general and, for that reason, usually turned out to be the first piece of Mission furniture people acquired for their homes. William Morris's firm had popularized the chair in England by re-

Drop-arm Morris chair of fumed oak, with leather cushions (height of back from floor, 40″; height of seat from floor, 15″; Seat: 23″ wide x 27″ deep). Circa 1909.

fining an older version called the Sussex chair; when Stickley traveled to England it immediately caught his attention. Ironically, Morris designed no furniture for Morris, Marshall, Faulkner and Co., though he supervised the firm's overall production. Philip Webb actually designed the so-called Morris chair about 1865 from a sketch sent to him based on a chair crudely executed by a Sussex carpenter. But so powerful was the Morris name that it attached itself to this particular chair.

Over the years, Stickley offered various models, the most substantial of which was a large, flat-armed monster, with slats under the arms and an adjustable back, and harnessed solidly together with mortise and tenon joints. Parents could flop themselves down on its ample cushions, kids could hoist themselves up on its broad arms—the Morris chair in its boxy defiance withstood whatever use or abuse it received.

Stickley presented just such a chair to Charles Wagner as a gift when Wagner visited the Craftsman Workshops and lectured at the Craftsman Hall. Wagner took the chair home to Paris and wrote Stickley to tell him how much he enjoyed the piece:

> *My new friend is an arm chair. . . . Such a chair is a real resource in the house. . . . It receives you when you come home tired out. And if you wish to taste the joys of domesticity in the chimney corner, a whole group of children can find place on its wide arms which are like two benches.*
>
> *. . . I have already tried several experiments: the first is that one can sleep admirably in the arms of my new friend; the second, that one naturally meditates there. It is a chair which induces reflection. For itself it is full of thoughts. It is not one of those pieces which can say nothing; it wants to say something.*
>
> *There are ideas of solidity, of character, of home, of venerated antiquity, of fidelity in this gigantic frame. It is not a frail piece of furniture, it is an honest one. It wants you to be an honest man.*[11]

The Craftsman Workshops had designed the chair to give pleasure. Most models had wide arms to accommodate books, pipes, or drinks—wide enough, in fact, to use as small writing desks. Stickley provided the chairs with huge stuffed cushions for further comfort, and in front of the Morris chair could usually be found a Craftsman footstool. Nearly all the Morris chairs sold well and remained in the catalogs over the years.

Stickley also manufactured a range of sheet music racks and cabinets, liquor cabinets, and a smoker's cabinet. He truly believed that because the wood and workmanship of the furniture were so fine, the colors so rich and warm, and the edges so sharp, people would naturally find the impulse to keep their rooms neat and tidy, their furniture clean and waxed. A room fitted with Craftsman furniture created an inviting, peaceful space.

In Stickley's scheme, restful environments could never be achieved with overstuffed couches and chairs. Cleanliness and health were principal concerns during the period, and Stickley believed that upholstered furniture harbored germs, especially tubercular germs. (For the same reason, he advised against wall-to-wall carpeting.) In the Arts and Crafts Movement, cleanliness held first rank with Godliness: Clean-lined furniture, clean hands, and a clean mind all went together. Elbert Hubbard, who started the arts and crafts community called the Roycrofters, began his entrepreneurial life as a soap salesman; Frank Lloyd Wright designed a factory for the Larkin Soap Company; and the architects Charles and Henry Greene designed a residence in Pasadena for William Gamble, President of Proctor and Gamble Soap Company. The settle, with removable cushions, represented the Arts and Crafts answer to the upholstered couch.[12] But settles were not nearly as comfortable as couches and were not meant for slouching or reclining. Recognizing that people would likely find the settle uncomfortable, Stickley recommended that people pad the backs and sides with loose pillows—available, of course, from the Craftsman Workshops.

Most of the settles that remained in Stickley's catalogs throughout the years were large, heavy-looking rectangles of wood. The largest of them measured eighty-four inches long; the shortest, fifty-six inches. They all came with loose cushions, constructed with painstaking care:

> *The removable cushions are made of selected Java floss encased in denim, and are so stitched at the edges that the shape is retained as long as the cushion lasts. They are covered with leather, canvas, or other material equally durable, and are as rich in effect as the best upholstery and as easily kept fresh and clean as sofa pillows. A delightful variation is secured by the use of soft leather or sheepskin, stained to any color that*

Single-door bookcase of fumed oak, with copper hardware
(56" high, 36" wide, 13" deep). Circa 1909.

Tea table of fumed oak (26″ high, 20″ diameter). Circa 1912.

harmonizes with the wood of the framework and with the color scheme of the room. With chairs and settles made of fumed oak in all its varying shades of brown and green, the cushions of leather may be of brown, green, bisquit color, dull orange, old blue, or any color that is found most desirable in a room. Very often the strongest color accent in the room is given by these leather cushions, and endless color combinations may be obtained by their use. Another excellent material for the coverings of loose chair cushions is an imported canvas of hemp and flax, woven together and dyed in the piece, a process which produces a delightful play of tones caused by the different degrees in which the dye is taken by the two materials. These come in all colors and wear "like iron."[13]

The living room would probably have one or two rockers—the sine qua non of Mission furniture. Stickley's 1909 catalog alone listed eighteen different models, including a children's version. In fact, Stickley made a rocker version of almost every straight-legged chair he produced. He made rockers with arms and without, large rockers for loose and lazy rocking, and low-seated rockers for knitting or sewing. Some came with hard leather seats, some with spring seat cushions, some with slip rush seats.

The Arts and Crafts Movement believed in bookcases. Literacy was on the rise in early twentieth-century America, and bookcases spoke of culture and erudition. The movement favored bookcases with doors inset with small glass panes so that the books could be shut away and remain dust free. The bookcases came in varying sizes—one, two, or three doors wide—some with mortise and tenon joints, and some with keyed joints. Corners were usually pegged, and shelves were stationary in line with the door mullions, the thin wooden strips used to divide the glass panes. Door pulls were either hammered iron or copper, shaped as circles or teardrops. In addition to these sturdy bookcases, Stickley also manufactured several kinds of magazine cabinets, as well as simple, freestanding book racks and small revolving and sliding book racks designed to sit on top of a library table, another standard piece of living room furniture.

The largest type of library table, the trestle table, was produced early on at the United Crafts, and a lighter version of it later came out of the Craftsman Workshops. The most popular version held two drawers, but the factory also produced tables with one drawer and with three drawers. (Designers stretched leather over some of the tops and decorated the edges with brass or copper brads.) A round wooden peg secured each joint on the library table, the top joints were double pegged, and a shelf was connected by a mortise and tenon joint to the thick side stretchers.[14] Long, curving corbels, pegged to the legs, supported the usually thick table top. Stickley showed these tables with a book or two spread out on them.

Craftsman interior.

Stickley paid careful attention to details most furniture manufacturers slighted. For instance, the factory constructed the desk drawers, though they were seldom seen, with the same care that it gave to an exposed table top or a leg joint. These drawers were, first of all, unusually deep, made out of the same oak—or sometimes maple—as the rest of the table. They had dovetail joints in front and back and ran on hardwood guides. Workmen stamped each drawer with a number, since they made a particular drawer to fit only one particular side of a library table or one particular tier of a cabinet.

Stickley also manufactured a round library table in forty- and forty-eight-inch diameters with a wooden or leather top, and a handsome hexagonal table. It measured twenty-nine inches high and forty-eight inches across from point to point and was decorated with copper brads around the edge. Stylized mortise and tenon, keyed joints echoed the pattern created by the sharp corners of the table, and the graceful curves on the table supports found their echo in the stretchers that connected to the flat legs. In this table—more sophisticated than most in terms of design—curves played against sharp angles, a design strategy that lightened the gravity of the table. Two modifications from the United Crafts version of the table are worth noting, both probably engineered by Harvey Ellis. First, he stylized the tenons to match the tabletop. Second, he reduced the legs in thickness. Both changes contribute to a much lighter-looking, more graceful piece of furniture.

Since Stickley paid so much attention to home interiors, and particularly to the great room—the living room as a gathering place for the family—it was perhaps inevitable that he would produce a piano. In November 1909 he advertised the first Craftsman piano, designed by the Craftsman Workshops and executed by the Everett Piano Company of Boston. Stickley's description of his piano, which included an inlay design reminiscent of Harvey Ellis, sounds more like a description of a painting than a musical instrument:

> The piano case is built of carefully selected fumed oak finished in a clear luminous tone of brown. Around the top we have put a narrow inlaid band of very dark green wood and dark brown English oak, both of which serve to emphasize the prevailing tones in the lighter oak of the case. The conventionalized plant forms that appear on either side of the music rack are inlaid with a combination of pewter and fine-grained wood that shows varying tones of green. Directly in the center of the dark blossom that appears in the square of pewter, is a fleck of brilliant vermillion which seems to accent the whole color combination.

Stickley wanted even something as large and boxy as a piano to carry a vegetal form, and the inlay met that need.

To accent his Craftsman furniture for the living room, Stickley offered for sale two Craftsman rugs, in colors to harmonize with everything else in the room.

121

Woven in Scotland, they came in several geometric designs. Stickley described one in an advertisement in the November 1909 issue of *The Craftsman:*

> *The design is worked out in three different color combinations, one rug showing a round work of deep leaf-green with a design in wood and leather tones and the other, with a ground work of dark brown, almost the color of old oak, with the design worked out in lighter brown and straw colors. The third with a ground work of dark blue with the design worked out in lighter shades.*

The second style carried out its design in varying combinations of colors such as "green on a background of deep brown, broken here and there with spots of a light golden brown." Stickley also sold Craftsman rugs woven in Ireland in odd sizes for "the buyer who cares to furnish his own design."

Fall-front desk, fumed oak with copper hardware
(52" high, 26" wide, 11" deep). Circa 1902.

Fall-front desk of fumed oak, with copper hardware (52″ high, 26″ wide, 11″ deep). Circa 1904.
Desk chair of fumed oak with leather cushion (height of back from floor, 40″;
height of seat from floor, 18″; seat: 15″ wide x 14″ deep). Circa 1904.

For all its talk to the contrary, the Arts and Crafts Movement developed along clearly traditional gender lines. The men in the Movement took as their own domain metalsmithing, cabinetmaking, and leather working, and left needlework exclusively to women. Architecture, as I have already pointed out, admitted virtually no women into its ranks. The results of this traditional view could be clearly seen in Craftsman houses. The Craftsman house had a study for a man, a kitchen and a sewing room for a woman. A man might be found reading books or writing poetry in the study; a woman, at her demure desk, with its reduced writing surface, jotting notes or paying bills.

Stickley pretended otherwise. He ran article after article arguing for the social and political equality of women. In one such article, Giles Edgerton, an art critic, pointed out that reviewers who assumed a polite and courteous stance toward women's art only humiliated female artists in doing so: "[Women] resent a sex distinction in art (not in the variation of art, but in the quality) and they honestly prefer just, discriminating criticism to this attitude of tender-hearted masculine protection."[15] Edgerton concludes that a "woman's exhibit is something out of the past. It is Eighteen-Thirty in expression and belongs to the helpless days of crinoline when ladies fainted if they were spoken to with undue harshness; when a sampler, at least in America, was the only field for feminine artistic endeavor."[16]

In practice, however, Stickley fell back on the same old, dreary Victorian attitudes toward women. He hired women in his factory but only to execute needlework designs. In the name of paying careful attention to women's needs, though, the Craftsman Workshops produced a series of delicate writing desks, or what Stickley called ladies' writing desks. The earliest of this type appeared in the first issue of *The Craftsman*. In this particular design, a wooden knob held the desk lid fast; when released with a turn of the wrist—no cold metal pull here—the lid dropped down on two invisible posts, revealing a complex of tiny compartments. Stylized mortise and tenon, keyed joints created an abrupt, rather pleasing interruption on the otherwise slim sides. A primitive but elegant-looking piece of furniture, Stickley built this particular desk on simple lines.

In volume 5 of *The Craftsman*, Stickley showed a larger writing desk inlaid with pewter and copper designed by Harvey Ellis. Though it bears some similarity to Stickley's own early desk, it clearly reveals Ellis's tasteful touches. He dramatically altered the desk's overall appearance by widening the slab legs, enlarging

Craftsman interior.

Left: occasional chair of fumed oak with rush seat (height of back from floor, 34″, height of seat from floor, 18″). Circa 1902. *Right:* occasional chair or dining chair of fumed oak, with leather seat (height of back from floor, 36″, height of seat from floor, 18″). Circa 1909.

the inset box on top, and removing the mortise and tenon joints and the base supports—in short, he broadened the silhouette to lend it more elegance. At the same time, he reinforced the feeling of delicacy by using inlay that would emphasize the vertical lines of the desk and so, according to Stickley, "give a certain slenderness of effect to a whole which was otherwise too solid and heavy." Ellis even improved on the original hinge system: "The closed desk shows a hinge which, by its placing and construction, does away with the brace usually employed to hold the door in horizontal position; permitting the latter, when let down, to pass under the body of the desk."[17] The lid thus became strong enough to be used as a writing surface.

Looking at this Ellis design, one has a hard time determining whether it was designed for a man or a woman, or, for that matter, in what room it belongs. This desk may be Stickley's most interesting piece of furniture up to this point, the most "androgynous." Bold and oddly disconcerting, it commands attention and demands definition from the viewer. Perhaps for those reasons, it did not sell well, and Stickley made the desk available only one year.

In October 1904, Stickley introduced yet another design for a lady's writing desk, this time in hazelwood. The hazelwood desk combines Stickley's first design with some of Ellis's elaborations. The overall size and proportions clearly belong to Ellis, as well as the hinge design, the top, and the general vertical thrust of the piece. But Stickley integrated into it his own original curves for the door and his earlier design for a pedestal base.

Stickley manufactured other writing desks, both men's and women's, and desks seemed to interest him more and more. While he showed five different models in the 1905 catalog, he expanded to eleven designs, including a large slant-top—the Mission version of the rolltop desk—in the 1909 catalog. Stickley still included eleven models in the 1912 catalog, some from 1909 and some new mod-

China cabinet of fumed oak, with copper hardware
(60″ high, 36″ wide, 15″ deep). Circa 1909.

els. What Stickley eliminated, generally, from his 1909 catalog were the flattop, uncovered desks. Perhaps living became more hectic in the twentieth century, and people wanted to quickly and easily shut away their mess, or perhaps people became more private—covered desks could hide belongings with a turn of a key. Stickley also made several kinds of desk chairs, including swivel chairs with adjustable springs and screws, to accompany his many desk designs.

The dining room also received the Stickley treatment. As Ellis described the dining room and its relation to Craftsman living, it ranked "second in importance in the house."[18] Stickley urged that, as much as possible, dining room furniture be built in as structural components of the house:

> *Nowhere more than in the dining room is evidenced the value of structural features. Almost all the decorative quality of the room depends upon them. In addition to wainscot and ceiling beams—or instead of them if the room be differently planned—the charm of well placed windows, large and small; of built-in cupboards, side-boards and cabinets for choice treasures of rare china or cut glass; of shelves and plate racks; of window ledge and window seat; and above all a big cheery fireplace, is as neverending as the ingenuity which gives to each beautiful room exactly what it needs.*[19]

The dining room table dominated the dining room in several ways. First, it was the largest, most dramatic piece in the room and usually sat smack in the center. Anyone walking through the dining room had to go around the table. But more important, all the activity took place there—eating, talking, laughing, and so on. The dining room table was the site of declarations of war and of peace treaties. Such a demonstrably important piece of furniture was bound to be loaded with symbolism. Stickley appreciated the table's importance.

Though Stickley showed both a round and a rectangular dining room table in his first catalogs, in those early years he seemed to favor the rectangular one. He chose to show the rectangular table rather than the round one in the first issue of *The Craftsman*. But over the years one version and then another of the round table became the most popular model, perhaps because, like King Arthur's, it spoke of a more democratic design. A rectangular table has a head and a foot, but a round table does not. Stickley produced two very early versions of the round table at the United Crafts. The first was a rather plain, five-legged version that came with a forty-eight-, fifty-four-, or sixty-inch top and would extend to either a ten-foot or a twelve-foot oval. He kept this design in the catalogs over the years but made the legs thinner and gradually phased out many of the sizes.

The most popular dining table eventually turned out to be a modification of the five-legged model. Instead of using five legs to support the round top, Stickley used a series of stretchers that radiated out from a center post and connected with each leg. Whereas a fifty-four-inch version of the simple five-legged table sold for $40.50 in 1902, the stretcher-leg table in the same size sold for $51.00—25 percent more. This table displayed Stickley's concern for craftsmanship, coupled with his own visual sense, in the long, gradual sweep of the stretchers emanating from the massive center post, the nicely rounded tenons, and the wide overhanging apron.

Stickley's most popular dining chair was a ladder-back design (see photo 125). Originally the chair came with either a rush or a roan leather seat. In the later version, Stickley widened the slats from 2¾ inches to 3 inches, and increased the width and depth of the front and rear posts by ¼ inch. Whereas the early United Crafts chair was held together by very small nails, all the joints in the later chairs were pegged. Craftsman designs, however, always cut chairs with the same acute angle; the rear legs on most of Stickley's chairs stand absolutely straight. The later chair, larger and better proportioned, seemed better suited to even the smaller tables that Stickley manufactured. In a manner of speaking, the ladder-back grew up, as Stickley's business matured, to stand solidly and authoritatively on its own four legs.

The dining room table and chairs would usually be complemented by a large sideboard, another piece modeled on a medieval design. The sideboard held silverware and perhaps some fancy plates and served as a supplemental table—a "side board"—to the main dining room table. Food could be kept warm there on a chafing dish. One of Stickley's showpieces, the Craftsman sideboard featured hammered copper or iron straps, hinges, and pulls. The top drawers usually came lined with what Stickley called "ooze leather," a kind of felt, for storing silverware without scratching it. These large dining room pieces required a house with large rooms. Over the years, Stickley produced smaller, more delicately proportioned, and less expensive sideboards.

Finally, a china cabinet might occupy a corner of the dining room. Stickley seemed less interested in china cabinets, however, than in bookcases. The latter he produced in a great many different designs and sizes over the years, but the china closet appeared in only two, sometimes three, designs each year. For example, in 1909 he showed only three china cabinets but eleven different bookcases. The living room and its activities, reading and writing, relaxing and talking, took over as principal arts and crafts images. The word *illiteracy* is a late nineteenth-century American coining: semischolarly publications, such as the *Massachusetts Journal of Education*, took up the cause of literacy. Cheap paper, efficient printing techniques, fairly inexpensive eyeglasses, and incandescent lighting all converged to make reading a much more popular activity after the turn of the century. Even Stickley himself had turned to words—the magazine—to bring his philosophic and aesthetic case to a large audience. It is one of the odd contradictions of the period that in a movement dedicated to hand work, publishers attributed the amazing growth in reading in America to the industrialization of printing and to innovations in printing technology.[20]

But in the Craftsman house books did not necessarily get read. They nestled neatly and tidily behind locked glass doors in hand-crafted cases. Image—display-

Chest of drawers of fumed oak, with mirror
(66″ high to top of chest, 48″ wide, 22″ deep). Circa 1906.

ing the proper books of great social significance—was important. Besides, lighting in a Craftsman house, calculated to produce a certain aesthetic, made reading difficult. Stickley believed that in order to be tolerable, electric light must be softened and diffused. In some houses he accomplished this through a method of indirect lighting devised by Frank Lloyd Wright: A bank of lights was concealed behind a cornice and the light allowed to bounce off the ceiling. Other houses used wall sconces with bulbs fitted with isinglass shades. But in the majority of cases, these proved unsatisfactory solutions for Stickley. And though he made some floor lamps with stately wooden bases and hammered copper fittings, Stickley believed that "the most beautiful fixture for the electric light is one form or other of the "chain-dropped lamp," or what Stickley called "Craftsman Shower Lights," comprised of a series of small hammered-copper fixtures suspended by chains from a ceiling plate. Usually these lights hung over a dining table, providing the soft, diffused light that Stickley demanded:

> *The arrangement of the lights, softened as they are by the opalescent globes, tends to do away with the sharp, unbecoming shadows cast by the ordinary electrolier. Whether it is a group of three, five, or eight lanterns, hanging at the same or at different heights, the decorative effect of the straight line of lights depending by chains from the beam above is always the same. It gives a feeling of simplicity and of unstudied freedom in the arrangement that does away with all idea of fixtures or of the need of any. All that is seen is a row of tiny, softly-glowing lanterns hanging straight and free from wrought-iron chains that themselves depend from a sturdy hook fastened to a small canopy of wrought-iron or dull copper, which in its turn is bolted to the beam. . . . With the use of the ceiling plate and the consequent grouping of lights, there comes a shower effect that reminds one of the downward flight of sparks from a rocket. In the center of a large room this shower effect is indescribably beautiful, and lacks entirely the stiffness of almost any set form of electrolier.*[21]

A Craftsman house glowed with a soft, diffused light, often filtered through amber glass or mica shades. In addition, the house contained a good deal of dark wood. Large overhanging eaves blotted out most of the sunlight. All in all, a Craftsman house did not collect a sufficiency of light. One would have difficulty reading for any stretch of time. Such a subdued, darkened atmosphere—not unlike that produced by low-powered gaslight—tends to foster subdued activities. The Arts and Crafts Movement did not even welcome "bright" colors. The clean, sharp-edged, earth-colored houses induced a kind of meditative state, as if the Arts and Crafts period were preparing—saving up its strength—for the brightness and roar of the 1920s.

A brown house, paneled inside with brown wooden walls and with brown floors, filled with brown furniture and brown cushions, lighted in brown and

Table or piano lamp of hammered copper. Circa 1906.

Andirons, of wrought iron (20″ high, 21″ deep). Circa 1905.

amber light—such an overwhelming sense of *brown!* For some cultural historians, the Arts and Crafts period captured the very essence of brown. The historian Lewis Mumford renamed the period following the Civil War to the turn of the century "the Brown Decades," a reference to autumn when leaves turn sere and fall. Mumford noticed that a brooding sense of death and despair had settled over America following the Civil War: young men returned home battered and mutilated, disillusioned about the slavery they had fought so bloodily to eradicate. Mumford dates the change from the death of Lincoln, which

> *made the deep note of mourning universal, touching even those who had stood outside the conflict. . . . In part, the change lay on the outside. Society was adapting its coloration to the visible smut of early industrialism: in the new coal towns, the national banner itself, after a few days' exposure to the air, changed its red, white and blue to brown, grey and black. But even more the Brown Decades were created by the brown spectacles that every sensitive mind wore, the sign of renounced ambitions, defeated hopes. The inner world coloured the outer world. The mood was sometimes less than tragic; but at bottom, it was not happy.*
>
> *Like all such historical changes, the colour had manifested itself, as a leaf turns here and there on a maple early in July, before the causes of the change itself had become dramatically apparent. Brownstone began to be used in New York on public buildings in the early fifties, and just on the eve of the war it was first used as a facing for brick houses. With this alteration came dark walnut furniture, instead of rosewood and mahogany, sombre wall papers and interiors whose dark tones swallowed up the light introduced slightly later by the fashionable bay window. By 1880 brown was the predominant note.[22]*

If Mumford sees things correctly, then we can place Stickley in a broader political context. He continues that dour, subdued palette through the 1890s but

Sideboard of fumed oak (37″ high, 48″ wide, 18″ deep). Circa 1902.

Spindle footstool of fumed oak, with leather seat
(height of seat from floor, 15″; seat: 20″ x 16″). Circa 1909.

Floor lamp with hammered copper harp and trim
(56″ high). Circa 1905.

also keeps hope alive in his essays by opposing the griminess of the Industrial Revolution with the integrity and individualism of handicrafts. Stickley could adopt such a high-minded, ministerial tone because he had co-opted brown and attempted to infuse that color with new meaning.

In hindsight, of course, his attempts seem nothing more than a failed, naive optimism. For the optimism of the 1920s comes roaring like a steam locomotive; it bursts on the scene not with the colors of nature, but with the bright chemical colors produced inside the factories. It is an optimism driven by the great grinding wheels of wealth, not one chiseled by the cautious hand of the craftsman.

WITH THE SOMBER TONE and light of the Craftsman period, it would have been a snap to follow Frank Lloyd Wright's famous dictum about the impossibility of designing a really comfortable chair: If you truly want to be comfortable, he advised, then go to bed. So Stickley manufactured a full line of bedroom furniture:

single beds, double beds, chests of drawers, armoires, full-length mirrors, clothes racks, nightstands, dressing cabinets, and table mirrors. His earliest dressing tables were made with hammered-copper handles and candleholders on either side of the mirror. By 1906, Stickley's chests of drawers and dressers could be ordered in a variety of sizes in oak, maple, or mahogany. Later, he made them available only in oak.

To round out the bedroom, Stickley made single and double beds in a variety of styles, along with nightstands, clothes trees, and dressing mirrors in different designs. And he also produced an extensive line of children's bedroom furniture. Today, collectors have a hard time finding much of Stickley's bedroom furniture. One reason, perhaps, is that people changed their bedroom furniture less frequently than they did other furniture in the house. Also, it was less visible than dining room or living room furniture, and so people bought less of it.

In 1907, Stickley also introduced a line of willow furniture in his New York showrooms—two large armchairs and two settles, handwoven in brown or green. Stickley recommended these willow pieces as a contrast to his heavier oak furniture. Over the years, Stickley also greatly favored Indian baskets, blankets, and pottery for their simplicity and promoted them as natural complements for willow and Craftsman furnishings. American Indians lived close to nature, Stickley argued, without the superfluities of modern civilization, as one could see in the simple shapes of their pottery and the natural designs of their rugs, pots, and blankets.

In fact, according to Stickley, Indians produced the only "real handicrafts" in America, for handicrafts alone represented "the spontaneous growth of necessity and therefore an absolutely natural expression of the individuality of the maker."[23] In each of the Indians' three principal crafts—blanket weaving, basket weaving, and pottery making—"primitive sincerity" distinguished their work from vulgar imitations. Stickley insisted that no other form of floor covering harmonized with the mellow tones of Craftsman furniture and woodwork as well as Navaho rugs; the geometrical lines of their designs worked perfectly in his decorative scheme. The Puma and Apache wove their baskets of willow, left in their natural, dull yellow state, and decorated them with religious or natural symbols in a "dull rusty black" from a plant known as devil's claw. Pottery was the oldest craft of the Southwest Indians, each piece absolutely original, hand molded, and colored with powdered potsherd. Stickley recommended these pots as perfect accessories for Craftsman houses. Over the years, more than two dozen articles on various aspects of Indian life, customs, and art appeared in the pages of *The Craftsman*, including a series of Indian portraits embossed in red carbon on heavy brown paper by Elbridge Ayer Burbank, a famous painter of Indians.

Stickley's tastes seemed eclectic—willow furniture, Indian handicrafts, oak furniture, oriental rugs—but everything he valued fit into his philosophy for the Craftsman Movement. And his production was as broad as his taste. Whenever

THE PRODUCTS OF THE CRAFTSMAN WORKSHOPS

Stickley became interested in a subject, the results fell naturally into a long list. By 1906, the Craftsman Workshops turned out close to one hundred separate furniture designs, including umbrella stands; sewing tables; floor, table, and hanging lamps; electric lanterns and newel post lamps; electroliers; sconces; hall seats; hall mirrors; dressing mirrors; daybeds; single and double beds; wardrobes; taborets; tea tables; lunch tables; drop-leaf tables; serving stands; plant stands; gout stools; telephone stands; dinner gongs; scrap baskets; bride's chests; hall and mantle clocks; and room screens. He manufactured virtually every conceivable piece of household furnishings. By 1909 the number of designs in the Craftsman repertoire had grown to a staggering 185!

This popularity existed despite the price of Stickley's objects. In 1902, one of Stickley's settles with leather cushions sold for $78; a sideboard for $84; a dining room table for $60; a bookcase for $108; and a dining chair for $7.25. In the same year flour sold for 12½ cents for five pounds; round steak, 15 cents a pound; pork chops, 14 cents a pound; milk, 7 cents a quart; potatoes, 1.8 cents a pound; and sugar, 28 cents for five pounds.

Just how democratic, then, was this purportedly democratic art? Wage earners certainly could not afford his furniture in 1902. Stickley was, at least in the beginning, appealing to a wealthy clientele, those who might also be inclined and able to buy Grueby pottery. After his furniture gained wide popularity, around 1909, he dropped his prices sharply. Some of that decrease resulted from more efficient production techniques. It appears, however, that Stickley was able to lower prices on some pieces because the higher-priced furniture sold so well; that is, the higher-priced line of furniture subsidized this new, less expensive line. By 1909 a bookcase sold for $28; a settle for $42; a chest of drawers for $28; and one could buy a modest sideboard for $40. Dining room chairs were available for $7.

In a sense, then, Stickley did build an egalitarian spirit into his line of Craftsman furnishings: the wealthy could still buy impressive items of Craftsman furniture by choosing, for example, from a line of large, heavily strapped sideboards, while the less wealthy could choose from among simpler styles. These smaller, less expensive pieces of furniture fit in with Stickley's argument that people should simplify their lives by reducing the size of their houses.

B Y NOVEMBER 1909, Stickley's furniture was selling in stores in forty-two cities across the country, and he was expanding. An enthusiastic description of his furniture in 1909 points up reasons for the enormous popularity of Craftsman furniture:

> *The one distinctive American style is commonly known by the name of Mission. . . .*
> *Mission is of comparatively recent origin, but its influence has been very great. . . .*
> *The favor with which it has met . . . has been a surprise to both manufacturers and*

dealers. Others may claim the distinction of having offered furniture built on the lines of what is now popularly known as Mission, but it attracted no attention until Gustav Stickley, of Syracuse, New York, made a modest exhibition of what he called Craftsman furniture at the semi-annual exhibition held in the summer of 1900 in Grand Rapids. But Mr. Stickley's offerings then differed materially from the standardized Mission of today, although containing the basic features of the present Mission school of design. He is entitled to the distinction of having originated and brought to recognition in the trade the one distinctively American school of design. . . . Not only was the furniture constructed along new lines, but it was finished with dull stains instead of with hard, highly polished finishes which were common to nearly all American made furniture up to 1900. . . . Since then the finish has undergone many changes, until at this writing the best examples of this school are done in a soft brown which does not disguise, as did the first finishes, the grain of the white oak which is most used in the manufacture of this class of furniture. Where upholstery of any sort was used Mr. Stickley substituted, in place of highly polished leathers, often elaborately tufted, plain thick leathers, with smooth surfaces, which apparently were first of all durable.

These first examples of Mission or Craftsman furniture were a reaction from the curved lines which had characterized the greater part of all the furniture which had been sold in America. They were a protest against the elaborate ornamentation which the introduction of the carving machine had made possible; a protest against the hard and high polishes which seem to have been characteristic of American furniture only. The pendulum of taste swung clear away from the polished and tufted leathers which up to that time were used wherever it seemed desirable to introduce leather at all. Mention is made of these things because there is abundant reason to believe that Mr. Stickley's departure won its way to favor quite as much because of its finish, and the other accessories, as because of the appeal which was made by the departure in design. The result was in any event harmonious, and it was new, and the American people have a way of running after the new, and so Mission furniture was fairly launched.[24]

8

CRAFTSMAN FARMS
SCHOOL

STICKLEY FIRST DISCUSSED his general theory of education fairly late in his career, in an article in the September 1910 issue of *The Craftsman* titled "A Visit to Craftsman Farms: The Study of an Educational Ideal." At that point, his own children had been educated, and he could stand back and critically assess the state of education in America. He presented his ideas through one of his favorite devices: the creation of a character. In this case, he created The Traveler, who comes to interview The Host, or the master of the farm. Although "A Visit" presented a romanticized version of the values of country living, family, and education, in it The Host described his vision of a school for boys that he planned to open at Craftsman Farms in Morris Plains, New Jersey. The Host (Stickley) spoke with certainty, urgency, and moral concern about the value of a proper education.

Stickley referred to Craftsman Farms as a "school for citizenship," what was usually called a normal school. Normal schools primarily produced teachers, but their goal, even for nonteachers, was to instill moral uprightness—to develop good, solid citizens. The ideal of such a school would have appealed, of course, to the moral, hard-working side of Stickley. But the idea would also have been attractive to him for other reasons. A "normal" was an architect's tool from the Middle Ages, used for making perfect right angles. An analogy can be made to human affairs. People need to take their place in society as upright citizens, upstanding members of the community. Thus, posture was an important visual expression of deportment: a youngster who held his or her head high displayed an attitude of moral self-righteousness that he or she could bring to daily affairs. Furniture could contribute to education, because chairs cut on severe lines encouraged the proper moral stance. Since slouching suggested a moral slovenliness, couches and overstuffed chairs were especially ill suited to a normal education.

Stickley believed that one's moral foundation came from the family. He there-fore intended Craftsman Farms to replicate the "ideal of the home" and referred to the farm itself as the "Mother-Home." Home life taught one principal lesson, according to Stickley—the value of human relationships—a lesson that would be intensified on the farm, where a young person could witness the relatedness of all life by watching the actions of farm animals. Reacting perhaps to his early aban-donment by his father, Stickley talked about the family with intensity: "The fam-ily, with all its loving duties, is the greatest institution humanity has yet produced. It is the most sacred heritage of evolution. No communistic theories will ever wholly supplant the ideal of family life in the individual family home. And, be-sides, if a boy learns to supply himself, the material wants of a simple home (bring-ing to the family table the fruits of his garden, even splitting wood for the fire), how much truer will be his attitude toward life and toward social problems and conditions! I want to teach fundamentals not for their practical value only, but for their ideals."[1]

Stickley believed he could achieve those ideals by reversing the generally ac-cepted educational order. Boys (and girls) usually received their first training from books and then, when "educated," went off to work. Stickley argued that instead boys should first be taught the "ideal and the practice of *doing something useful* with brains and hands, combined with abundant outdoor life." Through working, then, a child would learn the necessity for knowledge. Stickley summed up with words that would come back to haunt him: "Life without work is no life at all; whatever the man's fortune, his growth is dependent upon work, and to cease growing is to die, spiritually."[2]

Later in the same article, Stickley talked more specifically about the school he had in mind. He seemed uncertain about exactly what would take place at the school, but he knew that most of the learning would occur out-of-doors. Necessity would gradually dictate the details of his educational program. As usual, Stickley did not formalize the details of his idea and announce it to the public; rather, he worked out the idea as it proceeded. The Traveler asked, for instance, "What is the plan of the Farm-School?" The Host replied:

Begin by taking boys at the completion of the usual grammar school period and . . . give them a practical education on the Farm here between fourteen and twenty, the important years of change mentally and physically from boyhood to manhood, when in my opinion, boys should have the stimulus to body and soul of work in the open air. I want the boys to learn here to stand on their own feet and to work directly for re-sults, and above all, I want them to develop independence of thought and creative ini-tiative. I believe that the boy who has learned to work here will apply himself better later on to whatever his vocation than will the boy who has had book-education only. You understand, this school will be in no sense an agricultural college or a trade school.

We are not aiming to turn out expert farmers. The training here simply equips the boy with general education, only the education differs from that usually prescribed. Here we will not study half the year and play half the year. We will work and study and play alternately all the time. On the Farms, school will "keep" the year 'round, and thus the boy who is educated here will enter college—if he cares to—not much later than will other boys. These cottages that are going up are for the parents of the boys who will, it is hoped, spend their summers at the Farms to share in the life amid which the education of their sons is carried on. Also, the parents may want to come during the winter for weekends. The Club House will be a central building for meetings and social gatherings where also meals may be obtained by those who do not care to keep house at the cottages.[3]

By 1912, Stickley had formalized his ideas for the school a bit more. He had obviously thought a good deal about exactly what kind of school he wanted to open, but he had also, as was usual for him, met someone who helped shape his ideas and give them substance. Now, it was a thirty-five-year-old educator named Raymond Riordan, the superintendent of Interlaken, a boys' school similar to Craftsman Farms, in Rolling Prairie, Indiana. Stickley had published an article by Riordan, "Interlaken, An Outdoor School Where Boys through Their Own Efforts Learn How to Think and How to Work," in May 1912. The manuscript arrived unsolicited and so impressed him that correspondence promptly ensued between the two men. The result: "The scheme of organization will be thoroughly worked out, Mr. Riordan helping in all practical ways—most notable of which will be the manning of some of the departments of work at Craftsman Farms with young men trained at the Interlaken School, who will not only take charge of their own work, but immediately begin planning to make it of value to the fifty boys with whom the school will start."[4]

Drawing on Riordan's professional experience and expert ideas (Riordan had spent seventeen years training boys in the manual arts), Stickley was able, by October 1912, to articulate more clearly his plan for the school:

The boys will be taught to build, to care for the animals and the garden, to understand and help in the installation and running of our electric plant, as well as to learn road-making and landscape gardening in their various branches. Whatever is new and scientific in agricultural development in this country will be gathered for the benefit of the boys, and any information that is of real importance in stock-raising will be at their disposal. The newest systems of intensive farming will be taught in the most practical way. . . . The boys that we have in mind for this school in citizenship are the less fortunate youths of the land, those who have not had the right help from parents or friends and who have been left to face the difficult problems of boyhood at times when they had not the strength to come out whole. . . . We prefer the boys to be between nine and fourteen.[5]

That same month Stickley announced that fifty boys would be accepted at the Craftsman Farms School for Citizenship after June 15, 1913. They would have to be at least nine years old and must be willing to work on the Craftsman house they would eventually live in. Parents should not come expecting to find classrooms; classes would be conducted in the fields, in barns, in the orchards—wherever farming activities were going on. The products of the farm—vegetables, fruit, eggs, milk—would be sold in the local town to raise money for the ongoing operations of the school. Tuition, board, laundry, clothing, and lodging for the first twelve months totaled $1,000; for the second year, $800; for the third, $400; and for the fourth, $300. Since Stickley originally conceived of the school for the underprivileged, "after a boy has been at the school two years he will have the privilege of selecting some boy unable to pay the tuition charge, as a member of the school—this to ensure democracy." Stickley concluded the initial plans with this statement:

> *Mr. Riordan's present plan is to begin to send on his trained young men from the first of October, 1912, so that from month to month during the winter our plans for the school will crystallize. Then early in the summer he himself will come, bringing with him his wide experience of the mental, moral and physical training of the boys. He will stay long enough to help get the work thoroughly under way, and will keep in close touch with us afterward through correspondence and occasional visits. We feel that this association with a man who has tested his capacity and right to govern youth is one that will prove invaluable to such a school as we are hoping to develop at Craftsman Farms.*[6]

By 1912, one year before Stickley opened his grand building in the heart of Manhattan, Craftsman Farms consisted of the clubhouse—in which the Stickley family lived—fourteen shingle or log cottages, and other buildings such as a cow stable made of fieldstone, a horse stable, a garage, and chicken houses. Stickley had 150 acres under cultivation, including a large rose garden, a vegetable garden, pastureland, a cornfield, vineyards, an extensive peach orchard, an apple orchard, and a plum and cherry orchard. Stickley seemed to be carrying out his plan for Craftsman Farms in his typical manner—with abandon. Craftsman Farms, to all appearances, stood ready to accept its first pupils. Readers of *The Craftsman* magazine would have no reason to doubt that it had opened.

Indeed, the magazine did nothing to dispute that idea, choosing to remain silent on the issue. No announcement that any boys had arrived at the school can be found in the June or July, August or September 1913 issues of *The Craftsman*. But no announcement that they had not arrived, either! Stickley next mentioned Craftsman Farms in an October 1913 article entitled "Craftsman Farms: Its Development and Future" in which he described the farm in four detailed pages but made no mention of the school. In the photographs that accompany the arti-

Stickley's home in Morris Plains, New Jersey.

cle, not one boy appears. The school simply and totally disappeared. No one ever mentioned it again in *The Craftsman*. To the careful reader it should have been clear that the school never actually functioned, for if it had Stickley would surely have publicized it. Stickley changed his mind about the school for reasons he preferred not to reveal.

The first hint of a revision in his initial plans came in October 1913, in an article titled "The Evolution of a Hillside Home: Raymond Riordan's Indiana Bungalow," which focused on Riordan's home at the Interlaken School. The article made clear that Stickley still held an abiding interest in education and still admired the Interlaken School, but evidently found himself consumed, finally, not with architecture per se, but with the prestige that that profession carried with it. The short, opening section of the article passed quickly over Riordan and his school and shifted abruptly to focus on Riordan's bungalow. This shift revealed in large part what really interested Stickley:

> *That brings us to the most delightful feature of the lakeside bungalow — the fact that it is not only the home of the superintendent, but also a club house for the boys and teachers of the school community of a hundred and seventy people. And surely, this bungalow is an ideal gathering place for the inmates of such a school — a school that aims to develop body and mind in wholesome harmony.*
>
> *Turning to the plans and illustrations, we find that the design was adapted from a certain five-room, stone and shingle Craftsman bungalow, published about three years ago in* The Craftsman Magazine. *And it is interesting to note how carefully and at the same time with what pleasing originality the owner and his assistant architect, George W. Maher of Chicago, have adapted the Craftsman plan to meet the special needs of individual and site.*[7]

George W. Maher was a well-known architect who had apprenticed in the offices of J. L. Silsbie, where both Frank Lloyd Wright and George Grant Elmslie had also done their apprentice work, and had opened a practice in 1888. Maher, Wright, and Elmslie were three major figures of Prairie School architecture. Stickley places himself over Maher by suggesting that "the assistant architect" relied on Craftsman plans for Riordan's bungalow. Stickley's ego required continual feeding, and architecture, which he considered the premier activity among the arts and crafts, gave him the most nourishment. It is not unlikely that designing and building a skyscraper would have made him happiest.

A second, and more important, statement comes in April 1914, in "An Outdoor School for Boys, Where Development Is Gained from Work as Well as Books," by Raymond Riordan. In that article, Riordan discussed this theory of education: "Let the basis of education be life itself instead of mere book learning." So he proposed the Raymond Riordan School, which was scheduled to open in June 1914, "seven hundred feet above the Hudson, two hours and a half from New York, nestling on fertile acres of fruit and farm land, with a placid lake reflecting its beauties, the new school hopes to prove worthy of its ideals, worthy of its aim for a close kinship to Nature." Riordan's plan to attract boys to his 300 acres and to educate them through farming and handicrafts sounds remarkably close to Stickley's Craftsman Farms School. Riordan never mentioned Craftsman Farms, but he ended with these lines: "It was Gustav Stickley's friendly offer of cooperation when I presented the thought of the new school to him—he was the first to be approached—that gave further impetus and inspiration to what now has become a permanent reality."[8] When the plan for a school began to fade in his own mind, Stickley decided, it seems, to let Riordan carry on the idea in his stead. Stickley's daughter confirms that, contrary to popular belief, "Craftsman Farms school never opened. It was used only as a residence for the family."[9] But she confesses to not knowing why her father abandoned the idea for the school.

The evidence suggests that although he experienced two seeming failures—the loss of his dream house and the school—Stickley never expressed even a scintilla of disappointment. Why should he? He wanted no part of Morris Plains. For one thing, he planned his house at the same time he himself took up residence in New York City. The farm might be fine for his family, but Stickley opted for the big city. He planned to open his school three years later, at the same time he planned to open his new Craftsman Building in the heart of Manhattan. Stickley's daughter, Mrs. Wiles, points out that her father lived only for brief periods at Craftsman Farms. Most of the time, he lived in New York, involved with operations there.

Stickley may have abandoned the school because he did not want to leave Manhattan any more than he had to. Building the clubhouse and moving his family into it solved a vexing problem for him. The same daughter reported that her mother disliked everything that Manhattan represented and wanted no part of it. Her father, on the other hand, loved eating late in the evening in fancy restaurants, attending theater and opera, and generally enjoying the thrill of New York nightlife.

Stickley had not only abandoned his idea for a school, but also turned his back on his family. Craftsman Farms School was not a failure, it was a mistake. Stickley's repeated statements about the inviolability of the family sounded hollow when placed alongside his actions. According to Mrs. Wiles, Stickley's wife clearly fretted about her husband. How could he possibly open a normal school when he himself no longer stood upright and solid? He could no longer implement in his own life the ideals he had so cavalierly advanced about the family. The failure to open Craftsman Farms may have been a significant turning point in his business life, revealing for the first time the financial problems Stickley faced. In just two short years, he would be out of business, bankrupt and alone.

But for now Stickley stood on the threshold of his new office building in New York, ready to rise twelve stories into the air.

9

THE CRAFTSMAN
BUILDING

ON MARCH 9, 1913, Stickley celebrated his fifty-fifth birthday in his magazine. Filled with tremendous enthusiasm and optimism, he could be mistaken for a man half his age:

> *Having just passed my fifty-fifth birthday, I realize that I am facing the greatest responsibility of my life at an age when many men are "retiring from business." Yet I am quite sincere in saying that never since I designed and finished my first good stout piece of furniture have I felt a greater joy and interest in undertaking a new venture, or a fresher spirit to face whatever life may hold for me.[1]*

He had the luxury, of course, to face whatever life presented him with a broad smile. His newest and "greatest responsibility" turned out to be an extraordinary opportunity, in the form of an office building in New York City. No ordinary office building, this one towered twelve stories high and stood two hundred feet deep—large enough to house Gustav Stickley's retail sales operations and his publishing company.

Located at 6 East 39th Street, just east of Fifth Avenue, the Craftsman headquarters sat in the heart of Manhattan's prime shopping district: "On one side it faced Bonwit Teller, while the ultrarespectable Union League Club was its neighbor across Thirty-Ninth Street. Such fashionable stores as Lord and Taylor, Tiffany's and Franklin Simon were nearby."[2] Stickley rented the formidable building for $50,000 dollars the first year and $61,000 every year following, an astronomic sum for the time.[3] In characteristic fashion, he confessed to assuming that colossal burden for altruistic reasons; specifically, to satisfy the incessant demand "from all quarters of the globe . . . for a Craftsman center in New York."[4]

He planned to open his building on October 1, 1913, the twelfth anniversary of *The Craftsman*, but because of unexpected delays he formally opened it on

145

November 10. At that moment, Stickley made the following claim: "There seems to be no limit whatever to the things which the Craftsman Movement can accomplish." Unfortunately, Stickley allowed that dizzying euphoria to guide him over the next couple of years. By November 10, 1913, however, what held the world's attention was not first-rate craftsmanship, but the threat of war in Europe.

However, Stickley had risen above world affairs. Even the way he chose to describe his new, imposing building sounds weirdly out of place, as if he were standing on the brow of some high hill and from that height looked down to survey the scene below him:

> It looks out over the city, to the rivers beyond and the harbor, and with so much space that we cannot only show our furniture and our house fittings and all the accompanying beautiful things that go with them, but that we shall be able to install draughting rooms for the designing of Craftsman houses, editorial rooms for The Craftsman Magazine, circulation and advertising departments, as well as various harmonious enterprises that are closely allied with Craftsman achievement. Above all, literally above all because it will occupy the top stories of the building, we shall have a Craftsman restaurant, where we are planning to serve wholesome, delicious meals to our friends and patrons, and where we shall have waiting rooms, reading rooms, bureaus of information, resting places for women and children, flower stands, every comfort and convenience, in fact, that people living in New York would enjoy finding in the midst of a day's pleasure or work.[5]

The Craftsman Building functioned primarily as a sales and promotional headquarters. Stickley continued to manufacture his furniture in Syracuse, in what had become, in itself, a large operation. By the end of 1912, Stickley's payroll included 198 employees, some of them—millwrights and machinists—working seven days a week, ten hours a day. Job titles in his payroll ledger constitute yet another long list: yard men, mill workers, gluers, millwrights, rush seat weavers, metal trimmers, copper workers, machine men of various sorts, packers, shippers, drivers, cushion and pillow workers, sanders, leather workers, needle workers, and various office personnel. In addition, the factory employed nineteen cabinetmakers and twenty-five men in the finishing department, the firm's single largest department. The payroll for the week ending February 28, 1912, totaled $2,108.57.[6] The records for the entire year are incomplete, but if that one week is typical, Stickley's payroll for the year would have exceeded $100,000. The output, too, must have been staggering—something approximating mass production—even though most of the country equaled the name Gustav Stickley with handcrafted furniture.

By 1913, Stickley enjoyed a secure, national reputation and to some extent had made a name for himself in Europe, through C. F. A. Voysey, Charles Wagner, and Samuel Bing. He lived like a celebrity, spending time in Greenwich Village eating and drinking with friends, patronizing small cafes and expensive restaurants, attending plays, and, satisfying one of his many passions, going to the opera. As one daughter remembers, Gustav was very musical—he loved to sing, especially arias from famous German operas.[7] Stickley also loved to hobnob with the rich and famous: Sinclair Lewis was an especially good friend. As his daughter remarked, he was generous to them all, famous or not—sometimes to a fault. If a friend admired a piece of furniture or a hammered metal object, Stickley usually offered it as a gift. He almost always picked up the tab for lunch or dinner. He also spent time publicizing the Craftsman Building. The idea of a skyscraper—however modest—may not have been in keeping with his philosophy of the simple life, but it certainly fit with his personality. He had planned to build his house at Craftsman Farms high upon a hill, overlooking the surrounding cottages. Instead, he now had a perch high above the largest American city, a great place to command the Craftsman Movement.

In the October 1913 issue of *The Craftsman*—its thirteenth anniversary—Stickley reflected, perhaps from high on the twelfth floor, on the movement he had inspired with his simple furniture and his homey, philosophical magazine. Stickley no longer sounded like that folksy, romantic character, the Craftsman, but more like a politician reciting his accomplishments. And like a politician, Stickley took credit for an awful lot, including the reinvigoration of the moral heart of America:

> *Today the Craftsman Movement stands not only for simple, well made furniture, conceived in the spirit of true craftsmanship, designed for beauty as well as comfort, and built to last, it stands also for a distinct type of American architecture, for well built democratic homes, planned for and owned by the people who live in them. . . . It stands for too the companionship of gardens, the wholesomeness of country and suburban living and the health and efficiency which these imply. It aims to be instrumental in the restoration of the people to the land and the land to the people. It is always for progress, for scientific farming, for closer cooperation between producer and consumer, and less waste in both agricultural and industrial fields. It stands for the rights of children to health and happiness, through an education that will develop hands as well as heads; an education that will give them that love and enthusiasm for useful work which is every child's rightful heritage, and fit them to take their places as efficient members of a great democracy. Civic improvement is close to its heart, political, as well as social and industrial progress; it desires to strengthen honest craftsmanship in every branch of human activity, and strives for a form of art which shall express the spirit of the American people.*[8]

Later in the same article, Stickley falls into a personal reminiscence in which he explores the reasons for his new building. Once more he comes off sounding somewhat bizarre, almost egomaniacal, as if he were now some research physician working feverishly on a cure for cancer. He trumps up a conversation between himself and a mysterious visitor to his building, to whom Stickley responds humbly and flatly: his clamoring public will not permit him to stop producing and expanding and working his way into the hearts of Americans. The movement that Stickley had started just a dozen or so years before, a movement dedicated to the handicrafts, had broadened and deepened into a way of life. In a sense, it could no longer be called a movement. Besides, he no longer exercised control over it; it had now begun to control him:

> *A few weeks ago I was showing a friend of mine the new Craftsman Building, ex-plaining my plans for its development—describing all the interesting things I hoped to bring together there. And after listening to me for a while, he said: "Tell me, what makes you do this? Why do you want to move into this big place? Do you realize the enormous load you are shouldering, how many more problems you will have to solve, and what a difficult undertaking this will be to carry through? You're getting on in years; you've reached an age when a business man usually begins to think about re-tiring and settling down to a quiet life. Instead, you are taking on harder work and bigger responsibilities. Why do you do it?"*
> *"Because I can't help it," I told him. "A movement that has grown as this one has, must keep on growing. People need it; they wouldn't let me stop even if I wanted to."*

Stickley ends with a benign image of himself as a gentle gardener:

> *Like the tree, out of what seemed a small and insignificant beginning, has the Craftsman Movement grown. Not because I consciously planned it; not because of great capital or prestige; but simply because it had roots in the ground. It grew out of actual spiritual needs and physical conditions. It drew life from the warm, fertile soil of the people's interests and enthusiasm. And it depends upon their continued love and help, as well as upon my own endeavor, to keep its branches green, to make it grow into still farther-reaching strength and still wider efficiency.*[9]

The Craftsman Building did not represent the culmination, according to Stickley's analogy, but only the next stage in the organic development of the Craftsman Movement. Continuing the organic analogy, the movement would never reach a limit or end. It would simply continue, develop, grow, and mature. Thus, whatever Stickley presented would have to succeed, for it was naturally correct.

STICKLEY TRIED TO IMBUE THE BUILDING ITSELF with that organicism by devoting every floor of the Craftsman Building "to the service of the home-loving, home-building public." The first four floors served as showrooms for Craftsman furnishings: a complete furniture display; a general furniture display, including

THE CRAFTSMAN BUILDING

"Colonial Designs"; draperies and home furnishings; and rugs and interior decorating. The ninth floor contained the Craftsman Workshops, where workmen and women demonstrated woodworking, metalsmithing, and needleworking techniques. The tenth floor housed *The Craftsman*'s architectural and service departments, as well as the editorial offices of the magazine. The eleventh floor contained the Craftsman Club Rooms "for the use of the public; here are charmingly furnished rest rooms for men and women, a reference library, and a lecture hall in which lectures will be given on building and decorating." The Craftsman Restaurant crowned the building.

But Stickley felt most proud of floors five through eight, which housed what he called the Craftsman Permanent Homebuilders' Exposition. The Homebuilders' Exposition offered visibility to manufacturers who rented space in such categories as gardens and grounds, home equipment, home decoration, model rooms (with attention to wall finishes), and building materials. These four floors brought to a culmination Stickley's passion for architecture, a passion that appeared, if the Craftsman Building is any indication, to overtake his interest in furniture. That is perhaps to be expected: a house, when designed properly, requires intricate and complicated planning, a philosophy about space and the arrangement of rooms, and a grander sense of scale than is required to design a chair or a cabinet. Architecture seemed more suited to Stickley's monumental sense of himself. And so, on floors five through eight, Stickley proposed to present a wide range of building materials and fittings, in addition to the usual run of furnishings.

> In the Craftsman Building methods of building construction will be shown, as well as miniature buildings; various kinds of economical house-hold devices will be in operation; in fact, all phases of home building and home-living will receive as complete an exposition as our experience and knowledge will be able to present. I have in previous articles spoken of my own draughting room in the building for the planning of Craftsman architecture; here also my friends will be made welcome and advice will be given to those contemplating the putting up of their own houses, so that they may carry out their own ideas as successfully as possible.[10]

In his early and middle years as a businessman, Stickley used his magazine, *The Craftsman*, to promote his furniture and accessories. *Magazine* derives from the French word *magasin*, meaning "department store," and Stickley seems to have taken the idea seriously. The Craftsman Building allowed people to examine firsthand Stickley's ideas on all phases of the building process—each department in the magazine, that is, came alive. In a sense, a magazine produced anonymity: readers knew Stickley's voice in a limited way and his gestures and manner not at all. But Stickley needed to be noticed. He could not move to his Morris Plains residence because he had outgrown everything it represented. The Craftsman Building served as his new residence, a twelve-story living room into which he could welcome people from all across the country. He had managed to reverse the way a magazine works; he no longer needed to be delivered to people's homes. Instead, they could flock to see him. The Craftsman Building made Craftsman Farms seem like an impoverished shack.

Stickley also planned a series of lectures that would differ from his earlier series at the United Crafts Hall. In that hall, Stickley had offered topics of general interest in the arts and crafts. In New York, he limited the subjects mainly to architecture and technical matters such as the latest building materials; questions of building sites, land values, garden designs, home hygiene, and a scrutiny of the U.S. economy. H. S. Quillan, an expert on color harmony, delivered the first lecture on May 2, 1914, entitled "The Voice of the Wall and Its Message." A few days later, John Gutzon Borglum, internationally known for sculpting the faces on Mount Rushmore, gave a lecture called "American Art from an Individual Viewpoint." Stickley planned for other talks on disparate topics such as "The Story of the Oriental Rug," "Thrilling Experiences in the Air," "Vacation Activities for Your Children," and "The Songbird and Its Place in Our Lives." While newspapers covered the possibility of a world war, Stickley blithely offered lectures on songbirds and vacation activities. Perhaps such things took people's minds off impending disaster. But ensconced high on the twelfth floor, Stickley seems to have had his head literally in the clouds, removed from mainstream political life and detached from basic democratic concerns.

Yet people must have found these lectures if not useful, at least entertaining, for by June 1914, Stickley expanded his initial series and spoke of them as intimate get-togethers in his living room:

> I think perhaps it is the informality of these lectures, in addition to the subjects and speakers, that appeals to people. They are more like talks, friendly gatherings of men and women and young people who are interested in the same subject and who come together to hear the message of one who knows more about it than they do, and who can tell them, in a simple, earnest way, some practical fact that his own work as artist or craftsman has taught him. Up in one of our pleasant Club Rooms, on the eleventh floor, in that quiet, restful atmosphere that always clings about the open hearth, roomy settles and inviting bookshelves of a Craftsman room, these visitors of ours feel at home. They listen in comfort to the informal talk, and take part afterwards, if they feel inclined, in the general discussion of the topic—which is often even more illuminating and helpful than the lecture itself.[11]

Those informal talks, delivered on the eleventh floor in Manhattan, seem inconsistent with the Craftsman philosophy, for Stickley had up to that point run his Craftsman operations based on the idea of country living. From the heights of his big-city office building, Stickley, more strongly than ever, urged folks to move back to the soil "safely and sanely." He stated, "We do not intend to take up the question of country living in order to exploit any phase of it. We only want to make clear the kind of things that are good in country life for the people suited to lead that existence, and then we want to help people to lead it in the wisest happiest fashion."[12]

Despite his outlandish inconsistencies, Stickley functioned as a serious and financially successful reformer and businessman who wanted to educate people in what he considered the good life. His desire to instruct is clear from this description of the kinds of activities that would take place at the Craftsman Building:

> *Skilled craftsmen will be found making willow furniture, weaving baskets, binding books; the whirr of the potters' wheel will be heard and the sound of the metal worker's hammer. In these rooms will be found not only the opportunity to study the handiwork of the craftsmen, but to work with them, especially where students are anxious to perfect their crafts. Fabrics will also be designed here, and new ideas for embroidering sofa pillows, window curtains, portieres and bedroom sets will be furnished to order, harmonious in design, with color and furnishings of a well thought-out house.*[13]

Perhaps Stickley's most revealing project was the Craftsman Restaurant. All the butter, milk, eggs, poultry, fruit, vegetables, and flowers necessary for the operation were to be supplied by Craftsman Farms, so that "the food itself will be as near an ideal of good living as we know how to produce." The restaurant clearly represented the culmination, the climax, made absolutely concrete, of the movement. From that lofty position Stickley could feed his minions. More than that, food and the kitchen are associated with feelings of love and caring. Not only had Stickley assumed the role of father of the Arts and Crafts Movement: now he also served as its mother.

An article in the January 1914 issue of *The Craftsman*, attributed simply to "A Visitor," described the restaurant. Like Stickley's earlier Lecture Hall, from the days of the United Crafts, the new room brought together various aspects of Stickley's Craftsman ideal. It also marked the beginning of his last phase—the spiritual, evangelical father; the great provider of furniture, of homes, of crafts, of food.

> *The room is long and airy, with soft-textured walls of warm, rich Gobelin blue, brightened at the top by a frieze of conventionalized nasturtium leaves and blossoms in tones of light and dark green and deep red. Here and there are framed sepia photographs giving glimpses of the homestead and wooded hillsides, the grazing cattle and pasturelands of Craftsman farms . . .*
> *The floor is of maple, stained a mellow brownish-gray, and is dressed with rugs in soft tones of brown. The furniture, especially designed and built at the Craftsman Workshops, is of brown fumed oak, and the chairs have seats of brown and gold haircloth. The oak tables vary in size, some being round, some square, and some hexago-*

nal. Also in close harmony of browns are the handsome sideboard, china cabinets, leather-cushioned settles and piano, while over the windows are coffee-colored net curtains, with brown velour hangings at the sides, bearing a stenciled nasturtium border in dark green, dull red and orange.

One of the most attractive and homelike features of the room is the fireplace, which is faced with Grueby tiles of brownish-mauve, bound with bands of hammered iron. The hood, of iron-bound hammered copper, bears in raised letters the motto:

Where Young Men See Visions
And Old Men Dream Dreams.[14]

At fifty-five or -six, Stickley, it appeared, could not be toppled. His furniture had been selling well for more than a decade, his house designs dotted the countryside, his magazine enjoyed a healthy circulation, and his name was for many a household word. He could relax. Instead, in 1914, after ten years of heavy involvement in architecture, Stickley turned his attention, surprisingly, back to furniture. But the new designs he produced did not fit into the aesthetics of the Craftsman Movement. After a lifetime of arguing for simplicity, Stickley introduced an unusual line of modified Mission furniture colored with a paint he had perfected himself. Stickley possessed an uncanny business sense; perhaps he knew—before anyone else—that his original Mission designs were slowly falling out of favor and that other furniture styles, imitations of European styles, were coming into favor.

By January 1914 fifty stores throughout the country carried the Craftsman line. In addition, Stickley had Craftsman stores in Boston, at 468 Boylston Street, and in Washington, D.C., at 1512 H Street N.W. The signs of a slipping market can still be detected. A letter in the Winterthur Museum manuscript collection dated January 20, 1913, shows that the Boston store had lost more than $4,000 in 1912.[15] The tax return for the Craftsman Publishing Company for 1913 shows a gross income of only $86,806.02.[16] Mary Ann Smith points out that Stickley's son-in-law and business manager, Ben Wiles, had argued against the Craftsman Building as "too expensive for Stickley's resources[17]," but the old man would not hear of it. When the building finally opened, Wiles resigned and moved back to Syracuse. Something serious had begun to infect the Craftsman operations, but Stickley never uttered a word in print about his problems. He simply introduced a new line of furniture and hoped for the best.

In October 1914, Stickley began running articles in *The Craftsman* urging something shocking—a mixture of furniture styles and introducing yet another line of furniture in gumwood, mahogany, and oak, "which in their lighter proportion show graceful construction and a pleasing variation from our early models." These pieces resembled a simplified Chippendale Revival style, without the carving. In one issue, Stickley declared, rather feebly, that he did not intend these de-

Modified Morris chair, mahogany. Circa 1915.

signs to take the place of traditional Mission designs, but rather "to enrich the variety which the general style has produced." In the same issue he tried to correct what he called a misconception about the Craftsman style:

> There has been an impression that if Craftsman furniture be used in a house, every other kind must be denied place, as not appropriate. This is a mistaken idea. Articles of willow, Chinese Chippendale, or models of Jacobean suggestion give interest to a room and make for the comfortable sense of informality always brought about by the introduction of harmonious variety. . . . Thoughtfully chosen and well-placed furnishings emphasize the beauty of every separate piece; each is complementary to the other. An infinite variety of fittings may be so harmoniously arranged as to give the charm that flowers, ferns, and paths give to a woodland grove.[18]

In fact, Stickley had earlier argued against using European imports or American imitations of European styles. He had pushed for the development of a democratic, American furniture, one that would express "the American character." His answer, of course, was Craftsman furniture. Suddenly, he seemed desperate. By 1915, Stickley argued for exact and careful reproductions of historical models, and he began to feature his own versions of Jacobean and Chinese Chippendale. He also introduced a last-gasp series in *The Craftsman* called "The New Idea in Home Furnishing," designed "to show how the old-time method of living and home furnishing could be adapted to our present mode of life." He recognized that Mission furniture was now fast falling out of favor, and he began to develop a philosophy for this new style, just as he had for his Craftsman furniture: "Much of the charm of the old lay in the fact that the furniture was all individual pieces not made in sets, and that they were interchangeable, not intended for one room only."[19] Craftsman had become "old" furniture that needed to be enlivened for "our present mode of life." Stickley tried heroically to redirect the Craftsman Movement to keep pace with changing tastes, but more important, he wanted to save his toppling Craftsman empire. He suddenly found himself no longer setting the standard, but rather trying to catch up to it. He did not know that role at all. And he did not like it.

Modified armchair, mahogany. Circa 1915.

In article after article, for more than twelve months—from February 1915 to April 1916—Stickley and his staff advocated a mixture of styles to enliven each room of the house. In one article, "More Color in the Home: Painted Furniture Inspired by Peasant Art," Stickley even showed Craftsman furniture painted in black glaze and embellished with hand-painted floral decorations in brick red, blue, and green. These new chairs came with orange cushions or rush bottom seats. In July 1915 an article titled "New American Furniture: Its Variety and Beauty and Comfort" announced that the color choices had expanded to include Japanese blue and Chinese vermillion, and water green with silver trim. Stickley seemed to be trying to discover just what would sell.

In the middle of all this Chinese Chippendale, Sheraton, more delicate Craftsman, and Colored Craftsman, Stickley also introduced, in an article entitled "The Ethics of Home Furnishings" (January 1916), three pieces of oak furniture with lathe-turned legs, "designed and executed by Gustav Stickley." These pieces he colored too and introduced as a new line called Chromewald. Photo below shows two of the same Craftsman armchair; these photographs, both undated, come from Stickley's workshops. The chairs appear to be either mahogany or walnut. The chair on the right has a projection sketched in, perhaps by Stickley himself but more likely by some designer in the shop, of a leg for his new Chromewald. The new Chromewald chair looks like an earlier design with an elaborate series of turnings. This new furniture Stickley made available in "the brown of the pine cone, the gray of the misty air in green woods, the green of spring orchards," but he also favored bright orange and yellow.

Chromewald chair and rocker. Circa 1916.

Coming full circle, Stickley showed his Chromewald furniture at the 1916 Grand Rapids Furniture Exposition, and evidently received better treatment from the trade than he had at his first showing fifteen years before:

In view of the waning popularity, in some sections at least, of the straight-line stuffs that originally made Mr. Stickley, his factory and magazine famous, there was considerable conjecture as to what he would have to present to the trade to take the place, in some measure at least, of the Craftsman stuffs. It was fully appreciated by all well-informed furniture men that it would be something worth while, for Gustav Stickley is an artist in the manipulation of cabinet woods. Even when the Craftsman type of furniture was at the height of its popularity, and was being widely imitated, the intelligent furniture men appreciated that there could be just as much difference between two pieces, which to the eye are similar in style, as between two distinct periods. The difference might lie perhaps in the subtle lines, proportions, choice of materials, and application of the materials to advantage through artistic understanding. These features may not be so precisely marked that they can be pointed out, but they are there just the same, and the trained and experienced eye realizes it. The Gustav Stickley Craftsman furniture was never successfully imitated.

The anticipated innovation brought out by Mr. Stickley this season he has christened Chromewald furniture. The notable features are the decorative distinction and originality of design, and especially the beautiful finish, which is in fumed antique, as he terms it, in blue, gray, and brown. The characteristic style? When one sees the Chromewald furniture he does not think of a special type or period or school of design. He is impressed with the warmth, harmony and artistic ensemble of the furniture itself. There is a generous amount of cabinet wood. Perhaps the nearest comparison would be to that of a centuries-old violin.

The new process of finish was invented and perfected by Mr. Stickley himself, and it really reverses the usual course of finishing furniture. The first treatment of the wood is to wet it to bring up the loose fibers. It is then sanded and polished and rubbed with wood oil before it is fumed. After the fuming process the final finish is applied. It is doubtful if there is any finish now used on wood that possesses the permanency of this finish. And it is so rarely beautiful, with the lights and shadows of the grain, that one's hand involuntarily reaches out to touch and smooth its surface.[20]

Stickley boasted in the September 1916 issue of *The Craftsman* that the demand for Chromewald was so great that he had decided to confine his activities in the future to the wholesale business exclusively. Also in that issue, Mary Fanton Roberts, managing editor of *The Craftsman*, argued, after fifteen years of the Craftsman Movement, that Mission was just a phase in educating people to rid themselves of ornamental furniture and that Chromewald had assumed the place of the new, democratic furniture. At the time her comments appeared in *The Craftsman*, Stickley had been bankrupt for a year and a half.

10

BANKRUPTCY

On Wednesday, March 23, 1915, Gustav Stickley filed a petition of bankruptcy with the Metropolitan Trust Company of the City of New York, for his firm, Craftsman, Inc.[1] *The Craftsman*, which normally reported on the slightest movement within the company, gave no hint that Stickley faced the prospect of bankruptcy. The *New York Times*, however, a few days after the petition filing, revealed Stickley's financial condition to the entire country: the *Times* reported liabilities for Craftsman, Inc. of $175,000 and assets of $200,000. A month later, the *Times* printed more accurate figures, claiming liabilities of $229,705 and assets totaling no more than $123,000. Stickley's magazine did not cease publication until December 1916, more than a year and a half after the petition filing. So when Stickley introduced his new line of Chromewald furniture in 1915, he must have surprised, even shocked, the business community. Indeed, even those outside the business world—especially the readers of the *Times*—must have known how bizarre and brazen an act it was.

To the very end, *The Craftsman* remained silent on the subject of Stickley's finances. Its last issue still listed Gustav Stickley as editor, and the magazine advertised that, for 1917, readers could order bound volumes in Holly Red, Delft Blue, or Craftsman Brown sheepskin covers. Anyone reading the magazine would have concluded that Stickley's enterprises enjoyed robust health. In reality, by December 1916, Stickley had already gone out of business. George and Albert, two of his brothers, were by this time wealthy businessmen in Grand Rapids. Leopold and Julius George, two other brothers, had also achieved considerable financial success. Any of them could have rescued Gustav from financial ruin, but none did. Too much competitive spirit, even outright hostility, had developed over the years.

In January 1917 *The Craftsman* merged with a magazine, published in New York under the auspices of the Art Society of America, called *Art World*. The first issue pointed out cryptically that *The Craftsman* had been "for a number of years in other hands." Stickley had in effect lost the editorship of his own magazine. Those "other hands" belonged to Mary Fanton Roberts, associate editor and later (around 1912) managing editor of *The Craftsman*, and to the Metropolitan Trust, which had held the magazine in receivership. Although *Art World* began publishing Stickley's Craftsman home plans because of what it called "persistent demand," the magazine veered away from Stickley's editorial philosophy. Articles and essays in *Art World* were too scholarly and academic for *The Craftsman*'s general audience. The spirit of *The Craftsman* actually informed another monthly, *The Touchstone*, which Mary Fanton Roberts and many of the former staff of *The Craftsman* started in February 1917. The inside cover of *The Touchstone* carried a reserved, carefully worded note of congratulations from Stickley: "I believe there is a wide field for your magazine, and wish you every success." The magazine never again mentioned Stickley. If Mary Roberts could have offered Stickley a job as a writer, she apparently never did.

He received worse treatment from his immediate family, who picked over the carcass of Craftsman, Inc., for morsels. After Stickley declared bankruptcy, one of his sisters, Christine, and her husband bought all of Gustav's inventory and opened a retail outlet in Boston to sell Craftsman furnishings and metalwork at reduced prices—cut-rate Craftsman. Leopold and Julius George purchased Gustav's factory in Eastwood and continued their furniture business for a time both in Fayetteville, New York, and in Eastwood. By 1920, however, the firm no longer produced Mission furniture. Recognizing that tastes had markedly changed, they began manufacturing furniture based on variations of the Chippendale style. They were also eager, however, to capitalize on Gustav's phenomenal success: original layout sketches found in the L. and J. G. Stickley factory show Gustav's joiner's compass and L. and J. G.'s wood clamp merged into a new logo for a proposed firm, Stickley Products (see logo opposite title page).[2] Today, L. and J. G. Stickley, Inc. manufactures American colonial furniture in cherry wood, as well as reproductions of L. and J. G. and Gustav's Mission designs in oak. Mission designs constitute the overwhelming bulk of their sales. For a time, even the contemporary catalogs did not mention Gustav Stickley, but carried his well-known motto, "Als Ik Kan," as their title.

PERHAPS BECAUSE OF THE TREATMENT HE RECEIVED from his brothers and immediate family, Stickley's behavior during the last months of his career took bizarre turns. He seemed desperate for a solution, a hapless victim willing to go to any extreme to restore his position and reputation. The description of Stickley by Mary Fanton Roberts in the May 1916 issue of *The Craftsman* borders on the pathetic. From the powerful character called the Craftsman described in June 1904, sitting contentedly in his workshop "mindful of everything about him," Stickley had fallen into utter despair: "A man sat alone in a small room in a great city building, his world had fallen in around him, hope had flown past, her wings brushing him but for an instant. . . . He had dreamed too fast for the world, and suddenly in the midst of his accomplishment he found himself alone—broken, sad, with tragedy all about him in the little room in his great building."[3]

Mary Fanton Roberts's dramatization of Stickley's response to his fall borders on the ludicrous. According to her account, Stickley abandoned Craftsman furniture, along with its ideals and philosophy, in favor of something new and better. She describes a man struggling with aesthetic principles:

> *If I have failed, it is not because I have planned too high, it must be that I have not given the people enough. I must find something better. Perhaps I have not realized how deep in the heart of the whole world is the real desire for beauty. I shall not discredit the people or myself. I will rather aim to find something more significant, more worth while, more permanently beautiful. It will be possible I know to find it, and if I find it the world will forget my first failure.*[4]

Her portrayal of her boss appeared more than a year after Stickley had filed for bankruptcy. If she wanted to resurrect a positive image of Gustav or generate sympathy for him, she managed to do the opposite—she created an overblown, silly portrait of an inept designer. Astute readers of *The Craftsman*, who over the years came to know Stickley's personality well, would surely have read through the facade of her prose. Stickley was too strong a personality, too practical a businessman, too much the survivor to abandon everything in favor of something new—unless the old idea had petered out, and the new one would bring renewed fame and fortune. It is difficult to imagine Stickley saying, "I have not given the people enough," when he had argued for years that he had given his public everything they needed. Something else motivated Stickley—something close to fame or reputation or prestige. Craftsman, Inc. had failed, and he felt desperate. According to Mary Fanton Roberts's melodramatic account, however, through months of sorrow and failures and isolation, Stickley forged courageously ahead, experimenting with colors and stains and textures until he found what he thought the public needed—the Chromewald coloring process.[5] What he found was a gimmick—short-lived at that. Where once Stickley argued against coloring of any kind, he now advocated, with the same vigor, brightly colored furniture.

But in developing the Chromewald colors, Stickley merely pursued the one aspect of furniture design in which he had always actively engaged—finishes. He had long wanted to perfect a one-coat finish so that furniture would not have to be refinished or waxed for the life of the piece. Shortly after he declared bankruptcy, one of his daughters reports, Stickley believed he had finally perfected the finish, a treatment he called Kem-Tone. He was in the process of selling the formula to the Kestonia Company of New York when, before the papers could be signed, the president of Kestonia died. The new president decided not to enter into the contract, and Stickley of course received no money.[6]

Chromewald sold poorly. On top of that, according to business records for 1913 to 1916, Craftsman, Inc. showed "a gradual decrease in profits, attempts to consolidate debts, and a shrinkage of assets. *The Craftsman's* circulation had fallen from a high of 60,000 in 1909, to 22,500 in 1915. Gustav Stickley's salary, which in 1912 had been $5,000 a year plus 10 percent of annual sales, was reduced in 1914 to a flat $10,000 a year with no percentage of sales, certainly a dramatic change in personal income.[7] On May 20, 1915, the corporation sent a letter to all its creditors setting its liabilities at $229,705.64. Stickley offered to pay 33⅓ cents on a dollar, but creditors flatly refused.[8]

For LESS THAN A YEAR, IN 1917, Stickley moved to Kenosha, Wisconsin, to work for the Simmons Bed Company, which wanted him to design bedsteads for its hide-a-beds.[9] But Stickley could not work for someone else, and he soon returned to Syracuse to live with his daughter Barbara Wiles, in a house on Columbus Avenue that Stickley may have himself designed in 1900. Although only fifty-nine years old, he disengaged himself from the world for the next twenty years. He knew how to take the ideas of others—William Morris, John Ruskin, C. R. Ashbee, Ralph Waldo Emerson—and market them on a colossal scale. But he couldn't go it alone; he needed the inspiration and direction of inventive supporters. Suddenly, seemingly abandoned by every associate and without the Arts and Crafts Movement to impel him on a course, he turned passive and practically inert. Gustav Stickley was a "movement" person in all senses of the word: the Arts and Crafts Movement had set him in motion.

At the Wiles's he spent time in the garage making chairs and odds and ends out of scraps of lumber and helped design a couple of chairs for a small chair company, now forgotten, down the road from the Wiles's house. At times he would boil pots of chemicals on the stove for one of his many experiments in pursuit of the perfect finish. But he never worked a steady job again. After one year, in 1918, his wife died. He then passed the time playing with his grandchildren and taking walks through the countryside. After an initial bout of depression following bankruptcy—Mrs. Wiles says her father was hospitalized briefly with a nervous breakdown[10]—he always radiated good cheer and high spirits. He knew every gardener in the district and on his walks engaged each of them in long discussions about the character and properties of various local plants.

One day, after a particularly long stroll in the country, Stickley returned home to say that he had bought a parcel of land down the road. He shocked everyone, needless to say, since he was penniless. But the local bank, it turned out, did not know that. Stickley, the master of gab, had persuaded the bank president to lend him the money for the property. Though Mrs. Wiles made her father's financial condition clear to the bank, causing the bank to withdraw its offer, the story provides insight into Gustav Stickley's personality. Still dreaming about a parcel of land, he had taken immediate, practical steps to make his dream real. Once more he had promoted a scheme, though what he had planned to do with the land is anyone's guess. Stickley understood how to sell merchandise and ideas—and more important, even to the end he could still sell himself.

In his audacity, Stickley displays a marvelously American character. He dreamed wildly, but had the savvy to give his dreams practical application. When he seized on a new idea for a piece of furniture, he immediately marketed it. When he uncovered an interesting tool, he broadcast it in *The Craftsman*. Gustav Stickley moved with lightning speed—so fast that no one had time to discourage him. The great architect Louis Sullivan once remarked about the American people, "We practical and sensible Americans, as we like to term ourselves, are the most visionary and impractical of any people on earth." He could have been describing Gustav Stickley, a man who produced practical, sensible furniture and at the same time presided over a powerful romantic movement that captured the imagination of the entire country.

Stickley was not really *in* the furniture business; he had a *career* in furniture manufacturing. And he took the idea of career seriously. Stickley knew the power of language and frequently wrote about the original meanings of words; he would have enjoyed the early definition of *career*: "to gallop, run or move at full speed." Over time, the word came to describe a person's progress through life, especially when that life became publicly conspicuous. Stickley's desire to pursue a career determined the character of his life: intense, fast, perhaps too short. But his career had assumed too large a scale and required too much money and commitment from too many people to sustain. Once it had run its course, he found it impossible to start the race again. Stickley did not fall into despondency in his last years, however, for he had, as he told his children over and over, enjoyed the race.

Stickley's personality is perhaps best exemplified in the Emerson essay, "Self-Reliance," which reads, in many ways, like a blueprint of Stickley's life. We know that Emerson was one of Stickley's philosophical heroes. "There is a time in every man's education," Emerson begins, "when he arrives at the conviction that envy is ignorance; that imitation is suicide; that he must take himself for better or worse as his portion. . . . Trust thyself: every heart vibrates to that iron string." Emerson proclaims, "Whoso would be a man, must be a nonconformist. . . . A foolish consistency is the hobgoblin of little minds, adored by little statesmen and philosophers and divines. With consistency a great soul has simply nothing to do." Speak the truth, Emerson counsels, for "nothing is at last sacred but the integrity of your own mind." As I said at the outset of this book, no one could accuse Stickley of a "foolish consistency"; indeed, some of his family and friends would have been relieved if he had shown a bit more of it.

In a country as new as America in the early twentieth century, a country with few strong traditions, a person enjoyed a curious freedom—a chance to imagine freely, with no boundaries to break or limits to exceed. A person's ideas could expand as large as the country itself. There were few expectations to meet, few molds to break. So at one moment one idea seemed appropriate or ethical to Stickley, and the next moment he adopted a different stance—even when it stood opposed to an earlier position. His models provided him instruction and general direction, but he brought his own ingenuity and style and bold confidence to their ideas. Besides, he attracted people like Irene Sargent, Charles Wagner, C. F. A. Voysey, Harvey Ellis, George Wharton James, and Mary Fanton Roberts, all talented translators of ideas. In short, Stickley could not have reached such commanding success without the help of others. Even there, Stickley brings his inconsistency to bear—a communitarian spirit that found expression in a rugged individualism.

One can understand just how badly he needed those people after seeing Stickley's own handwriting—not many examples of which exist. No one in his family remembered ever having seen one of his letters. He left no rough drafts of his many articles and editorials. His daughters all insisted that their father never wrote letters. He didn't like to, Barbara Wiles said: "If Gus had anything to say, he wrote it in *The Craftsman*." However, the Joseph Downs Manuscript Collection in the Henry Francis du Pont Winterthur Museum contains one item in Stickley's own handwriting, a small, two-line note, dated September 8, 1902: "I hereby tender my resignation as tresurer [sic] of the Gustave Stickley Co To take efect [sic] at once."[11] Unschooled, virtually untutored, unable to spell, perhaps able to read only with difficulty, he pushed and shoved and persevered until he reached financial success. In America, you don't have to be able to spell "treasurer" to become one.

11

ANALYSIS OF
THE BANKRUPTCY

IT IS TEMPTING TO EXPLAIN Stickley's bankruptcy by standard theories of competition. The moment Craftsman furniture became popular, other furniture manufacturers quickly moved in to replicate Stickley's designs. Firms like Come-Packt, Quaint, Roycroft, Macey, Gunn, Limbert's Arts and Crafts, Cincinnati Crafters, Retting, Ridenour, Life-Time, Handcraft, Hawthorne, and Sears, Roebuck and Company—not to mention Stickley's own brothers—all manufactured Mission furniture at various times during the Arts and Crafts period. Some of the furniture matched the quality of Gustav Stickley's pieces, but most did not. Where Stickley used dowels to pin his joints together, others used nails and screws; where Stickley avoided dark stains and bright varnishes, others piled on the chemicals; where Stickley demanded quartersawn, seasoned oak, others used straight cut, green woods, or worse yet, veneers and plywood; where Stickley fastened with real mortise and tenon joints, other glued on mortise and tenons as ornamental embellishments. Other companies simply used cheaper methods of construction to sell furniture at cheaper prices to a mass market. They knocked off designs and knocked down prices. Thomas Pelzel, an art historian, believes that Stickley was "so widely imitated that his less committed competitors (including his own brothers) were soon to prove Morris's thesis of the competition of cheapness versus excellence, driving Stickley eventually into bankruptcy."[1]

But Pelzel's argument that cheap furniture will eventually drive the more expensive out of existence does not hold up. Stickley's imitators may have cut into his market, but Stickley enjoyed great success during the time when people were imitating his styles and undercutting his prices. A market always seems to exist for quality—for "the real thing." Price comparisons between the 1911 Come-Packt catalog and the 1909 Stickley catalog reveal shocking differences: A Stickley armchair sold for $19, while the comparable Come-Packt chair sold for $6; Stickley charged $53 for a fifty-four-inch, round dining table, while the same Come-Packt model retailed for $19.25. (Come-Packt furniture was also called sectional furniture; that is, it came disassembled, allowing the buyer to save some money by assembling the furniture at home. All pieces, however, left the factory hand-finished and hand-stained.) One would have a difficult time reconciling Stickley's prices with his desire for a "democratic household art," but Morris had faced the same problem with his high prices. Nonetheless, Stickley enjoyed strong sales in 1909. His high prices only served to bolster his reputation for high-quality furnishings. In short, Stickley's furniture sold well against Come-Packt and other low-priced competitors.

Other historians have argued that competitors' use of efficient mass-production techniques drove him out of business. But Stickley employed some of those same techniques. Aside from his first couple of years in business as the United Crafts, Stickley's factory employed workers who cut out furniture parts with power slides and rough finished them with broad planes. True, the factory used no gravity slides or conveyor belts, but nonetheless Stickley ran a fairly large business. In a 1902 photograph of the employees of the United Crafts factory, one can count more than one hundred workers, and there must have been more who could not crowd into the picture. By 1912, Stickley owned his own lumber mills near Star Lake in the Adirondack Mountains. When he incorporated on September 15, 1912, Gustav Stickley/The Craftsman, Inc. issued capital stock valued at $300,000—a large sum of money for the period.[2]

If economic reasons forced Stickley into bankruptcy, they were reasons of his own creation. In a real sense, he forced himself out of business. Seduced by his rapid and major success, Stickley overextended himself, blinding himself to the realities of changing taste, and fell into financial ruin. At the end of his career, he continually crowed about owning a Craftsman Building near all the exclusive New York shops, and he loved to point out that New York's elite, on their way to those fancy shops, would have to pass his building,

> . . . located practically in the heart of New York. The great flood of the city's finest trade passes past its doors; the Bryant Park Public Library, the beautiful Morgan Library, the new Grand Central Station, the most famous art galleries, the Union League Club, Tiffany's, McGreery's, Altman's, Lord and Taylor's, Kurzman, Simon and Co., one and all within less than five minutes' walk; on the highest point of land, touching the Murray Hill restricted district, it crowns that portion of New York which is the most beautiful, most vital center of business and social life.[3]

He seemed to have all the markings of a successful businessman. And yet, his story at this point can be read as an early twentieth-century fable about the dangers of greed. Success and money and skyscrapers—the possibility of dominating the public's imagination and the city's horizon—began to consume him, distorting perception and judgment. The Craftsman Building and Trump Tower stand as bookends in an all too familiar, twentieth-century story—a classical tragedy practically—of greed.

The history of the Craftsman Workshops not only describes the trajectory of fine craftsmanship in this country—a rebellion against mediocre, mass-produced goods—but also traces the way unmitigated success can derail powerful ideals and goals. Stickley had enough business savvy and acumen to respond wisely to changing tastes in 1914 and 1915—his brothers certainly did—but Stickley had come to believe in a most dangerous idea: his own invulnerability. Like Donald Trump or Ivan Boesky, he had drifted into an otherworldly life where he operated beyond the rules followed by run-of-the-mill businesspeople.

By 1915, three short years after he had opened his Craftsman Building, a New York bank held a $50,000 mortgage on his 600-acre farm in Morris Plains, New Jersey, and he owed local metal and lumber suppliers. The total liabilities of Craftsman, Inc. in 1915 amounted to $229,705.[4] The turn-of-the-century medieval guild known as the United Crafts, a romantic profit-sharing collective, was just a dim memory.

ONE OF STICKLEY'S NIECES advanced a radically different reason for her uncle's demise. Mrs. Monny Nitchie says she remembers well the Stickley family discussing those critical years preceding 1916. She maintains that by 1911 Stickley's own name came to haunt him, because it sounded so clearly Germanic. Gustav believed that the Americans and the Germans would never find themselves at war, and he proudly defended the Germans in public, extolling the virtues of their language and culture. He loved all German music and favored German opera. A good friend of Stickley's, John Wanamaker, the founder of the grand department store of the same name, brought a piano from Germany—which made the finest pianos, in Wanamaker's opinion—and presented it to Stickley. (It was that piano for which Harvey Ellis designed the inlay, as an example of the pianos the United Crafts might offer for sale.) The Austrian composer Anton Weber said, in August 1914, "An unshakeable faith in the German spirit, which indeed has created, almost exclusively, the culture of mankind, is awakened in me," and that view typified the feeling of Germanophiles like Gustav Stickley. But a good many Americans accepted those views with something less than enthusiasm. Even in a 1906 homage to Stickley in the principal trade publication, *The Furniture Journal*, the author dismisses Stickley's flirtation with politics by saying, "Oh, that is simply the German of it"—something of a backhanded compliment to Stickley's flamboyance or quixotic German character. Over time, Stickley's own pro-German views became unpopular with his friends. As anti-German sentiment increased in the United States, Stickley became more stridently outspoken until, by 1916, according to Mrs. Nitchie, he had severely and irreparably damaged his reputation.[5]

The war years contributed in other ways to Stickley's business failure. In 1914, by the start of World War I, America had truly rolled into the Modern Age. Some literary historians date modernity from the publication in 1914 of William Butler Yeats's volume of poetry titled *Responsibilities*. Some art historians date it with the opening of the Armory Show in 1912. Virginia Woolf pointed to the start of World War I as the significant moment. Whatever date one chooses, during World War I the pulse of the Modern Age beat hard and steady. Mission furniture smacked of an archaic past. After 1917, *The Touchstone* no longer mentioned Mission furniture. More to the point, perhaps, after the first issue, the magazine no longer mentioned Gustav Stickley, because people had grown tired of his missionary zeal beckoning them to return to the dreamy past. Americans had grown weary of the past and of the present as well. They wanted to climb inside a time machine that would take them to a rich and prosperous future.

Indeed, the country grew wealthier during the war, and furniture and accessories provided one immediate and concrete way to put that wealth on exhibit. Antique furniture seemed exotic and interesting, and, most significant, it looked expensive.[6] *Art World* magazine, which had absorbed *The Craftsman* in 1917, emphasized antique, European furnishings for the "modern" home. It dismissed Mission furniture as stark, severe, and hence no longer modern. Plain oak furniture did not smack of prosperity. On the contrary, it signaled an Appalachian, backwoods thriftiness—cabin furniture suitable for weekend retreats in the woods.

BETWEEN 1919 AND 1929, industrial production doubled in America, and as wages rose, a good many Americans found themselves with more buying power. The American household changed radically, as people, especially housewives, sought ways to save time. Industrial engineers, scientists, and designers responded with new items that instantly became standard household fixtures. The number of telephones increased from 1,355,000 in 1900 to 20,200,000 by 1930. The consumption of canned foods doubled between 1914 and 1929. The electrification of homes increased dramatically, from 24 percent in 1917 to almost 90 percent in 1940. Dark craftsman interiors gave way to bright and cheery open spaces—to rooms dotted with floor lamps and table lamps, wall sconces and chandeliers. Americans craved light, light, and more light!

Electricity ushered in its own revolution in home appliances: radios, vacuum cleaners, washing machines, toasters—all of which could be purchased by even the most middle of middle-income families. The year of *The Craftsman*'s final issue, 1916, marked the introduction to American homes of the electric refrigerator; five years later, 5,000 Americans had installed them in their kitchens. By 1929 an astonishing 890,000 Americans had purchased electric refrigerators; by 1934 the number had skyrocketed to 7 million. *The Craftsman's* interest in air-cooled pantries and pie safes seemed so far out of step as to be laughable.

At the end of the nineteenth century, Stickley had stood on the brink of a new era that had harkened back to a simpler, more dignified time of work with the hands; his temperament and ideas had fit that period perfectly. In 1916, with the demise of his Craftsman enterprises, Stickley once again stood at the brink of another, more industrial era. But he continued to walk with the same methodical, medieval step, while the band had switched to a fast-paced jazz tune. Stickley responded to the new tempo by introducing gussied-up, redecorated Craftsman designs. He missed the point, seemingly incapable of peering past the most immediate design horizon.

It would not be accurate to call him a failure. Rather, he represents in broad outlines the best of the nineteenth century. His interests were every bit as all-encompassing as that great nineteenth-century invention, the encyclopedia. In addition, he had a charismatic personality, magnetic in its ability to draw people to him. Personal magnetism was also a nineteenth-century innovation, used to describe the towering new cultural heroes such as Stickley, Frank Lloyd Wright, and Henry Ford. Finally, Stickley rose as high as the earliest high-rise, a building style made really viable by the introduction of reinforced concrete, the first such building reaching into the sky just after the turn of the century, in 1903.

What made concrete high-rise buildings possible was yet another nineteenth-century invention, cement—the glue that gave concrete its rock-hard solidity. First used in the United States when Gustav Stickley turned fourteen, in 1871, cement quickly turned America into a solid, mercantile reality: concrete locks and walls instantly turned the Erie River into a commercial shipping channel and soon after worked the same transformation on the Richmond, Allegheny, Chesapeake, Ohio, and Lehigh rivers. America's cash flow could be observed coursing through its concrete river beds. The first reinforced concrete bridge was built in 1889, and the first concrete steel in 1891.

America seemed to internalize the ideal of solidity, or more accurately, the idea of maintaining solidity in structures that rose in defiance of gravity. In moral terms, it meant standing strong and tall in solid opposition against the odds, against all attacks by enemies, at home or abroad. That ideal was literally embodied in the philosophy of the turn-of-the-century "Father of the Physical Culture Movement," Bernarr McFadden, whose magazine *Physical Culture* proclaimed across the top of each issue, "WEAKNESS IS A CRIME." He proposed "building" the body into a solid wedge through proper diet and exercise.

McFadden's life bears striking resemblances to Stickley's. Born in 1868 in the Midwest, he, like Stickley, barely learned to read and write but developed both physical and psychic strength from hard work on the farm. Like Stickley, he pounded out his message in his monthly magazine and built a $30 million-a-year business out of body building and health tonics; during the 1920s and 1930s one in every four Americans was reading a McFadden publication. Why shouldn't people be as towering as a high-rise, as strong as cement, as practical as concrete? Like Stickley, McFadden built himself into a towering figure of larger-than-life proportions and promised to take everyone along on the ride to Paradise.

Stickley came out of the same set of ethical and moral assumptions. His own sense of moral solidity and uprightness he designed into every chair and sideboard and table and desk. A Stickley chair cannot be easily tipped. Solidity, however, has its disadvantages. A tall, solid structure can withstand a great deal of shock, but its very solidity—its immovable, implacable presence—by definition excludes it from malleability and adaptability. When, in about 1909, the massive wheels of the new Machine Age began to roll, Stickley turned a deaf ear. When the noise increased and the machine made its presence absolutely clear, Stickley responded feebly by offering his old styles in new dress. His customers began shopping elsewhere.

Sitting on the twelfth floor of his Craftsman Building, he maintained—against the financial advice of his son-in-law Ben Wiles—that his ways were right, and the world was flat-out wrong. The world would come around, he predicted, to see his point of view. His very success, his formidable independence and unwavering commitment, ironically doomed him to inevitable destruction.

Stickley's career can be read as a forerunner, an early precursor, to today's fallen capitalist giants such as Michael Milken, Charles Keating, Boesky, and, to some extent, Trump. Stickley blinded himself by constructing an image of himself that grew larger and larger. What fueled him, as it fueled Milken and others, was greed—the acquisitive appetite for more and more beyond all reasonable restraints: more money, fame, power, and control. In classical dramaturgy, such characters would troop across the stage as tragic heroes. Aristotle hoped that audiences would undergo a cathartic experience by feeling pity and terror for those characters. Translated into the world of business, such tragedies of rampant capitalism might induce terror, but they generate very little pity in the average American.

WHEN GUSTAV STICKLEY DIED on April 21, 1942, he left no will. He had no estate. A small obituary appeared in the *New York Times* the following day, which spelled his name *Gustave*. The headline read: "G. Stickley Dies; Furniture Maker. Designed 'modern' pieces 50 years ago and was founder of a national magazine. Had first trolley line." John Crosby Freeman, who dubbed Stickley the "forgotten rebel," described the funeral:

> *At his funeral his old workmen made a touching display of affection for their old friend who had maintained his friendship with them after his bankruptcy. Many had continued to work for Leopold Stickley at the old Craftsman factory which Leopold*

had bought from Gustav in 1918. During work-days Stickley ate lunch with these men. Stickley's funeral took place on a work-day. Leopold had refused to give Stickley's friends the day off. In a body they took the day off anyway and appeared at the funeral. It was a fitting last tribute to a man who was one of the final representatives of an old tradition of comradeship between owner and worker.[7]

Living out his life with his daughter in Syracuse, Stickley had plunged rapidly into obscurity. Public life lay beyond his reach. He traded the macrocosm for the microcosm. Stickley puttered in the garden and worked in the garage. He showed some children down the road from his daughter's house how to build a chair out of broom handles. He played with his grandchildren. Though his family claims he was in good spirits, Mary Fanton Roberts may have caught some truth when she says Stickley felt he had failed miserably. But if he could only grab the right thread again, seize on the right idea, deep in his heart he must have believed, he would be able to raise himself back up to a position of authority and power. As the years passed and he grew older, however, he lived out the motto that had been displayed in his restaurant, and only dreamed his dreams: Where Young Men See Visions and Old Men Dream Dreams.

NOTES

INTRODUCTION

1. C. R. Ashbee, "Memoirs," 1938, vol. 1, page 228, Victoria and Albert Museum, London.

2. The Transcendental Club established Brook Farm as a cooperative community near West Roxbury, Massachusetts; it lasted from 1841 to 1847. Nathaniel Hawthorne lived there for a time and wrote about his experiences in *The Blithedale Romance* (1852).

CHAPTER ONE

1. As others have already indicated, the details of Stickley's early life are hard to sort out. Some sources say that Leopold and Barbara had nine children. The name of Barbara Schlaegel's minister brother has disappeared from history, and Barbara's maiden name is sometimes given as Brandt. The chair factory in Brandt, Pennsylvania, where Stickley received his first training in chair making, may have been owned by Schuyler Brandt. One of Gustav's early backers, Schuyler may have actually been a relative. Stickley may have been born in 1857, but most likely in 1858. (He said in the May 1913 issue of *The Craftsman* that he had just celebrated his fifty-fifth birthday.)

2. Gustav Stickley, *Chips from the Craftsman Workshops*, Number 1 (New York, 1906), 6.

3. Stillwater was the home of the Minnesota State Prison. Established in 1851, the Prison employed a progressive system of parole with a graded diminution of sentences and maintained a school and library for the inmates. It was perhaps in Stillwater that Gustav's life-long interest in prisons and prison reform began.

4. "The Craftsman Movement: Its Origin and Growth," *The Craftsman* 25, no. 1 (October 1912): 18–23.

5. This subject is taboo: No one in the family would admit to knowing or would conjectre why Leopold abandoned his family.

6. Gustav Stickley, *Chips from the Craftsman Workshops* (New York: Kalkoff Co., 1906), 1.

7. Mrs. Benjamin Wiles, Sr., interview with author, May 16, 1979.

8. John Crosby Freeman, *The Forgotten Rebel: Gustav Stickley and His Craftsman Mission Furniture* (Watkins Glen, N.Y.: Century House, 1966), 12.

9. Mrs. Benjamin Wiles, Sr., interview with author, May 19, 1976.

10. *Chips*, Number 1, 5.

11. Mrs. G. W. Flaccus, interview with author, July 15, 1977.

12. Some sources give the date, erroneously I believe, as September 5, 1887.

13. Mrs. G. W. Flaccus, interview with author, May 15, 1977.

14. Mrs. Benjamin Wiles, Sr., interview with author, July 15, 1979.

15. Binghamton *Daily Republican*, May 15, 1884.

16. Binghamton *Daily Republican*, October 21, 1885.

17. Binghamton *Daily Republican*, November 27, 1884.

18. *Chips*, Number 1, 12–15.

19. When the Stickley-Brandt Company began to manufacture Mission furniture in the early part of the twentieth century, the signature of Charles Stickley appeared by itself on the furniture, in an effort, perhaps, to capitalize on the Stickley name. Charles Stickley declared bankruptcy in 1918, when it became too difficult for him to acquire raw materials.

In 1892, Albert left Binghamton for Grand Rapids, Michigan. With another brother, George, he formed a new furniture manufacturing company known as Stickley Brothers Company. They acquired a lumber company in Grand Rapids and retired wealthy.

20. Gustav himself had only gone to elementary school.

21. Joseph Downs Manuscript Collection, 76x101.2350, Henry Francis Du Pont Winterthur Museum, Winterthur, Delaware.

22. Freeman, *The Forgotten Rebel*, 15. Mary Ann Smith notes in her book *Gustav Stickley, The Craftsman* that "apparently the New York legislature passed a law c. 1894 prohibiting the sale of convict-made products to the public; this exclusion of Stickley's main market was surely a reason for him to leave Auburn and start the Eastwood factory. Although the Stickley-Simonds Company factory was located in Eastwood, the company's stock certificates indicate Auburn as the location of incorporation." (Syracuse, New York: Syracuse University Press, 1983), 170.

23. Ibid.

24. *Decorator and Furnisher* pointed out, in 1895, that "the firm manufactures a large line of artistic and parlor chairs in the English and French styles."

CHAPTER TWO

1. "The Arts and Crafts Exhibition," *House Beautiful* 3, no. 6 (May 1898): 203–204.

2. David Howard Dickason, *The Daring Young Men: The Story of the American Pre-Raphaelites* (Bloomington, Indiana: Indiana University Press, 1953), 166.

3. Ibid., 165.

4. David A. Hanks, *The Decorative Designs of Frank Lloyd Wright* (New York: E. P. Dutton and Company, 1979), 63.

5. "Notes," *House Beautiful* 3, no. 3 (February 1898): 103.

6. See Carol Bohden and Todd Volpe, "The Furniture of Gustav Stickley," *The Magazine Antiques* (May 1977), 984–989.

7. Gustav Stickley, "Thoughts Occasioned by an Anniversary: A Plea for Democratic Art," *The Craftsman* 7, no. 1 (October 1904): 43.

8. Ibid., 48.

9. Mrs. G. W. Flaccus, interview with author, June 15, 1977.

10. Mrs. Monny Nitchie, interview with author, July 17, 1979.

11. Around 1904, Stickley dropped the *e* from his first name. No one in the family knows why, for Stickley never talked about it.

CHAPTER THREE

1. This popular book featured a decorative frontispiece by designer and painter Walter Crane, who founded the Arts and Crafts Exhibition Society in England in 1888. The South Kensington Museum later showed Crane's work, an exhibition that Stickley had seen on his European trip. Years later Scribner's displayed photographs of Crane's furnishings from their own collection, at Stickley's Craftsman Building.

2. Clarence Cook, *The House Beautiful: Essays on Beds and Tables, Stools and Candlesticks* (New York: Charles Scribner's, 1877), 187.

3. H. Isabelle Williams, "The Swan Furniture," *House Beautiful* 11, no. 6 (May 1900).

Notes

4. Margaret Edgewood, "Some Sensible Furniture," *House Beautiful* 7, no. 5 (October 1900): 653.

5. Williams, "Swan Furniture."

6. J. W. Dow, "A Wyoming Cottage," *House Beautiful* 11, no. 12 (November 1900): 670.

7. Advertised in *House Beautiful*, December 1899, page xii.

8. Advertised in *House Beautiful*, November 1900, page 706.

9. Hanks, *Decorative Designs*, 42.

10. Bruce Pfeiffer, telephone interview with the author, July 28, 1979.

11. Wright was in Buffalo in 1903 to see Darwin D. Martin, vice president of the Larkin Company. Wright designed the company's office building in Buffalo and was planning a house for Martin. The Larkin Company, a soap manufacturer, was started by John Larkin and Elbert Hubbard. On one particular stay with the Martins, Wright traveled to East Aurora, New York, to see Hubbard.

12. Freeman, *The Forgotten Rebel*, 28.

13. Frank Lloyd Wright, *An Autobiography* (New York: Longman's, Green and Company, 1932), 48.

CHAPTER FOUR

1. *Catalog of Craftsman Furniture* (Syracuse: Craftsman Publishing Co., 1910), 3–4.

2. Stickley, "Thoughts Occasioned by an Anniversary," 45.

3. March 1907 advertisement, quoted in Robert Judson Clark, ed., *The Arts and Crafts Movement in America, 1876–1916* (Princeton: Princeton University Press, 1976), 40.

4. June 30, 1900, p. 55.

5. Margaret Edgewood, "Some Sensible Furniture," *House Beautiful* 7, no. 5 (October 1900): 653–654.

6. "A Visit to the Workshop of the United Crafts at Eastwood, New York," *The Craftsman* 2, no. 1 (October 1902): 61.

7. *Grand Rapids Furniture Record*, October 1900.

8. Mary Ann Smith, *Gustav Stickley*, 24–26.

9. Stickley's magazine, *The Craftsman*, is discussed at length in Chapter 5.

10. *The Craftsman* 1, no. 1 (October 1900), Foreword.

11. Ibid.

12. Gustav Stickley, *Things Wrought by the United Crafts* (January 1902), 7.

13. *The Craftsman*, 1, no. 2 (November 1901), Foreword.

14. Gustav Stickley, "Foreword," *The Craftsman* 1, no. 3 (December 1901).

15. Gustav Stickley, "Notes," *The Craftsman* 4, no. 1 (April 1903): 62.

16. Gustav Stickley, "Epigraph," *The Craftsman* 2, no. 2 (May 1902).

17. Joseph Downs Manuscript Collection, No. 76x101.2350, Henry Francis Du Pont Winterthur Museum.

18. *Descriptive Price List of Craftsman Furniture* (New York, 1907), 2.

19. *Craftsman Furniture Made by Gustav Stickley* (New York, 1909), 12.

20. Gustav Stickley, *The Craftsman* 3, no. 3 (December 1902): 198–199.

21. Gustav Stickley, "Announcements," *The Craftsman* 3, no. 5 (February 1903): 326.

22. The Stickley family still owns some of the objects that Stickley brought back from Europe: a French oak hanging bookshelf with brass mounts, a bronze lamp base decorated with a stylized motif, and two bronze Art Nouveau candlesticks by Georges de Feure. (See Carol Lauraine Bohdan and Todd Mitchell Volpe, "The Furniture of Gustav Stickley," *The Magazine Antiques* (May 1977): 989, footnote 2.)

23. Irene Sargent, "A Recent Arts and Crafts Exhibition," *The Craftsman* 4, no. 2 (May 1903): 70–71.

24. From the *Guild Catalog*, p. xviii. The catalog represented a consortium of Mission furniture manufacturers: Grand Rapids Chair Company, Grand Rapids Fancy Furniture Company, Imperial Furniture Company, Luce Furniture Company, Macey Company, Nelson Mather Furniture Company, John D.

NOTES

Raab Chair Company, Stickley Brothers Company.

25. George Wharton James, *In and Out of the Old Missions of California* (Boston: Little, Brown and Company, 1905), 342.

26. Thomas Pelzel, *The Arts and Crafts Movement in America*, Exhibit, University of California, Riverside, California, May 8–31, 1972, 6.

27. Gustav Stickley, "How Mission Furniture Was Named," *The Craftsman* 16, no. 2 (May 1909): 225. See also Virginia Robie, "Mission Furniture: What It Is and Is Not," *House Beautiful* (May 1910): 162–75; and "San Francisco: The Home of Mission Furniture," *Architect and Engineer* (August 1906): 68.

28. Alwyn T. Covell, "The Real Place of Mission Furniture," *Good Furniture* 4, no. 6 (March 1915): 360. McHugh began his business in 1878 in New York City.

29. Robert Judson Clark, *Introduction to Mission Furniture: How to Make It*, by H. H. Windsor (Salt Lake City, Utah: Peregrine Smith Publishers: 1976), 6.

30. Gustav Stickley, "Structure and Ornament in the Craftsman Workshops," *The Craftsman* 5, no. 4 (January 1904): 396.

31. Stickley, "Thoughts Occasioned by an Anniversary," 53.

32. Gustav Stickley, "Home Training in Cabinet Work: The Qualities and Textures of Natural Woods: Their Individuality and Friendliness: Fifth of the Series," *The Craftsman* 8, no. 4 (July 1905): 533–534.

33. Gustav Stickley, "Cabinet Work for Home Workers and Students Who Wish to Learn the Fundamental Principles of Construction," in *Craftsman Homes* (Eastwood, New York: Craftsman Publishing, 1909), 175.

34. Stickley, "Structure and Ornament," 369.

35. Rod W. Horton and Herbert W. Edwards, *Backgrounds of American Literary Thought* (New York: Appleton-Century-Crafts, 1967), 264.

36. Henry Farnham May, *The End of American Innocence* (New York, 1959), 29.

37. *The Book of the Roycrofters, Being a Catalog of Copper, Leather, and Books*, 47. This facsimile of two catalogs was published by Nancy Hubbard Brady (East Aurora, N.Y.: Roycrofters, 1977).

38. *The Craftsman* 4, no. 2 (May 1903): 138.

39. Edgewood, "Some Sensible Furniture," 655.

40. Mrs. Benjamin Wiles, Sr., interview with author, July 15, 1979.

41. Gustav Stickley, "The Use and Abuse of Machinery, and Its Relation to the Arts and Crafts," *The Craftsman* 11, no. 2 (November 1906): 2.

42. *Things Wrought by the United Crafts* (Eastwood, N.Y.: The United Crafts Publishers, 1902), 22.

43. *The Craftsman* 1, no. 1 (October 1901): vii.

44. Gustav Stickley, "The Structural Style in Cabinet-Making," *House Beautiful* 15, no. 1 (December 1903): 21.

45. Quoted in Claude Fayette Bragdon, *Merely Players* (New York: Afred Knopf, 1929), 64.

46. Ibid., 72.

47. Roger G. Kennedy, "The Long Shadow of Harvey Ellis," *Minnesota History* 40, no. 3 (Fall 1966): 97.

48. Purcell to Roger G. Kennedy, February 19, 1965, quoted in Kennedy, "The Long Shadow," 98.

49. Barry Sanders, "Harvey Ellis: Architect, Painter, Furniture Designer," *Antiques* (February 1981): 59.

50. *A Rediscovery: Harvey Ellis, Artist, Architect*, catalog of a joint exhibition of the Memorial Art Gallery of the University of Rochester and the Margaret Woodbury Strong Museum, December 8, 1972, to January 14, 1973.

51. Kennedy, "The Long Shadow," 104.

52. Stickley, "Structure and Ornament," 396.

53. Sanders, "Harvey Ellis," 64.

54. Mrs. Benjamin Wiles, Sr., interview with author, July 15, 1979.

55. Gustav Stickley, "Chips from the Craftsman Workshops," *The Craftsman* 6, no. 3 (June 1904): 315–317.

CHAPTER FIVE

1. Mrs. Benjamin Wiles, Sr., interview with author, July 20, 1979.

2. Cleota Reed Gabriel, "Irene Sargent: Rediscovering a Lost Legend," *Courier* (Syracuse University Library Associates) 16, no. 2 (Summer 1979): 4–5.

3. *Things Wrought by the United Crafts* (Eastwood, N.Y.: The United Crafts, Publishers, 1902), 35.

4. Gabriel, "Irene Sargent," 9.

5. The format increased over the years to 8 by 10½ inches and then to 8¼ by 11 inches. Stickley sacrificed the format to his need to say more and more.

6. Stickley, "Thoughts Occasioned by an Anniversary," 56.

7. Gustav Stickley, "The Craftsman Movement: Its Origin and Growth," *The Craftsman* 25, no. 1 (October 1913): 18.

8. Reprinted in the February 1902 catalog of the United Crafts.

9. Randell Makinson, *Greene and Greene: Furniture and Related Designs* (Salt Lake City, Utah: Peregrine Smith Publishers, 1979), 15–16.

10. Ibid., 17.

11. Gustav Stickley, "Foreword," *The Craftsman* 3, no. 1 (October 1902): vii.

12. *The Craftsman* 3, no. 3 (December 1902): vii.

13. Quoted in Marcia Andrea Early, "The Craftsman (1901 to 1916) as the Principal Spokesman of the Craftsman Movement in America, with a Short Study of the Craftsman House Projects" (master's thesis, Institute of Fine Arts, New York University, 1963), 42.

14. " 'The Simple Life' by Charles Wagner, a Review," *The Craftsman* 2, no. 5 (August 1902): 256.

15. Ibid., 255.

16. Stickley may have gotten his idea for the persona of the Craftsman from Wagner that very night.

17. "M. Wagner's Lecture: "My Books and My Occasions for Writing Them," *The Craftsman* 6, no. 1 (October 1904): 138.

18. George Wharton James, "Two Days with M. Wagner," *The Craftsman* 7, no. 2 (November 1904): 191.

19. Ibid., 195. Wagner's comment may have prompted Stickley to introduce a new series in 1905 in *The Craftsman*, "Home Training in Cabinet Work: Practical Talk on Structural Wood-Working," in which he printed lumber lists, blueprints, and plans for the building of Craftsman furniture.

20. Timothy Andersen, Eudorah Moore, and Robert Winter, eds., *California Design 1910* (Pasadena: California Design Publications, 1974), 53.

21. John Spargo, "Edward Carpenter, The Philosopher: His Gospel of Friendship and Simplicity," *The Craftsman* 11, no. 1 (October 1906): 44–56. Much of the biographical information here comes from Spargo.

22. Ibid, 52.

23. "What Edward Carpenter Says About Walt Whitman in His Latest Book," *The Craftsman* 10, no. 6 (September 1906): 737–746.

24. M. Irwin MacDonald, "A Visit with Edward Carpenter," *The Craftsman* 17, no. 2 (November 1909): 123.

25. Gustav Stickley, Introduction to " 'The Simplification of Life': A Chapter from Edward Carpenter's Book Called 'England's Ideal,' " in *Craftsman Homes* (Eastwood, New York, Craftsman Publishing, 1909), 1–2.

26. Ibid., 2.

27. Spargo, "Edward Carpenter," 55.

28. Reprinted in the April 1905 issue of *The Craftsman*, page 130.

29. Gustav Stickley, "Als Ik Kan," *The Craftsman* 8, no. 6 (April–September 1905): 688–690.

30. Gustav Stickley, "Als Ik Kan," *The Craftsman* 12, no. 1 (April 1907): 113.

31. Gustav Stickley, *Craftsman Homes*, 2.

32. Stickley, "Als Ik Kan," *The Craftsman* 9, no. 4 (January 1907): 65.

CHAPTER SIX

1. Stickley, "The Structural Style in Cabinet Making," 21. In the Middle Ages, architecture informed discussions of education, *edifica-tion*—"building".

2. Anthea Callen, *Women in the Arts and Crafts Movement*, has resurrected the names of twelve women who functioned as architects during that time (New York: Pantheon Books, 1979).

3. Stickley, *Craftsman Homes*, 195.

4. Gustav Stickley, "Chips from the Craftsman Workshops," *The Craftsman* 5, no. 2 (November 1903): 199.

5. Mary Ann Smith, *Gustav Stickley the Craftsman* (Syracuse: Syracuse University Press, 1983), 82–83.

6. Craftsman catalog, 1912.

7. Stickley, *Craftsman Homes*, 196.

8. Ibid., p. 1.

9. Stickley, "Halls and Stairways: Their Importance in the General Scheme of a Craftsman House," in *Craftsman Homes*, 125.

10. Morris Plains has no connection to William Morris; the township got its name from Lewis Morris, a governor of New Jersey in the eighteenth century. I have often wondered, though, if Stickley did not make his own romantic connections to William Morris or if he did not at least enjoy the coincidence.

11. Gustav Stickley, "The Craftsman's House: A Practical Application of All the Theories of Home Building Advocated in This Magazine," *The Craftsman* 5, no. 1 (October 1908), 79.

12. Ibid, 80.

13. Gustav Stickley, "The Craftsman's House: A Practical Application of Our Theories of Home Building," in *Craftsman Homes* (Eastwood, New York: Craftsman Publishers, 1909), 4.

14. Ibid, 85.

15. Ibid, 78.

16. Ibid, 87.

17. Ibid, 88.

18. Ibid, 89.

19. Smith, *Gustav Stickley*, 111.

20. Gustav Stickley's personal record, April 26–July 9, 1910, Joseph Downs Manuscript Collection, 76x101.54, Winterthur Museum.

21. "Craftsman Farms: Its Development and Future," *The Craftsman* 25, no. 1 (October 1913): 8.

22. Ledger 1901–05, 76x101.11, Henry Francis Du Pont Winterthur Museum.

23. Natalie Curtis, "The New Log House at Craftsman Farms: An Architectural Development of the Log Cabin," *The Craftsman* 21, no. 2 (November 1911): 196.

24. Gustav Stickley, "Three of the Craftsman Farms Bungalows That May Prove Useful for Summer or Weekend Cottages," *The Craftsman* 15, no. 2 (November 1908), 220.

25. Stickley "The Craftsman's House," 344.

26. Gustav Stickley, "A Craftsman House That Shows the Development of a New Idea," *The Craftsman* 17, no. 4 (January 1910): 430.

27. Gustav Stickley, "The Cost of the Craftsman House: Why These Designs Do Not Lend Themselves to What is Called 'Cheap Building,' " *The Craftsman* 17, no. 6 (March 1910): 683.

28. Isabelle Anscombe and Charlotte Gere, *Arts and Crafts in Britain and America* (New York: Rizzoli International Publications, 1978), 54.

29. Gustav Stickley, *More Craftsman Homes* (Eastwood, New York, Craftsman Publishers, 1912), 1.

30. "The Value of Craftsman Service," *The Craftsman* 23, no. 6 (March 1912): 729.

CHAPTER SEVEN

1. That Stickley applied for a patent on an element of furniture design—a series of spindles—attests to his almost obsessive need to set his furniture apart from every other competitor.

2. Gustav Stickley, "Home Training in Cabinet Work: The Texture and Qualities of Natural Wood: Their Individuality and Friendliness: Fifth of a Series," *The Craftsman* 8, no. 4 (July 1905): 525–556.

3. Gustav Stickley, "Als Ik Kan," *The Craftsman* 8, no. 6 (September 1905): 835.

4. Gustav Stickley, "Als Ik Kan," *The Craftsman* 9, no. 1 (October 1905): 133.

5. Gustav Stickley, *The Craftsman's Story* (Syracuse, N.Y., n.d.), 3. Though *The Craftsman's Story* is not dated, Stickley announced its publication in July 1905, "after some unavoidable delays."

6. When I visited Mrs. Wiles in her home in New Jersey, she placed in my hands what she called her prize possession from her father, a large copper charger. "Gus made this," she said, "when he was a very young man." It looked slightly rough—a youngster's work—but the color and feel clearly connected it with what he would later offer for sale in his own workshops.

7. Some collectors insist that Stickley's furniture can be dated by its metal trim: Iron, they say, was used only on the early designs, copper on the later ones. I have seen pieces, however, that date from the United Crafts period with copper hardware, and the earliest United Crafts catalog says that hardware on a sideboard is available in "either copper or iron." Type of metal thus does not provide a reliable way to date Stickley's furniture.

8. Gustav Stickley, "Als Ik Kan," *The Craftsman* 9, no. 3 (December 1905): 434.

9. The Craftsman Workshops also offered a commercial line of furniture for businesses and offices that could be special ordered.

10. Stickley, *Craftsman Homes*, 196.

11. Charles Wagner, "In the Arms of a New Friend," *The Craftsman* 8, no. 2 (May 1905): 261–262.

12. The name *settle* had Anglo-Saxon and medieval roots. Like the Sussex chair, this piece was popularized by Morris through his firm.

13. Stickley, "Home Training in Cabinet Work," *The Craftsman*, 8, no. 4 (September 1905), p. 531.

14. Wooden pegs hold joints securely over time because the post and peg expand and contract at the same rate; nails, however, tend to loosen joints over time since metal and wood expand and contract at different rates.

15. Giles Edgerton, "Is There a Sex Distinction in Art? The Attitude of the Critic Toward Women's Exhibits," *The Craftsman* 14, no. 3 (June 1908): 204.

16. Ibid, 205.

17. Stickley, "Structure and Ornament," 396.

18. Harvey Ellis, "A Craftsman House Design," *The Craftsman* 4, no. 4 (July 1903): 271–72.

19. Gustav Stickley, "The Craftsman Idea of the Kind of Home Environment That Would Result from More Natural Standards of Life and Work," in *Craftsman Homes*, (Eastwood, New York: Craftsman Publishers, 1909), 196.

20. See Ronald Zboray, "Antebellum Reading and the Ironies of Technological Innovation," in *Reading in America: Literature and Social History*, ed., Cathy N. Davidson (Baltimore: The John Hopkins University Press, 1989), 180–200.

21. Gustav Stickley, "Our Home Department: Craftsman Shower Lights," *The Craftsman* 10, no. 4 (July 1906): 546.

22. Lewis Mumford, *The Brown Decades: A Study of the Arts in America, 1865–1895* (New York: Harcourt, Brace and Company, 1931), 7–9.

23. "Indian Blankets, Baskets, and Bowls: The Product of the Original Craftworkers of This Continent," *The Craftsman* 17, no. 5 (February 1910): 588.

24. Herbert E. Binstead, *The Furniture Styles, with Chapters on Modern Mission and Craftsman Furniture* (Chicago: Trade Periodical Company, 1909), 344–346.

CHAPTER EIGHT

1. "A Visit to Craftsman Farms: The Study of an Educational Ideal," *The Craftsman* 18, no. 6 (September 1910): 645–646.

2. Ibid., 647.

3. Ibid., 643. I emphasize the words "stand on their own feet" to call attention to a "normal" architectural/moral phrase, one that had worked its way into education. In effect, Stickley was engaged in building young people—even designing them—as if they were so many cabinets. Recall the Boy Scout credo, an institution developed during the Arts and Crafts period: "It is better to build boys than it is to mend men."

4. Gustav Stickley, "Als Ik Kan: A School for Citizenship," *The Craftsman* 23, no. 1 (October 1912): 121.

5. Ibid., 121.

6. Ibid., 121.

7. Gustav Stickley, "The Evolution of a Hillside Home: Raymond Riordan's Indiana Bungalow," *The Craftsman* 25, no. 1 (October 1913): 53.

8. Raymond Riordan, "An Outdoor School for Boys, Where Development Is Gained from Work as Well as Books," *The Craftsman* 26, no. 1 (April 1914), p. 94.

9. Mrs. Benjamin Wiles, Sr., interview with author, July 15, 1979.

CHAPTER NINE

1. Stickley, "Als Ik Kan: The Craftsman's Birthday Party," *The Craftsman* 24, no. 2 (May 1913): 254.

2. Smith, *Gustav Stickley*, 152.

3. Lease for 6 East 39th Street, Joseph Downs Manuscript Collection, 76x101.2355, Winterthur Museum.

4. Smith, *Gustav Stickley*, 152.

5. Stickley, "Als Ik Kan," 252.

6. Joseph Downs Manuscript Collection, 76x101.31, Winterthur Museum.

7. Mrs. G. W. Flaccus, interview with author, July 17, 1977.

8. Stickley, "The Craftsman Movement," 18.

9. Ibid., 26.

10. Gustav Stickley, "Als Ik Kan: More Plans for the New Craftsman Building," *The Craftsman* 24, no. 5 (August 1913): 550.

11. Gustav Stickley, "Als Ik Kan: Lectures and Talks at the Craftsman Building," *The Craftsman* 26, no. 3 (June 1914): 352.

12. Ibid., 551.

13. Gustav Stickley, "The Craftsman Building," *The Craftsman* 24, no. 2 (May 1913): 254.

14. "The Craftsman Restaurant: By a Visitor," *The Craftsman* 25, no. 1 (January 1914): 362–367.

15. Letter from Edward S. Wood to Howard E. Brown, Joseph Downs Manuscript Collection, 76x101.2356, Winterthur Museum.

16. Joseph Downs Manuscript Collection, 71x101.2391, Winterthur Museum.

17. Smith, *Gustav Stickley*, 154.

18. "The Development of an American Style of Home Furnishing Founded upon Beauty, Comfort and Simplicity," *The Craftsman* 27, no. 1 (October 1914): 77–78.

19. "The New Idea in Home Furnishing: No. 1: The Dining Room," *The Craftsman* 29, no. 2 (November 1915): 201.

20. *Grand Rapids Artisan-Record*, quoted in "A Progresive Step in American Cabinet-Making," *The Craftsman* 30, no. 6 (September 1916): 624–627.

CHAPTER TEN

1. Joseph Downs Manuscript Collection, 76x101.2358, Winterthur Museum.

2. Some historians claim that Leopold and Julius George would have included Gustav in their new firm. I find the claim hard to believe. According to every family member I interviewed, Leopold in particular had no use for Gustav and treated him accordingly.

3. Mary Fanton Roberts, "One Man's Story," *The Craftsman* 30, no. 2 (May 1916): 188.

4. Ibid.

5. Stickley relied on a German noun, *wald*, meaning "forest" or "woods," for his new furniture line, a play perhaps on *Schwarzwald*, the Black Forest. Stickley imagined a *wald* filled with color.

6. Mrs. Benjamin Wiles, Sr., interview with author, July 15, 1979.

7. Smith, *Gustav Stickley*, 157.

8. Joseph Downs Manuscript Collection, 76x101.2359, Winterthur Museum.

9. Mrs. Benjamin Wiles, Sr., interview with author, July 15, 1979.

10. David M. Cathers, *Furniture of the American Arts and Crafts Movement; Stickley and Roycroft Mission Oak* (New York: New American Library, 1981), 254, based on interviews with Barbara Wiles. David Cathers asks, "We have seen late L. and J. G. Stickley furniture marked with your father's joiner's compass and their Handicraft clamp conjoined. Did he work for them after he went bankrupt?" She answers, "I think he did, but it couldn't have been for very long. All the brothers in that family were too strong-willed to work for anybody, except George, who was really just a salesman for Lee." In my own interviews with Barbara Wiles, however, she never alluded to her father's working for Leopold (Lee) or Julius (George). In fact, she made a point of saying "Gus" could never work for anyone. He had to be his own boss.

11. Joseph Downs Manuscript Collection, 76x101.2350, Winterthur Museum.

CHAPTER ELEVEN

1. Pelzel, *The Arts and Crafts Movement in America*, 6.

2. The entire capital stock issue consisted of 3,000 shares of par value priced at $100 a share. Joseph Downs Manuscript Collection, 76x101.2350, Winterthur Museum.

3. Stickley, "The Craftsman Building," 254.

4. *New York Times*, May 16, 1915.

5. Mrs. Monny Nitchie, interview with author, July 18, 1979.

6. The English designer, architect and writer, C. R. Ashbee, deplored the antique industry in High Wycombe, England, where "a special study is made of the fashion for antiquity, and where the Chippendale and Sheraton frets hang in rows along the factory walls, and the antique chairs and settees are turned out in the hundreds to the hum of the *latest American machinery*" (*Craftsmanship in Competitive Industry* [London: Essex House Press, 1909], 53; emphasis added). The Hampton Shops, meanwhile, fancy Manhattan furniture stores, were already advertising reproductions of "old Sheraton and Heppelwhite Masterpieces" in the *New York Times* in 1915. The times had changed.

7. Freeman, *The Forgotten Rebel*, page 20.

BIBLIOGRAPHY

THE DETAILS OF STICKLEY'S LIFE many times contradict themselves—especially from his own accounts or from the accounts of others, even family members. Some pertinent details—number of siblings, date of marriage, uncle's name—have disappeared altogether. I have had to snoop and probe, surmise and suspect. To find Stickley, one must turn detective. Such is the history of a man who created an entirely new persona for himself—particularly of a man who continually reinvented and reshaped that persona.

I am indebted, however, to Mrs. Benjamin Wiles, Sr., Mrs. G.W. Flaccus, and Ms. Monny Nitchie for their willingness to talk to me about "Gus." I have found some clues in the *National Cyclopedia of American Biography*; *Who's Who in America, 1906–1907*; John Crosby Freeman's Master's Thesis, *The Forgotten Rebel*, at the University of Delaware, 1964; the Stickley Collection, Archives and Library, Edison Institute, Henry Ford Museum and Greenfield Village, Dearborn, Michigan; and the Henry Francis Dupont Winterthur Museum, Winterthur, Delaware.

For historical background, certain trade journals and periodicals have proved useful: *American Cabinet Maker and Upholsterer, Decorator and Furnisher, Furniture Journal, Furniture World, House Beautiful, International Studio, Ladies Home Journal,* and *Studio*. The Binghamton *Daily Republican*, the New York *Times*, the Syracuse *Herald*, and the Syracuse *Post-Standard* carried articles on and off about Stickley. City directories for Binghamton and Syracuse gave up a few leads.

I have not listed Stickley's articles from *The Craftsman* in the bibliography: I have of course consulted them all and, in one way or another, incorporated them all in this book. In addition, I have relied on the following Stickley catalogs and ephemera for production details of his workshops:

Stickley, Gustav. *Cabinet Work from the Craftsman Workshops*. Furniture Catalog, 1905.

———. *Catalog of Craftsman Furniture*. 1909.

BIBLIOGRAPHY

———. *Chips from the Craftsman Workshops* (New York: Kalkoff, 1906).

———. *Chips from the Craftsman Workshop.* Number 11, 1907.

———. *Chips from the Workshops of Gustav Stickley.* 1901 Catalog.

———. *The Craftsman Department of Home Furnishings* (New York: Craftsman Publishing Co., no date).

———. *Craftsman Furnishings.* 1906 Catalog.

———. *Craftsman Furniture.* 1912 Catalog.

———. *Craftsman Furniture.* 1913 Catalog.

———. *Craftsman Homes* (New York: Craftsman Publishing Co., 1909).

———. *Craftsman Houses* (New York: Craftsman Publishing Co., 1913).

———. *The Craftsman's Story* (Syracuse: Mason Press, 1905).

———. *Descriptive Price List of Craftsman Furniture.* 1907 Catalog.

———. *More Craftsman Homes* (New York: Craftsman Publishing Co., 1912).

———. *A Summary of Craftsman Enterprises* (New York: Craftsman Publishing Co., no date).

———. *Things Wrought by the United Crafts* (Eastwood, New York: The United Crafts Publishers, 1902).

———. *Twenty-Four Craftsman Houses with Floor Plans* (New York: Craftsman Publishing Co., no date).

———. *What Is Wrought in the Craftsman Workshops* (Syracuse: Gustav Stickley, 1904).

ADDITIONAL READING

Adams, Mary. "The Chicago Arts and Crafts Society." *House Beautiful* IX (January 1901): 96–101.

Addams, Jane. *Twenty Years at Hull House* (New York: Signet Classics, 1960).

Andersen, Timothy, Eudorah Moore, and Robert W. Winter, eds. *California Design 1910* (Pasadena: California Design Publications, 1974).

Anon. "The Arts and Crafts Movement at Home and Abroad." *Brush and Pencil* VI (June 1909): 110–121.

———. "The Boston Society of Arts and Crafts." *The Craftsman* 11 (August 1902): 258–259.

———. *Forms From the Earth: 1000 Years of Pottery in America* (New York: Museum of Contemporary Crafts, 1962).

———. *Grueby.* Exhibition Catalog of the Everson Museum of Art, Syracuse, New York. March 21–May 31, 1981.

———. "Mission Furniture." *Country Living* (August/September 1981): 68–95.

———. *A Rediscovery: Harvey Ellis, Artist, Architect.* Catalog of the Joint Exhibition of the Memorial Art Gallery of the University of Rochester and the Margaret Woodbury Strong Museum, Rochester, New York. December 8, 1972 to January 14, 1973.

————. "A Revival of Pen and Ink Rendering: The Work of Harvey Ellis." *Western Architect* XVIII (March 1912): 31–37.

————. "Rookwood at the Pan-American." *Keramic Studio* III (1901): 146–148.

————. *A Souvenir of the Great Pan-American Exposition—May 1, 1901 to November 1, 1901* (Grand Rapids, Michigan: James Hayne Co., 1901).

————. "Structure and Ornament in the Craftsman Workshops." *The Craftsman* V (January 1904): 391–396.

Anscombe, Isabelle, and Charlotte Gere. *Arts and Crafts in Britain and America* (New York: Rizzoli International Publications, Inc., 1978).

Balch, David Arnold. *Elbert Hubbard: Genius of Roycroft* (New York: F.A. Stokes, Co., 1940).

Barber, Arthur A. "Cincinnati Women Art Workers." *Art Interchange* XXXVI (February 1896): 29–30.

Bartinique, A. Patricia. *Gustav Stickley, His Craft*. Exhibition at Craftsman Farms, Parsippany, New Jersey, November 15, 1992 to January 31, 1993 (New York: Turn of the Century Editions, 1993).

Bavarro, Joseph J., and Thomas Mossman. *The Furniture of Gustav Stickley: History, Techniques, Projects* (New York: Von Nostrand Reinhold, 1982).

Beisner, Robert L. " 'Commune' in East Aurora." *American Heritage* XXII (February 1971): 72–77, 106–109.

Bing, Samuel. *La Culture artistique en Amérique*. Paris, 1895.

Binns, Charles F. "The Arts and Crafts Movement in America: Prize Essay." *The Craftsman* XIV (June 1908): 275–279.

Binstead, Herbert E. *The Furniture Styles* (Chicago: Trade Periodical Co., 1909).

Blackall, C.H. "The Grueby Faience." *Brickbuilder* VII (August 1898), 162–163.

Blasberg, Robert. *Fulper Pottery: An Aesthetic Appreciation 1909–1929* (New York: The Jordan Volpe Gallery, 1979).

————. "Grueby Art Pottery." *The Magazine Antiques* C (August 1971): 246–249.

Bohdan, Carol L., and Todd M. Volpe. "The Furniture of Gustav Stickley." *The Magazine Antiques* (May 1977): 989–998.

Boulden, Jane L. "Rookwood." *Art Interchange* XLVI (June 1901), 129–131.

Bowdoin, W.G. "The Grueby Pottery." *Art Interchange* XLV (December 1900): 137–138.

Bowman, Leslie Greene. *American Arts and Crafts: Virtue in Design*. Los Angeles County Museum of Art Exhibition 1990 (Boston: Little, Brown and Company, 1990).

Bragdon, Claude. "Harvey Ellis: A Portrait Sketch." *Architectural Review* XV (December 1908): 173–183.

Bray, Hazel V. *The Potter's Art in California, 1885 to 1955*. Catalog of Exhibition at Oakland Museum, August 22–October 1, 1978 (Oakland, California: The Oakland Museum Art Department, 1980).

Brener, Carol. "Move Over, Deco—Here Comes Mission Furniture. *New York* (January 24, 1977): 49–56.

Brooks, H. Allen. "Chicago Architecture: Its Debt to the Arts and Crafts." *Journal of the Society of Architectural Historians* XXX (December 1971): 312–317.

————. *The Prairie School: Frank Lloyd Wright and His Midwest Contemporaries* (Toronto: University of Toronto Press, 1972).

Callen, Anthea. *Women Artists of the Arts and Crafts Movement* (New York: Pantheon Books, 1979).

Caruthers, J. Wade. "Elbert Hubbard: A Case of Reinterpretation." *Connecticut Review* L (October 1967): 67–77.

Cathers, David. *Furniture of the American Arts and Crafts Movement: Stickley and Roycroft Mission Oak* (New York: New American Library, 1981).

Champney, Freeman. *Art and Glory: The Story of Elbert Hubbard* (New York: Crown Publishers, 1968).

Clark, Robert Judson, ed. *The Arts and Crafts Movement in America 1876–1916*. Catalog of show at The Art Museum, Princeton University, 21 October–17 December, 1972. (Princeton: Princeton University Press, 1972).

————, ed. *Aspects of the Arts and Crafts Movement in America*. Record of the Art Museum of Princeton University, Vol. 34, no. 2, 1975.

Cobden-Sanderson, T.J. *The Arts and Crafts Movement* (London: Hammersmith Publishing Society, 1905).

Coulter, Mary J. "History of the Arts and Crafts Movement in America." *California's Magazine* II (1916), 169–178.

Covell, Alwyn T. "On the Relation of Furniture to Its Architecture (Craftsman Interior)." *Good Furniture* IV, ii (November 1914): 70–76.

————. "The Real Place of Mission Furniture." *Good Furniture* IV, vi (March 1915): 358–366.

Cumming, Elizabeth, and Wendy Kaplan. *The Arts and Crafts Movement* (New York and London: Thames and Hudson, 1991).

Darling, Sharon. *Chicago Furniture: Art, Craft, and Industry, 1833–1983* (New York: W.W. Norton and Company, 1984).

————. *Chicago Metalsmiths* (Chicago: Chicago Historical Society, 1977).

Davidoff, Donald A. "Sophisticated Design: The Mature Work of L. and J.G. Stickley." *Antiques and Fine Art*, Vol. VII, no. 1 (December 1989): 84–91.

Denison, Lindsay. "Elbert Hubbard's Shop: An American William Morris at Work in East Aurora." New York *Sun*, October 29, 1899, 6.

Dickason, David Howard. *The Daring Young Men: The Story of the American Pre-Raphaelites* (Bloomington: Indiana University Press, 1953).

Early, Marcia Andrea. "The Craftsman (1901–1916) as the Principal Spokesman of the Craftsman Movement in America, With a Short Study of the Craftsman House Projects." Master's Thesis, Institute of Fine Arts, New York University, 1963.

Edgewood, Margaret. "Some Sensible Furniture." *House Beautiful* VIII (October 1900), 653–655.

Edwards, Robert. "The Roycrofters: Their Furniture and Crafts." *Art and Antiques*, Vol. 4, issue 6 (November/December, 1981: 80–87.

Elliott, Maud Howe, ed. *Illustrated Art and Craft in the Woman's Building of the Columbian Exposition, Chicago* (Paris and New York: Goupil and Co., 1893).

Ellis, Harvey. "An Adironack Camp." *The Craftsman* IV (July 1903), 281–284.

———. "A Craftsman House Design." *The Craftsman* IV (July 1903), 269–277.

———. "A Note of Color." *The Craftsman* V (November 1903), 153–163.

———. "A Summer Chapel." *The Craftsman* IV (September 1903), 401–414.

———. "An Urban House." *The Craftsman* IV (August 1903), 313–327.

Evans, Paul. *Art Pottery of the United States* (New York: Charles Scribner's Sons, 1974).

Farrar, Francis, and Abigail Farrar. *The Book of the Roycrofters* (East Aurora, New York: Roycrofters, 1907).

Fidler, Patricia J. *Art with a Mission: Objects of the Arts and Crafts Movement* (Seattle: University of Washington Press, 1993).

Freeman, John Crosby. *The Forgotten Rebel: Gustav Stickley and His Craftsman Mission Furniture* (Watkins Glen, New York: Century House, 1966).

Gabriel, Cleota Reed. "Irene Sargent: Rediscovering A Lost Legend." *The Courier* (Syracuse University Library Associates), Vol. XVI, Number 2, Summer 1979: 3–14.

Garden, Hugh M.G. "Harvey Ellis, Designer and Draughtsman." *Architectural Review* (Boston) XV (December 1908), 184–186.

Gebhard, David. "C.F.A. Voysey—To and From America." *Journal of the Society of Architectural Historians* XXX (December 1971), 304–312.

Hanks, David A. *The Decorative Designs of Frank Lloyd Wright* (New York: E.P. Dutton, 1979).

Henzke, Lucille. *American Art Pottery* (Camden, New Jersey: Thomas Nelson, 1970).

Howe, Samuel. "A Visit to the Workshops of the United Crafts." *The Craftsman* III (October 1902): 59–64.

Hubbard, Elbert. *The Roycroft Shop: Being a History* (East Aurora, New York: Roycrofters, 1908).

Kalec, Donald. "The Prairie School Furniture." *Prairie School Review* I (Fourth Quarter 1964): 5–21.

Kaplan, Wendy, ed. *Art That Is Life, the Arts and Crafts Movement in America 1875–1920.* (Boston: Museum of Fine Arts, 1987).

Kaufmann, Edgar, Jr. "Some American Architectural Ornament of the Arts and Crafts Era." *Journal of the Society of Architectural Historians* XXIV (December 1965): 285–291.

Kennedy, Roger G. "Long Dark Corridors: Harvey Ellis." *Prairie School Review* V (First and Second Quarter 1968): 5–18.

———. "The Long Shadow of Harvey Ellis." *Minnesota History* XL (Fall 1966): 97–108.

Key, Mabel. "A Review of the Recent Exhibition of the Chicago Arts and Crafts Society," *House Beautiful* VI (June 1899): 3–12.

BIBLIOGRAPHY

Kinsey, Sally J. *Gustav Stickley and the Early Years of The Craftsman*. Master's Thesis, Syracuse University, 1972.

Koch, Robert. "Elbert Hubbard's Roycrofters as Artist–Craftsmen." *Winterthur Portfolio* III (1967): 67–82.

Lancaster, Clay. "The American Bungalow." *Art Bulletin* 40 (September 1958): 239–253.

Lears, Jackson. *No Place of Grace: Antimodernism and the Transformation of American Culture, 1880–1920* (New York: Pantheon Books, 1981).

Lucic, Karen. *Charles Sheeler and the Cult of the Machine* (Cambridge: Harvard University Press, 1991).

Lynes, Russell. *The Tastemakers* (New York: Harper and Brothers, 1955).

MacMasters, Dan. "The Craftsman House: An Architectural Heritage." Los Angeles *Times*, Home Section, October 6, 1974, no page numbers.

Macomber, H. Percy. "The Future of the Handicrafts." *American Magazine of Art* IX (March 1918): 192–195.

Makinson, Randell L. *Greene and Greene: Architecture and Fine Art* (Salt Lake City, Utah: Peregrine Smith, Inc., 1977).

———. *Greene and Greene: Furniture and Related Designs* (Salt Lake City, Utah: Peregrine Smith, Inc., 1979).

Manning, Eileen. "The Architectural Designs of Harvey Ellis." Master's Thesis, University of Minnesota, 1953.

Marck, Don. *Arts and Crafts Furniture Design, the Grand Rapids Contribution 1895–1915*. Exhibition Catalog. Grand Rapids Art Museum, 1987.

Mayer, Barbara. *In the Arts and Crafts Style*. (San Francisco, California: Chronicle Books, 1992).

McGann, Patricia. "Arts and Crafts Corpets." *Antiques West* (May 1980): 4–6.

Moffitt, Charlotte. "The Rohlfs Furniture." *House Beautiful*, VII (January 1900): 81–85.

Moore, Eudorah. "The Surprising Diversity of California's Early Designers." Los Angeles *Times*, Home Section, October 6, 1974, no page numbers.

Naylor, Gilian. *The Arts and Crafts Movement* (London: Studio Vista, 1971).

19th-Century America: Furniture and Other Decorative Arts (New York: Metropolitan Museum of Art, 1970).

Otto, Celia Jackson. *American Furniture of the Nineteenth Century* (New York: Viking Press, 1965).

Parris, Leslie, ed. *The Pre-Raphaelites* (Seattle: University of Washington Press, 1993).

Peck, Herbert. *The Book of Rookwood Pottery* (New York: Crown Publishers, 1968).

Pevsner, Nicholas. *Pioneers of Modern Design* (Hammondsworth: Penguin Books, 1960).

Pond, Theodore Hanford. "The Arts and Crafts Exhibition at the Providence Art Club." *House Beautiful* X (June 1901): 98–101.

Priestman, Mabel Tuke. "History of the Arts and Crafts Movement in America." *House Beautiful* XX (October 1906): 15–16; (November 1906): 14–16.

Reif, Rita. "Shedding Light on a Viennese Designer." New York *Times*, March 13, 1983, 31.

———. "The Master of Mission." New York *Times*, July 9, 1978, 27.

Roberts, Mary Fanton. "One Man's Story." *The Craftsman* XXX (May 1916): 188–200.

———. "The Grain of Wood." *House Beautiful* IX (February 1901): 147–148.

Robie, Virginia. "Mission Furniture: What It Is and Is Not." *House Beautiful* XXVII (May 1910): 162–163, 175.

Rohlfs, Charles. "May Adventures in Wood Carving." *Arts Journal* (October 1925): 21–22.

Russell, Arthur. "Grueby Pottery." *House Beautiful* V (December 1898): 3–9.

Sanders, Barry, ed. with an introduction. *The Best of Craftsman Homes* (Salt Lake City, Utah: Peregrine Smith, Inc., 1979).

———, ed. with an introduction. *The Craftsman: An Anthology* (Salt Lake City, Utah: Peregrine Smith, Inc., 1978).

———. "Gustav Stickley: A Craftsman's Furniture." *American Art and Antiques*, Vol. 2, Issue 4: 46–53.

———. "Harvey Ellis: Architect, Painter, Furniture Designer." *Art and Antiques* Vol. 4, Issue 1 (January/February 1981): 58–67.

Sargent, Irene. "William Morris." *The Craftsman* I (October 1901): 1–14.

———. "A Recent Arts and Crafts Exhibition." *The Craftsman* IV (May 1903): 69–83.

———. "Some Potters and Their Products." *The Craftsman* IV (August 1903): 328–337.

Shay, Felix. *Elbert Hubbard of East Aurora* (New York: Wise and Co., 1926).

Smith, Katherine Louise. "An Arts and Crafts Exhibition at Minneapolis." *The Craftsman* III (March 1903): 373–377.

Smith, Mary Ann. *Gustav Stickley: The Craftsman* (New York: Syracuse University Press, 1983).

Stein, Roger B. *John Ruskin and Aesthetic Thought in America, 1840–1900* (Cambridge: Harvard University Press, 1967).

Stern, Madeleine B. "An American Woman First in Textiles and Decoration: Candace Wheeler." In *We The Women* (New York: Schulte Publishing Co., 1963).

Swales, Francis S. "Master Draftsman, III: Harvey Ellis." *Pencil Points* V (July 1924): 49–55, 79.

Thompson, E. P. *William Morris, Romantic to Revolutionary* (London: Lawrence and Wishart, 1955).

Thompson, Paul. *The Work of William Morris* (London: Quartet Books, 1967).

Trapp, Kenneth, ed. *The Arts and Crafts Movement in California: Living the Good Life.* Oakland Museum Exhibition February 27–August 15, 1993 (New York: Abbeville Press Publishers, 1993).

———. *Ode to Nature: Flowers and Landscapes of the Rookwood Pottery, 1880–1940.* Catalog of Show, April 15–June 30, 1980, Jordan-Volpe Gallery, New York.

Triggs, Oscar Lovell. *About Tobey Handmade Furniture* (Chicago: Press of Metcalf, 1906).

———. "The Arts and Crafts." *Brush and Pencil* (December 1897): 47–55.

BIBLIOGRAPHY

———. *Chapters in the History of the Arts and Crafts Movement* (Chicago: Bohemia Guild of the Industrial Art League, 1902).

Twyman, Joseph. "The Art and Influence of William Morris." *Inland Architect and News Record* XLII (January 1904): 43–45.

Valentine, John. "Rookwood Pottery." *House Beautiful* IV (September 1898): 12–29.

Vidler, Virginia. "Hubbard's Roycroft." *Antiques Journal* XXIV (July 1969): 10–12.

Volk, Douglas. "The Human Element in Arts and Crafts." *Brush and Pencil* II (March 1903): 443–444.

Whiting, Frederic Allen. "The Arts and Crafts at the Louisiana Purchase Exposition." *International Studio* XXIII (October 1904): cccixxxiv–ccixxxix.

Williams, Raymond. *Culture and Society, 1780–1950* (Hammondsworth: Penguin Books, 1963).

Winter, Robert. *The California Bungalow* (Los Angeles: Hennessey and Ingalls, 1980).

———. "Southern California Architecture and Crafts: Early 20th-Century Works." *Historic Preservation* XXIV (April–June 1972): 12–15.

Wright, Gwendoline. "On the Fringe of the Profession: Women in American Architecture." In *The Architect: Chapters in the History of the Profession*, Spiro Kostof, ed. (New York: Oxford University Press, 1976).

Zueblin, Rho Fisk. "The Arts and Crafts Movement." *Chautauquan* XXXVI and XXXVII (October 1902–June 1903).

INDEX

INDEX

INDEX